SECRET PLACE

LEARN TO DWELL IN THE HOLY OF HOLIES

VINCE BAKER

Editor: Eunice Baker

Printed in the United States of America

Table of Contents

Dedication V

Foreword VII

CHAPTER 1: Secret Place 9

CHAPTER 2: Tabernacle and Temple 29

CHAPTER 3: Ark of the Covenant 53

CHAPTER 4: Tabernacle of David 81

CHAPTER 5: Second Temple 105

CHAPTER 6: Knowing God.......................................129

CHAPTER 7: Making Vows 159

CHAPTER 8: Crucified with Christ 181

CHAPTER 9: Better Promises...................................205

CHAPTER 10: Asking God..233

CHAPTER 11: Boldness...261

CHAPTER 12: Final Secret Thoughts 289

About the Author...323

DEDICATION

I dedicate this book to my Heavenly Father, Jesus, and the Holy Spirit. You have always been there for me and have taught me about the *Secret Place*. I don't know where I would be today if You had not revealed Yourself and Your Kingdom to me. Thank you for allowing me to dwell with You in the *Secret Place* and have fellowship with You. The communion I have shared with You has been priceless and changed my life. I love You with all my heart, mind, soul, body, and strength. I will never forget what You have done for me. I THANK YOU from the bottom of my heart!

I also dedicate this book to my wonderful wife, Eunice. How you love and care for me does not go unnoticed. You also played a significant role in getting this book out. Thank you for always supporting me, my walk with God, and the ministry God has given me. You are not only my wife but also my companion and friend.

FOREWORD

Vince has become one of my best friends and stayed with me during the spiritual war for my daughter's healing. I have spent many hours and weeks in fellowship with Vince as he taught me Biblical truths on the subject of faith. Vince has learned from God how to walk in unwavering faith and healing.

Vince Baker is a prophetic teacher who operates in the gift of prophecy, the word of knowledge, accurately hearing from the Holy Spirit, and seeing things before they happen. Vince is a gift to the Body of Christ, especially to those who need to learn how to walk in strong faith. My wife and I are grateful to God for our friendship with Vince and his wife, Eunice.

I highly recommend reading his new book, *Secret Place,* and all his other books. His teachings are absolutely sound and Biblical. If you want to grow in your walk with Christ and be ready to face a crisis with no fear but faith, you need to read his books.

Bishop Vasyl I. Pechko
New Life Worship Center

CHAPTER
ONE

SECRET

PLACE

The Bible reveals there is a hidden sacred location called the **Secret Place** *of the Most High* in reference to a private relationship we can have with the Lord. This place is shrouded in mystery when it is mentioned in the Word of God. The fact it is called the *Secret Place* lets you know that it is a spiritually hidden location that is only revealed to those who are privileged by God to know about it. The *Secret Place* is glorious and brings to light that there is something deeper we can seek in our relationship with the Lord. The deeper you go in God in the *Secret Place*, the deeper He will go in you. There is no place on the Earth like the *Secret Place*. Those called by God to be granted access to the *Secret Place* are blessed beyond measure to experience the most supernatural and captivating relationship with God they could ever imagine.

God has called me to reveal the mysteries of the *Secret Place* to His chosen people. If you are reading this book, God has graced you with the privilege of a lifetime to enter into a Divine Place of a closer relationship with Himself.

Let's begin this adventure by reading the famous verse from Psalm 91 that mentions the *Secret Place*.

Psalm 91:1 (KJV)
*1 He that dwelleth in the **secret place** of the most High shall abide under the shadow of the Almighty.*

Psalm 91:1 (AMPC)
*1 He who dwells in the **secret place** of the Most High shall remain stable and fixed under the shadow of the Almighty [Whose power no foe can withstand].*

As you consider the subject of the *Secret Place* in the Holy Scriptures, you will find the *Secret Place* is portrayed in different ways. God describes the *Secret Place* with mysterious imagery in His Word. God uses mysterious imagery to challenge His people to seek Him and research the Scriptures to learn His secrets about this Holy Place. Those who know the Lord understand that God doesn't just come out and tell everyone His deepest thoughts. God knows people won't value the mysteries of His Kingdom if it costs them nothing. Spiritual value comes from things you have to seek God for in His Word to discover their hidden meanings. It has taken me decades of seeking God in prayer and studying His Word to find the mysteries of the *Secret Place*, which I highly value.

Once you learn the mysteries of the *Secret Place*, developing a close and private relationship with the Lord will still take time. Some people reading this book may already dwell in the *Secret Place*, while others may still be on their journey to finding this hidden location. Either way, God led me to author this book to help anyone desiring to dwell in the *Secret Place* and to know Him more intimately.

Let's examine some insightful Bible verses to see how God portrays the *Secret Place*. Through diligent study and meditation on God's Word, I have found that God uses different terminologies to describe the *Secret Place*. As you explore the Scriptures, a picture begins to be painted within you that helps you to understand this sacred location. Once this picture is painted within you, you will become aware of what God is trying to unveil about the *Secret Place*. I will now share some verses that expand the thoughts of God on what precisely the *Secret Place* is. If you can perceive with your spiritual eyes what the *Secret Place* is, you can start to discover how to find this *Heavenly Place*.

The *Secret Place* is described as a **Pavilion** and the **Secret of His Tabernacle** in the following verses:

Psalm 27:4-5 (KJV)

*4 One thing have I desired of the Lord, that will I seek after; that I may dwell in the house of the Lord all the days of my life, to behold the beauty of the Lord, and to enquire in his temple. 5 For in the time of trouble he shall hide me in his **pavilion**: in the **secret of his tabernacle** shall he hide me; he shall set me up upon a rock.*

A *Pavilion* is a covering, hut, lair, hiding place, tent, and place where a person can dwell undetected. God's *Pavilion* is a place where He dwells. The *Secret of His Tabernacle* refers to the Tabernacle God instructed Moses to build on Mount Sinai (The Mountain of God). The Tabernacle of Moses consisted of the *Outer Court*, *Inner Court*, and *Holy of Holies*. More details regarding the Tabernacle of Moses and the Temple that King Solomon built will be given in the next chapter.

Psalm 31 talks of this place as the **Secret of Thy Presence** and uses the word **Pavilion** again to describe the *Secret Place*.

Psalm 31:19-20 (KJV)

*19 Oh how great is thy goodness, which thou hast laid up for them that fear thee; which thou hast wrought for them that trust in thee before the sons of men! 20 Thou shalt hide them in the **secret of thy presence** from the pride of man: thou shalt keep them **secretly in a pavilion** from the strife of tongues.*

This Scripture references the *Secret Place* as being in the very *Presence of God*. The word for *Presence* also means Face. We are instructed to seek the Face of God. Although we can't physically look at the actual Face of God, we can come into His *Presence* and hear His Voice. The Voice of God can also represent God's Face. After Adam sinned in the Garden, when he heard the

Voice of God walking in the Garden, he and his wife Eve hid from the *Presence of the Lord.*

Genesis 3:8 (KJV)
8 And they **heard the voice of the Lord God** *walking in the garden in the cool of the day: and Adam and his wife hid themselves from the* **presence of the Lord God** *amongst the trees of the garden.*

Psalm 32:6-7 refers to the *Secret Place* as **My Hiding Place**. In the **Hiding Place**, God surrounds you with Songs of Deliverance. The *Hiding Place* is a *Secret Covering Place* in God where the Lord provides protection. God Himself is the Covering over the *Hiding Place* as a refuge when we need His help. Songs of Deliverance are prophetic songs from the Lord that defeat the enemy when sung in the *Secret Place*.

Psalm 32:6-7 (KJV)
6 For this shall every one that is godly pray unto thee in a time when thou mayest be found: surely in the floods of great waters they shall not come nigh unto him. 7 Thou art **my hiding place;** *thou shalt preserve me from trouble;* **thou shalt compass me about with songs of deliverance.** *Selah.*

Psalm 81 describes the *Secret Place* as the **Secret Place of Thunder**. His Mighty Works and His Power define the word, Thunder. Thunder is also symbolic of the noise of warfare. Here, we can see that God uses His voice like *Thunder* to awe all of Creation as He acts out punishments against the enemies of those who dwell in His *Secret Place*.

Psalm 81:7 (KJV)

*7 Thou calledst in trouble, and I delivered thee; I answered thee in the **secret place of thunder:** I proved thee at the waters of Meribah. Selah.*

Psalm 119:114 describes God as our **Hiding Place** and **Shield**. In the *Secret Place*, God is your *Hiding Place* and *Shield*. I want to point out that God is a *Hiding Place* for those who are being attacked with the backbiting words of their enemies. Backbiting is malicious talk and slander about someone who is not present. When you are in the *Secret Place,* God becomes your shelter of protection against those who would slander and backbite against you. The *Shield* symbolizes God Himself as a shield of protection and a refuge of escape for the one in the *Secret Place.*

Psalm 119:114 (KJV)

*114 Thou art my **hiding place** and my **shield:** I hope in thy word.*

In His preaching, Jesus used language that referenced the *Secret Place* to describe someone who had a secret walk with God. We know Jesus was dwelling in the *Secret Place* in His Divine relationship with the Father. When Jesus preached the famous Sermon on the Mount, He taught us how to have a private walk with God.

First, Jesus said we should secretly give the poor gifts (alms). Jesus said our Father would reward us openly if we gave secretly. I believe the open reward would be the Heavenly Father supernaturally taking care of our needs because we gave gifts to the poor privately. Anyone dwelling in the *Secret Place* understands the importance of secretly giving to help the needs of others because it is in the heart of God to help those in need. The closer you get to God, the greater your desire to help others will be, but this must be done privately to please God.

Matthew 6:1-4 (KJV)

1 Take heed that ye do not your alms before men, to be seen of them: otherwise ye have no reward of your Father which is in heaven. 2 Therefore when thou doest thine alms, do not sound a trumpet before thee, as the hypocrites do in the synagogues and in the streets, that they may have glory of men. Verily I say unto you, They have their reward. 3 But when thou doest alms, let not thy left hand know what thy right hand doeth: 4 That thine alms may be in **secret***: and thy Father which* **seeth in secret** *himself shall reward thee openly.*

Secondly, Jesus taught us that we should pray in secret. Jesus said those who prayed in secret to God would be rewarded openly. I believe the open reward would be answers to prayers for everyone to see. Whatever you prayed about in secret, God would openly answer your prayers so that it was undeniable that God heard and answered you. Anyone who wants to dwell in the *Secret Place* must have a private place to go to and pray to God. There is a mountain in a park near my home where I spend alone time with God. I go there as many times as I can during the day. I have spent years at this private place of prayer, and I can't even tell you all the holy, life-changing moments I have had with my Heavenly Father.

Jesus referred to people going to a closet in their house to pray secretly, which can also symbolize anywhere private. We know this to be true because when Jesus was on the Earth, He didn't have a house to live in while traveling during His ministry but would still find a private place to pray to His Heavenly Father.

Matthew 6:5-8 (KJV)

5 And when thou prayest, thou shalt not be as the hypocrites are: for they love to pray standing in the synagogues and in the corners of the streets, that they may be seen of men. Verily I say unto you, They have their reward. 6 But thou, when thou prayest, enter into thy closet, and when thou hast shut thy door, pray to thy Father which is in secret; and thy Father which seeth in secret shall reward thee openly. 7 But when ye pray, use not vain repetitions, as the heathen do: for they think that they shall be heard for their much speaking. 8 Be not ye therefore like unto them: for your Father knoweth what things ye have need of, before ye ask him.

The famous Lord's Prayer is one of the most important prayers we must secretly pray. This is a prayer I pray every day. When I wake up, I go into my kitchen and spend alone time with God. During this time, I pray the Lord's Prayer. When you wake up, you should always give your first fruits to God. I do this by praying, and then I get into God's Word before doing anything else. If you are going to dwell in the *Secret Place*, you need to start your day off right. I have spent years praying in the *Secret Place*. I don't want anyone around when I pray, and I don't want anyone to hear me when I am praying.

This is the Lord's Prayer that Jesus commanded us to pray.

Matthew 6:9-13 (KJV)

9 After this manner therefore pray ye: Our Father which art in heaven, Hallowed be thy name. 10 Thy kingdom come, Thy will be done in earth, as it is in heaven. 11 Give us this day our daily bread.

12 And forgive us our debts, as we forgive our debtors. 13 And lead us not into temptation, but deliver us from evil: For thine is the kingdom, and the power, and the glory, for ever. Amen.

Another vital prayer I pray daily is found in the Book of Luke, where Jesus taught His disciples that we should always pray. This is a crucial prayer regarding the Last Days and the things that will happen on the earth.

Luke 21:36 (KJV)

36 Watch ye therefore, and pray always, that ye may be accounted worthy to escape all these things that shall come to pass, and to stand before the Son of man.

Lastly, Jesus taught us that fasting was to be done secretly, and the Father would reward us openly for fasting privately. This open reward can manifest in our prayers being answered because the Bible often mentions prayer and fasting together. The open reward may also refer to God promoting and honoring you. People living in the *Secret Place* would never try to promote themselves but wait for the Lord to advance them. I would rather stay in the *Secret Place* alone with God than attempt to promote myself.

Matthew 6:16-18 (KJV)

*16 Moreover when ye fast, be not, as the hypocrites, of a sad countenance: for they disfigure their faces, that they may appear unto men to fast. Verily I say unto you, They have their reward. 17 But thou, when thou fastest, anoint thine head, and wash thy face; 18 That thou appear not unto men to fast, but unto thy Father which is in **secret**: and thy Father, which **seeth in secret**, shall reward thee openly.*

In the four Gospels, we can observe that Jesus had a very private prayer, giving, and fasting lifestyle because the Father continuously rewarded Him openly for all to see. Jesus was not a hypocrite, and He practiced what He preached. Jesus often withdrew from the crowds and prayed alone to His Heavenly Father. If you desire a close walk with God, you must spend many hours praying alone. A person who loves the *Secret Place* will love to pray. Praying and spending time with God are my favorite things to do. The Bible teaches that those who wait upon the Lord will renew their strength (Isaiah 40:31). You will find supernatural spiritual strength by praying and spending alone time with God. Jesus was strengthened in His Spirit as He spent alone time in the *Secret Place* with His Father and the Holy Spirit.

Mark 1:35 (KJV)
*35 And in the morning, rising up a great while before day, he went out, and **departed into a solitary place, and there prayed.***

Mark 6:45-46 (KJV)
*45 And straightway he constrained his disciples to get into the ship, and to go to the other side before unto Bethsaida, while he sent away the people. 46 And when he had sent them away, **he departed into a mountain to pray.***

Luke 5:15-16 (KJV)
*15 But so much the more went there a fame abroad of him: and great multitudes came together to hear, and to be healed by him of their infirmities. 16 **And he withdrew himself into the wilderness, and prayed.***

Luke 6:12 (KJV)

12 And it came to pass in those days, that he went out into a mountain to pray, and continued all night in prayer to God.

Luke 22:39-46 (KJV)

39 And he came out, and went, as he was wont, to the mount of Olives; and his disciples also followed him. 40 And when he was at the place, he said unto them, Pray that ye enter not into temptation. 41 And he was withdrawn from them about a stone's cast, and kneeled down, and prayed, 42 Saying, Father, if thou be willing, remove this cup from me: nevertheless not my will, but thine, be done. 43 And there appeared an angel unto him from heaven, strengthening him. 44 And being in an agony he prayed more earnestly: and his sweat was as it were great drops of blood falling down to the ground. 45 And when he rose up from prayer, and was come to his disciples, he found them sleeping for sorrow, 46 And said unto them, Why sleep ye? rise and pray, lest ye enter into temptation.

Jesus referred to the *Secret Place* as the *Abiding* when teaching His disciples. The *Abiding* and the *Secret Place* are the same place. Jesus used the word *Abiding* because this is a location you are not supposed to leave. The *Secret Place* is not a place you bounce in and out of. Once you gain access to this Heavenly place, never leave it. Just like in **Psalms 91**, the *Secret Place* is where we are to *dwell* and *abide* all the days of our lives.

Psalm 91:1 (KJV)

1 He that dwelleth in the secret place of the most High shall abide under the shadow of the Almighty.

Dwell means to inhabit, remain, endure, stay, sit down with, be fully present, and live as a permanent resident. When we *Dwell* in the *Secret Place,* we are sheltered by God's protection. *Abide* means to reside, dwell, remain stable in a fixed state, continue, endure, live, and be present. *Abide* describes the secure and peaceful rest of one living close to the Lord. Your life will never be the same when you *Dwell* in the *Secret Place of the Most High* and *Abide under the shadow of the Almighty.*

I have been living in the *Secret Place* for years and have learned to practice staying in God's Presence. God showed me the secrets of how to *Dwell* and *Abide* in the *Secret Place.* You never want to leave this place once you enter this wonderful secret relationship with the Lord. No matter where I am or what I am doing, I stay conscious of Christ in me, my hope of glory.

Jesus often taught His disciples about the *Secret Place* during His ministry. The *Secret Place* is a very real private spiritual location, and Jesus lived there all the days of His life. It was always in the heart of God to teach His people how to dwell in a sacred relationship with Him. Here is a powerful passage of Scripture in the Book of John, where Jesus talks about the **Abiding**, which is the *Secret Place.*

John 15:4-10 (KJV)

*4 **Abide** in me, and I in you. As the branch cannot bear fruit of itself, except it **abide** in the vine; no more can ye, except ye **abide** in me. 5 I am the vine, ye are the branches: He that **abideth** in me, and I in him, the same bringeth forth much fruit: for without me ye can do nothing. 6 If a man **abide** not in me, he is cast forth as a branch, and is withered; and men gather them, and cast them into the fire, and they are burned. 7 If ye **abide** in me, and my words **abide** in you, ye* *shall ask what ye will, and it shall be done unto you. 8 Herein is my Father glorified, that ye bear much fruit; so shall ye be my disciples. 9 As the Father hath loved me, so have I loved you: continue ye in my love. 10 If ye keep my commandments, ye shall **abide** in my love; even as I have kept my Father's commandments, and **abide** in his love.*

The *Secret Place* and the *Abiding* in Christ is a place of love. God is love, and anyone who wants to draw closer to God and dwell in the *Secret Place* must be walking in the love of God. Keeping the Commands of Christ is how you *Abide* in His love. The closer you get to God, the more you will learn He is very loving, thoughtful, and caring. He answers our prayers and works miracles because He loves us. Whatever you are going through, know that God cares for you. When you are in the *Secret Place*, you will experience a satisfying love like you never have before. Multitudes of people are lonely, discouraged, and afraid, but when you enter the *Secret Place*, all loneliness, discouragement, and fear will leave you. The commitment to enter and *Abide* in the *Secret Place* is challenging but well worth it. ***Once I started dwelling in the Secret Place, I found the one whom my soul loves, and I won't let Him go (Song of Solomon 3:4).***

1 John 4:7-8 (KJV)
*7 Beloved, let us **love** one another: for **love** is of God; and every one that **loveth** is born of God, and knoweth God. 8 He that **loveth** not knoweth not God; **for God is love.***

Psalms 91, where the *Secret Place* is mentioned, ends with saying that God will deliver those who set their love upon Him. Setting your love upon the Lord means you are devoted, clinging, relying, delighting, focused, and longing for His Presence while obeying all of the Commands of Christ. A person dwelling in the *Secret Place* doesn't just love the Lord but is in love with the Lord. This means He is their everything, and they don't want to live without Him. They are not satisfied with anything this life has to offer. *Secret Place* love takes you out of this world and brings you to the Throne Room of God, where you lose yourself in Him.

> *Psalm 91:14-16 (KJV)*
>
> *14 Because he hath set his love upon me, therefore will I deliver him: I will set him on high, because he hath known my name. 15 He shall call upon me, and I will answer him: I will be with him in trouble; I will deliver him, and honour him. 16 With long life will I satisfy him, and shew him my salvation.*

Now that we have read multiple Scriptures that describe the *Secret Place*, I will gather all of these thoughts together to gain more insight into this fascinating location created by God. Below is a list of prophetic Divine thoughts about the *Secret Place*.

THE SECRET PLACE IS:

1. A Place Where You Live, Dwell and Remain

2. A Place That You Never Leave

3. A Pavilion

4. His Tabernacle

5. In His Presence

6. A Hiding Place

7. A Place of Thunder (His Power)

8. A Shield

9. A Place of Protection When Under Attack

10. A Place of Protection from Slander and Backbiting

11. Secret Giving to the Poor

12. Secret Prayer

13. Secret Fasting

14. A Place of Abiding in Christ

15. A Place of Abiding in the Words of Christ

16. A Place of Keeping All the Commands of Christ

17. A Place of Abiding in the Love of Christ

The *Secret Place* is revealed in the Scriptures as a Holy Place where a believer sets their love upon God by obeying the Words of Christ. This place is where the believer gives in secret, prays in secret, and fasts in secret. There is no hypocrisy in the *Secret Place* because this faithful believer is in a constant state of humbleness and serving God in the privacy of their heart. This believer also never leaves this location but continuously communicates with God. This is called *praying without ceasing* (1 Thessalonians 5:17).

Once God and the believer enter the *Secret Place* of this special relationship, God promises to protect them from any danger. The *Secret Place* becomes a unique relationship where the believer relies on the Lord to be there for them in their time of need. When the believer hides in the secret *Pavilion* of God's *Presence*, God surrounds them with songs of deliverance.

In this private place, the believer enters a close relationship with the Lord, and they can see the invisible God with their eyes of faith and hear His voice with their ears of faith. This is a sacred *Pavilion* where only the believer and God are allowed to dwell together through Holy Communion in the Spirit. The *Secret Place* is an intimate private relationship with God where He promises to protect believers from harm as they set their love upon Him. Below is a list of words that describe this unique and sacred place of *Holy Communion* only found in God.

THE SECRET PLACE IS A PLACE OF:

1. Lordship
2. Love
3. Trust
4. Commitment
5. Selflessness
6. Loyalty
7. Purity
8. Holiness
9. Righteousness
10. Obedience
11. Servanthood
12. Respect
13. Gentleness
14. Intercession
15. Communication
16. Covenant
17. Communion
18. Truth
19. Honor
20. Openness
21. Kindness
22. Thoughtfulness
23. Giving
24. Devotion
25. Peace
26. Rest
27. Reverence
28. Praise
29. Worship
30. Prayer
31. Intimacy
32. Protection
33. Courage
34. Boldness
35. Strength
36. Inspiration

Anyone given the privilege of accessing the *Secret Place* with God is highly favored. This holy refuge was created so God's people could commune with Him in the *Secret Place* of their hearts. The fact that it is secret reveals that this place is *Extraordinary*. Nothing is more important in this life than entering the **Secret Place of the Most High** and dwelling there all the days of your life.

For many years, I didn't live in the *Secret Place*. I wandered the Earth like countless others, not knowing that God had a special place where I could fellowship with Him. Once I found the *Secret Place*, my life was never the same. I received answers to my questions, and my life made more sense. Rather than running around looking for happiness in fleeting earthly things or people, I found joy in my relationship with God. The world lost all its allure. I realized there was nothing I wanted or needed in this world anymore. Sure, I need things to survive and live, but it is meaningless without God. My private walk with God can never be taken from me. I desire nothing more than to dwell in the house of the Lord all the days of my life to behold the beauty of the Lord and to enquire in His Temple (Psalm 27:4). It's not worth gaining the whole world only to find out you lost your soul.

Matthew 16:26 (KJV)
26 For what is a man profited, if he shall gain the whole world, and lose his own soul? or what shall a man give in exchange for his soul?

This book will be a holy pilgrimage for those who want God more than what this life has to offer. God is calling out to you from the *Secret Place*, and now is the time to leave the world behind and find Christ within you. *The Lord said that if you would seek Him with all of your heart, you would find Him (Jeremiah 29:13).* In this book, I will bring to light from the Scriptures numerous secrets about the *Secret Place* that God has taught me over the years. There are hidden mysteries in this book you may not have known before but prepare yourself to be expanded and challenged. Some of you may already be dwelling in the *Secret Place*, and this book will serve to strengthen your relationship with God. Either way, thank you for the opportunity and privilege to share the secrets of the *Secret Place*.

HE SHALL COVER THEE WITH HIS FEATHERS,
AND UNDER HIS WINGS SHALT THOU TRUST...
PSALM 91:4A

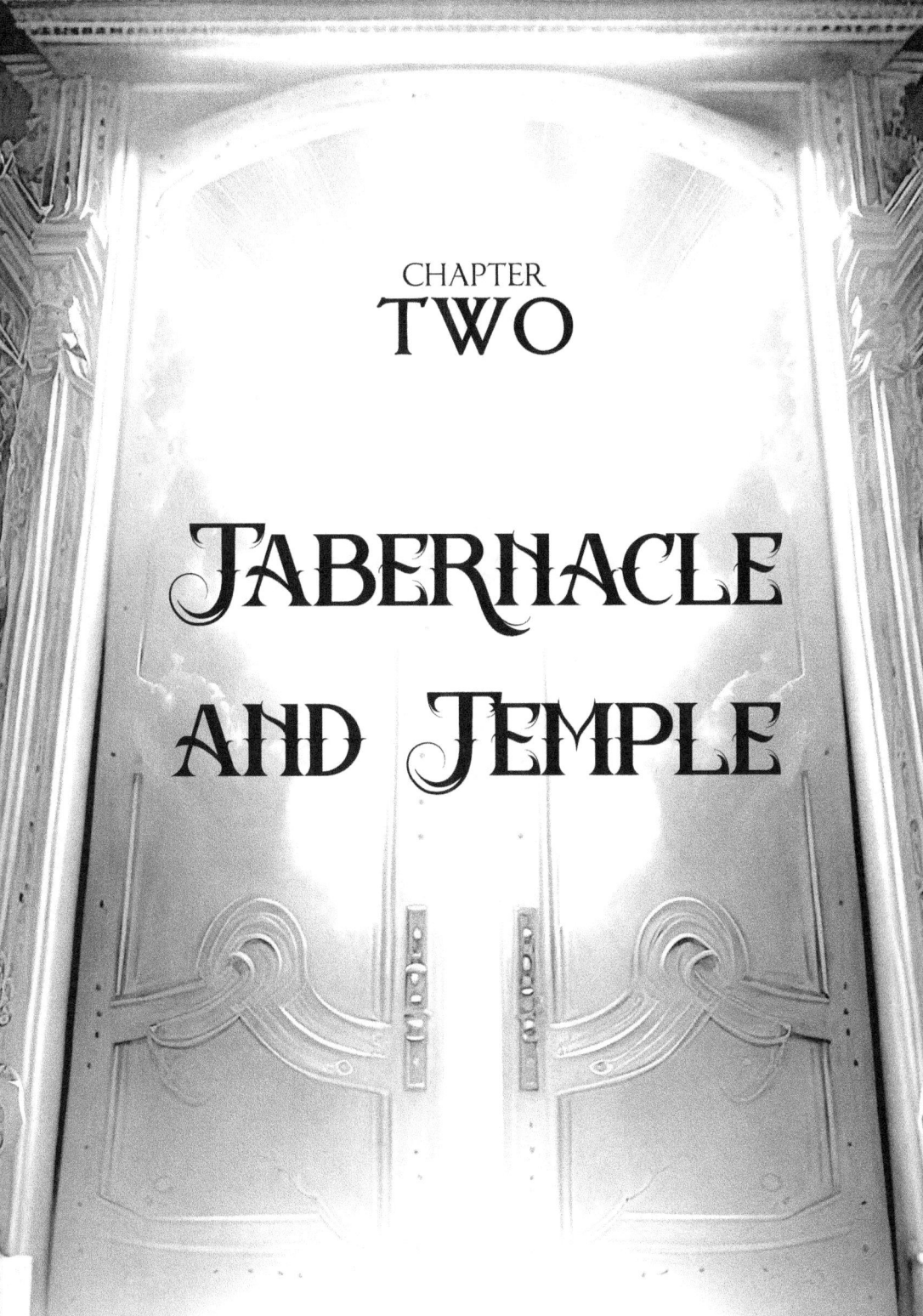

CHAPTER
TWO

TABERNACLE AND TEMPLE

N ow that I have established **WHAT** the *Secret Place* is, we need to know **WHERE** it can be found. The locality of the *Secret Place* was purposely hidden in plain sight by God in the Scriptures. God hid the *Secret Place*, so people must seek Him to discover it. God only allows those searching, hungry, and obedient to find this sacred place. In this chapter, I will reveal where the *Secret Place* is and how you can find its invisible location.

Let's read a verse from the last chapter to gain prophetic insight to discover the location of the *Secret Place*.

> *Psalm 27:4-5 (KJV)*
>
> *4 One thing have I desired of the Lord, that will I seek after; that I may dwell in the **house of the Lord** all the days of my life, to behold the beauty of the Lord, and to **enquire in his temple**. 5 For in the time of trouble he shall hide me in his pavilion: in the **secret of his tabernacle** shall he hide me; he shall set me up upon a rock.*

These insightful verses reveal that the *Secret Place* can be found in the House of the Lord, His Tabernacle, and Temple. We know from the Scriptures that Moses built the Tabernacle from a vision he saw from God when he was on Mount Sinai.

> *Hebrews 8:5 (KJV)*
>
> *5 **Who serve unto the example and shadow of heavenly things**, as Moses was admonished of God when he was about to make **the tabernacle**: for, See, saith he, that thou **make all things according to the pattern shewed to thee in the mount**.*

King Solomon later built the Temple after the pattern of the Tabernacle of Moses with some new additions. The Holy Spirit revealed additional patterns of this New Temple to his father, King David.

> *1 Chronicles 28:11-12 (KJV)*
> *11 Then David gave to Solomon his son the pattern of the porch, and of the houses thereof, and of the treasuries thereof, and of the upper chambers thereof, and of the inner parlours thereof, and of the place of the mercy seat, 12 And **the pattern of all that he had by the spirit**, of the courts of the house of the Lord, and of all the chambers round about, of the treasuries of the house of God, and of the treasuries of the dedicated things:*

Moses was in the *Secret Place* learning about the *Secret Place* as he communed with God for forty days and forty nights on Mount Sinai. Moses was Divinely chosen to understand the mystery of how to dwell with God in the *Secret Place*. God revealed to Moses the pattern of the sacred Tabernacle with its holy artifacts that would conceal the hidden mystery of the *Secret Place*.

> *Acts 7:44 (KJV)*
> *44 Our fathers had the **tabernacle of witness** in the wilderness, as he had appointed, **speaking unto Moses, that he should make it according to the fashion that he had seen.***

The Tabernacle that God instructed Moses to build included an *Outer Court*, *Inner Court*, and *Holy of Holies*. The Tabernacle was constructed to be a *Holy Place* where the children of Israel could come and meet with God by offering sacrifices in the Outer Court. However, the Inner Court was only accessible to certain priests from the tribe of Levi, and the Holy of Holies could only be entered once a year by a High Priest. A thick Veil separated the Holy of Holies from the Inner Court. The Holy of Holies was the most sacred *Secret Place* within the Tabernacle of Moses and in the Temple that King Solomon built.

Let's examine the Divine pattern of the Tabernacle and what was found in the *Outer Court, Inner Court*, and *Holy of Holies.* God prophetically instructed Moses to build the Tabernacle for Divine purposes, which later would be revealed in the New Testament. These Divine Purposes have everything to do with the *Secret Place.* Once your spiritual eyes have been opened, you will understand why God built the Tabernacle of Moses and Temple of King Solomon.

Let's explore each holy location in the Tabernacle that Moses was instructed to build and what was in each place.

THE OUTER COURT

Only two holy artifacts were found in the Outer Court. The first artifact was the *Bronze Altar,* just inside the gate. The second artifact was the *Bronze Laver,* where the Priests of the Lord washed themselves before entering the Inner Court. The holy artifacts found in the Outer Court were made of bronze, representing God's righteous judgment when dealing with sin. God's righteous judgments are perfectly just while being tempered with mercy.

BRONZE ALTAR

The Bronze Altar (Brazen Altar) was an altar where the ancient Israelites sacrificed animals to atone for their sins. The fire in the Bronze Altar could never go out. Animals were first sacrificed and then burned on the Bronze Altar. Sin is a serious matter, and only the shedding of blood, which stands for life, could pay for the penalty of sin. The Israelites were required to lay their hand on the animal before it was sacrificed to atone for their sins. Today, before you can enter the Holy of Holies of your own Temple *(Secret Place)*, your sins must be atoned for by the sacrifice of Christ.

Exodus 27:1-2 (KJV)

*1 And thou shalt make an **altar** of shittim wood, five cubits long, and five cubits broad; the altar shall be foursquare: and the height thereof shall be three cubits. 2 And thou shalt make the horns of it upon the four corners thereof: his horns shall be of the same: **and thou shalt overlay it with brass.***

Leviticus 1:1-4 (KJV)

*1 And the Lord called unto Moses, and spake unto him out of the tabernacle of the congregation, saying, 2 Speak unto the children of Israel, and say unto them, If any man of you bring an offering unto the Lord, ye shall bring your offering of the cattle, even of the herd, and of the flock. 3 If his offering be a burnt sacrifice of the herd, let him offer a male without blemish: **he shall offer it of his own voluntary will at the door of the tabernacle of the congregation before the Lord.** 4 And he shall put his hand upon the head of the burnt offering; and it shall be accepted for him to make atonement for him.*

BRONZE LAVER

The Bronze Laver (Brazen Laver) was located between the Inner Court (The Holy Place) of the Tabernacle of Moses and the Bronze Altar in the Outer Court. The Bronze Laver was filled with water, and because of the bronze, the water reflected like a mirror. The priests had to look at themselves as they washed their hands and feet to prepare to enter the Holy Place (Inner Court). We, as New Testament priests, have to look into the mirror of the Word of God and cleanse ourselves before we can enter the Holy Place of our own Temple.

Now it makes sense when Jesus washed the Apostles' feet the night before He went to the Cross and said they were clean. Jesus cleaned the Apostles' feet and continually washed them with the Word of God as He taught them the Truth. This is called the washing of the water of the Word (Ephesians 5:26-27 KJV). Priests had to bathe their hands and feet in the water from Bronze Laver before offering sacrifices and entering the Inner Court of the Tabernacle. The washing of their hands and feet represented sanctification or becoming holy. The Bronze Laver was only for the priests of the Lord, and if they didn't wash themselves beforehand, they could die when entering the Inner Court of the Tabernacle.

Exodus 30:17-21 (KJV)

*17 And the Lord spake unto Moses, saying, 18 Thou shalt also make a **laver of brass**, and his foot also of brass, to wash withal: and thou shalt put it between the tabernacle of the congregation and the altar, and thou shalt put water therein. 19 For Aaron and his sons shall wash their hands and their feet thereat: 20 When they go into the tabernacle of the congregation, they shall wash with water, that they die not; or when they come near to the altar to minister, to burn offering made by fire unto the Lord: 21 So they shall wash their hands and their feet, that they die not: and it shall be a statute for ever to them, even to him and to his seed throughout their generations.*

35

THE INNER COURT – THE HOLY PLACE

Three Holy artifacts were found in the Inner Court. The Inner Court was also called the Holy Place. The three Holy artifacts in the Holy Place (Inner Court) were *The Table of Showbread, The Golden Candlestick,* and *The Altar of Incense.* These three Holy artifacts were made of gold, representing God's *Divinity, Kingship, Royalty, Holiness,* and *Righteousness.* Before the priests entered The Holy Place, they had to sacrifice an animal on the *Brazen Altar* to atone for their sin(s) and wash themselves with the water from the *Brazen Laver.*

TABLE OF SHOWBREAD (SHEWBREAD)

The Table of Showbread was constructed of acacia wood overlaid with pure gold, and the bread on this Holy Table was called "The Bread of His Presence." The priests had to place twelve loaves of bread made from fine flour daily on this Holy Table with frankincense. The twelve loaves represented the twelve tribes of Israel, and the frankincense symbolized the priesthood. The "Bread of His Presence" was a reminder of God's provision, and it also represented the Word of God because God said, *"That man shall not live by bread alone but by every word that proceeded out of His mouth."* *Deuteronomy 8:3 (KJV).* As priests of the Lord, we must feed on the revelation of God's Word daily.

> *Exodus 25:23-30 (KJV)*
> *23 Thou shalt also make a table of shittim wood: two cubits shall be the length thereof, and a cubit the breadth thereof, and a cubit and a half the height thereof. 24 And thou shalt overlay it with pure gold, and make thereto a crown of gold round about. 25 And thou shalt make unto it a border of an hand breadth round about, and thou shalt make a golden crown to the border thereof round about.*

*26 And thou shalt make for it four rings of gold, and put the rings in the four corners that are on the four feet thereof. 27 Over against the border shall the rings be for places of the staves to bear the table. 28 And thou shalt make the staves of shittim wood, and overlay them with gold, that the table may be borne with them. 29 And thou shalt make the dishes thereof, and spoons thereof, and covers thereof, and bowls thereof, to cover withal: of pure gold shalt thou make them. 30 And thou shalt set upon the **table shewbread** before me alway.*

Leviticus 24:5-7 (KJV)
5 And thou shalt take fine flour, and bake twelve cakes thereof: two tenth deals shall be in one cake. 6 And thou shalt set them in two rows, six on a row, upon the pure table before the LORD. 7 And thou shalt put pure frankincense upon each row, that it may be on the bread for a memorial, even an offering made by fire unto the LORD.

GOLDEN CANDLESTICK

This unique Golden Candlestick was designed with seven branches and handcrafted from one piece of beaten pure gold. The bowl on the top of each branch was filled with olive oil to be lit to give light in the Holy Place (Inner Court). The purpose of this Golden Candlestick was to provide light for the priests because no natural sunlight was allowed in the Holy Place. The olive oil also represented the holy anointing of the Spirit of God. The Light from the Golden Candlestick represented Christ being the Light of the world. Without the Light of Christ, we would all be walking in the darkness of sin. The Light of Christ and His teachings brought Light to this dark world and represents illumination, revelation, truth, holiness, justice, and righteousness (John 3:19-21; Ephesians 5:8-14).

Exodus 25:31-40 (KJV)

*31 And thou shalt make a **candlestick** of pure gold: of beaten work shall the **candlestick** be made: his shaft, and his branches, his bowls, his knops, and his flowers, shall be of the same. 32 And six branches shall come out of the sides of it; three branches of the **candlestick** out of the one side, and three branches of the **candlestick** out of the other side: 33 Three bowls made like unto almonds, with a knop and a flower in one branch; and three bowls made like almonds in the other branch, with a knop and a flower: so in the six branches that come out of the **candlestick**. 34 And in the **candlesticks** shall be four bowls made like unto almonds, with their knops and their flowers. 35 And there shall be a knop under two branches of the same, and a knop under two branches of the same, and a knop under two branches of the same, according to the six branches that proceed out of the **candlestick**. 36 Their knops and their branches shall be of the same: all it shall be one beaten work of pure gold. 37 And thou shalt make the seven lamps thereof: and they shall light the lamps thereof, that they may give light over against it. 38 And the tongs thereof, and the snuffdishes thereof, shall be of pure gold. 39 Of a talent of pure gold shall he make it, with all these vessels. 40 And look that thou make them after their pattern, which was shewed thee in the mount.*

The Golden Candlestick also represents the Seven Spirits of God before the Throne of God.

Revelation 1:4 (KJV)

*4 John to the seven churches which are in Asia: Grace be unto you, and peace, from him which is, and which was, and which is to come; **and from the seven Spirits which are before his throne;***

Each of the seven branches of the Golden Candlestick symbolizes a different characteristic and facet of the Spirit of God. The number seven in the Bible refers to perfection and completion. The Spirit of the Lord is perfect and complete, as identified in the Book of Isaiah by His Seven attributes. *(Isaiah 11:2 - 1. The Spirit of the Lord 2. The Spirit of Wisdom 3. The Spirit of Understanding 4. The Spirit of Counsel 5. The Spirit of Might 6. The Spirit of Knowledge 7. The Spirit of the Fear of the Lord)* The Seven Spirits of God, which are the attributes of the Anointing of the Holy Spirit, were and are upon the ministry of Jesus. When you dwell in the *Secret Place,* these Seven Spirits will be present in your life as they were in the life of Jesus.

Isaiah 11:1-3 (KJV)

*1 And there shall come forth a rod out of the stem of Jesse, and a Branch shall grow out of his roots: 2 **And the spirit of the Lord shall rest upon him, the spirit of wisdom and understanding, the spirit of counsel and might, the spirit of knowledge and of the fear of the Lord;** 3 And shall make him of quick understanding in the fear of the Lord: and he shall not judge after the sight of his eyes, neither reprove after the hearing of his ears:*

ALTAR OF INCENSE

The Altar of Incense was made of acacia wood overlaid with pure gold and was positioned in the Inner Court before the Veil that separated the Holy of Holies from the Holy Place (Inner Court). The Lord required that a special incense be burned on this Altar. The High Priest also offered blood on the horns of the Altar of Incense once a year to atone for the sins of the children of Israel.

Exodus 30:1-10 (KJV)

*1 And thou shalt make an **altar** to burn incense upon: of shittim wood shalt thou make it. 2 A cubit shall be the length thereof, and a cubit the breadth thereof; foursquare shall it be: and two cubits shall be the height thereof: the horns thereof shall be of the same. 3 And thou shalt overlay it with pure gold, the top thereof, and the sides thereof round about, and the horns thereof; and thou shalt make unto it a crown of gold round about. 4 And two golden rings shalt thou make to it under the crown of it, by the two corners thereof, upon the two sides of it shalt thou make it; and they shall be for places for the staves to bear it withal. 5 And thou shalt make the staves of shittim wood, and overlay them with gold. 6 And thou shalt put it before the vail that is by the ark of the testimony, before the mercy seat that is over the testimony, where I will meet with thee. 7 And Aaron shall burn thereon sweet incense every morning: when he dresseth the lamps, he shall burn incense upon it. 8 And when Aaron lighteth the lamps at even, he shall burn incense upon it, a perpetual incense before the Lord throughout your generations. 9 Ye shall offer no strange incense thereon, nor burnt sacrifice, nor meat offering; neither shall ye pour drink offering thereon. 10 And Aaron shall make an atonement upon the horns of it once in a year with the blood of the sin offering of atonements: once in the year shall he make atonement upon it throughout your generations: it is most holy unto the Lord.*

The smoke that arose from the Altar of Incense represented the prayers of God's people. Holy prayers come up before God as a sweet fragrance. The prayers of New Testament believers come up before God as a sweet fragrance in the Temple of their own bodies before the Throne of God.

> *Revelation 8:3-4 (KJV)*
>
> *3 And another angel came and stood at the altar, having a golden censer; **and there was given unto him much incense, that he should offer it with the prayers of all saints upon the golden altar which was before the throne. 4 And the smoke of the incense, which came with the prayers of the saints, ascended up before God out of the angel's hand.***

THE VEIL (VAIL)

The Veil separated the Holy Place from the Holy of Holies. Priests from the Tribe of Levi were allowed to minister daily in the Holy Place (Inner Court) but were not allowed permission to enter the Holy of Holies. Only the High Priest could go into the Holy of Holies once a year on the Day of Atonement to make atonement for the sins of God's people. The Veil was a large curtain made of the finest twined linen of costly blue, scarlet, and purple dye. It was also skillfully crafted and interwoven with images of Cherubims, the angels of God.

> *Exodus 36:35 (KJV)*
>
> *35 And he made a vail of blue, and purple, and scarlet, and fine twined linen: with cherubims made he it of cunning work.*

The New Testament says the Veil was hung to show that man could not access the Holy of Holies in the Old Covenant.

Hebrews 9:6-8 (KJV)

*6 Now when these things were thus ordained, the priests went always into the first tabernacle, accomplishing the service of God. 7 But into the second went the high priest alone once every year, not without blood, which he offered for himself, and for the errors of the people: 8 **The Holy Ghost this signifying, that the way into the holiest of all was not yet made manifest, while as the first tabernacle was yet standing:***

When Jesus died on the Cross, the Veil in the Temple was torn in half, signifying we could now have access to God. Understanding what happened with Christ on the Cross is significant regarding the *Secret Place*.

Matthew 27:50-51 (KJV)

*50 Jesus, when he had cried again with a loud voice, yielded up the ghost. 51 **And, behold, the veil of the temple was rent in twain from the top to the bottom;** and the earth did quake, and the rocks rent;*

THE HOLY OF HOLIES

The Holy of Holies was the most sacred place in Moses' Tabernacle and King Solomon's Temple. The Holy of Holies was where the Ark of the Covenant rested. The Presence of God hovered between the two Cherubims in the center of the Mercy Seat, which sat on top of the Ark of the Covenant. The Ark of the Covenant was fashioned of acacia wood covered in pure gold, representing God's *Divinity, Kingship, Royalty, Holiness,* and *Righteousness.*

ARK OF THE COVENANT

The Ark of the Covenant was a golden chest which contained the two tablets with the Ten Commandments written on them. The Ten Commandments were the Ten foundational Laws that God spoke from His mouth on Mount Sinai to the children of Israel. This experience was so terrifying to the children of Israel that they asked Moses not to let God talk to them anymore. They wanted God to speak to Moses, and then Moses could tell them what God said. In his anger, Moses broke the first set of Ten Commandments written on stone tablets by the finger of God when he saw God's people worshipping a golden calve as he came down from Mount Sinai. Moses had to cut out two more stone tablets, and God rewrote the Ten Commandments on these two new stone tablets. These are the second and final copies of the Ten Commandments placed inside the Ark of the Covenant. Later, Aaron's rod that budded, and a golden pot of manna was placed in the Ark of the Covenant.

Hebrews 9:3-5 (KJV)

*3 And after the second veil, the tabernacle which is called the Holiest of all; 4 **Which had the golden censer, and the ark of the covenant overlaid round about with gold, wherein was the golden pot that had manna, and Aaron's rod that budded, and the tables of the covenant;** 5 And over it the cherubims of glory shadowing the mercyseat; of which we cannot now speak particularly.*

God said He would meet and commune from above the Mercy Seat, positioned on top of the Ark of the Covenant.

Exodus 25:10-22 (KJV)

*10 And they shall make an **ark** of shittim wood: two cubits and a half shall be the length thereof, and a cubit and a half the breadth thereof, and a cubit and a half the height thereof. 11 And thou shalt overlay it with pure gold, within and without shalt thou overlay it,* *and shalt make upon it a crown of gold round about. 12 And thou shalt cast four rings of gold for it, and put them in the four corners thereof; and two rings shall be in the one side of it, and two rings in the other side of it. 13 And thou shalt make staves of shittim wood, and overlay them with gold. 14 And thou shalt put the staves into the rings by the sides of the **ark**, that the **ark** may be borne with them. 15 The staves shall be in the rings of the **ark**: they shall not be taken from it. 16 And thou shalt put into the **ark the testimony** which I shall give thee. 17 And thou shalt make a mercy seat of pure gold: two cubits and a half shall be the length thereof, and a cubit and a half the breadth thereof. 18 And thou shalt make two cherubims of gold, of beaten work shalt thou make them, in the two ends of the mercy seat. 19 And make one cherub on the one end, and the other cherub on the other end: even of the mercy seat shall ye make the cherubims on the two ends thereof. 20 And the cherubims shall stretch forth their wings on high, covering the mercy seat with their wings, and their faces shall look one to another; toward the mercy seat shall the faces of the cherubims be. 21 And thou shalt put the mercy seat above upon the **ark**; and in the **ark** thou shalt put the testimony that I shall give thee. 22 And there I will meet with thee, and I will commune with thee from above the mercy seat, from between the two cherubims which are upon the **ark of the testimony**, of all things which I will give thee in commandment unto the children of Israel.*

Now, we must ask what the Tabernacle and its holy artifacts have to do with the *Secret Place?* The Tabernacle of Moses and the Temple of King Solomon have everything to do with the *Secret Place*. **THIS IS WHERE IT GETS FASCINATING!** If you are going to dwell in the *Secret Place*, you will have to understand what the Tabernacle of Moses and the Temple of King Solomon represented.

The New Testament reveals that the bodies of believers in Christ now become the Temple of God. It was 40 years after the death of Christ that the Romans in 70 A.D. destroyed the Second Temple in Jerusalem. There has not been a Temple in Jerusalem for around 2,000 years. Jesus prophesied, during His earthly ministry, the destruction of the Second Temple that King Herod expanded.

Matthew 24:1-2 (KJV)

*1 And Jesus went out, and departed from the **temple:** and his disciples came to him for to shew him the buildings of the **temple.** 2 And Jesus said unto them, See ye not all these things? verily I say unto you, **There shall not be left here one stone upon another, that shall not be thrown down.***

When Christ died, He fulfilled and did away with the Old Covenant with its Temple (Hebrews 8:13). New Testament believers have become the very Temple of God, which is essential to know if you are going to understand the mysteries of the *Secret Place.*

1 Corinthians 3:16-17 (KJV)

*16 **Know ye not that ye are the temple of God,** and that the Spirit of God dwelleth in you? 17 If any man defile **the temple of God,** him shall God destroy; for **the temple of God** is holy, **which temple ye are.***

1 Corinthians 6:19-20 (KJV)

*19 What? **know ye not that your body is the temple of the Holy Ghost which is in you,** which ye have of God, and ye are not your* *own? 20 For ye are bought with a price: therefore glorify God in your body, and in your spirit, which are God's.*

Now you can see the importance of why I walked you through each location and the artifacts of the Tabernacle of Moses. At the beginning of this chapter, I showed you the verse where the *Secret Place* is revealed as the Tabernacle of God, which later became the Temple that King Solomon built.

Psalm 27:4-5 (KJV)

*4 One thing have I desired of the Lord, that will I seek after; that I may dwell in the **house of the Lord** all the days of my life, to behold the beauty of the Lord, and to **enquire in his temple**. 5 For in the time of trouble he shall hide me in his pavilion: in the **secret of his tabernacle** shall he hide me; he shall set me up upon a rock.*

When Jesus died, the Veil that separated the Holy Place (Inner Court) from the Holy of Holies was torn in two. This means the Temple of your body, the Holy Place (Inner Court), and the Holy of Holies have become one place within you. This place is called the *Secret Place* within the Temple of your own body. The *Secret Place* is where God resides within the body of the believer. However, with this being said, there were laws that governed the Tabernacle of Moses, and there are also laws that govern the *Secret Place* within the New Testament believer. The Law of Moses was written as a shadow of things to come, and we need the Law to help us understand the *Secret Place*. Even though we are no longer under the Old Testament Law, it still contains secrets we can learn about how to dwell in the *Secret Place of the Most High*.

Hebrews 10:1 (KJV)

*1 **For the law having a shadow of good things to come**, and not the very image of the things, can never with those sacrifices which they* *offered year by year continually make the comers thereunto perfect.*

You can learn powerful mysteries about the *Secret Place* by understanding The Tabernacle of Moses and The Temple of King Solomon because your body is now the Holy Temple of God. The Old Testament was written as a shadow of the good things to come in the New Covenant. To know God and the *Secret Place*, you need the Old Covenant (Old Testament) and the New Covenant (New Testament). The entire Christian Bible is required to understand the *Secret Place*.

I have gone into great detail about what the *Secret Place* is and where it is located; now, we can move into the deep mysteries of God concerning this Holy Place. Your *Secret Place* relationship with God is taking place in your body. The rest of this book will be a discovery of what God intended for you from the very beginning and how to have a *Secret Place* relationship with Himself within the Temple of your own body. The *Secret Place* is not visible to the naked eye because it is a place deep inside your spirit where the Lord manifests Himself to you in the Holy of Holies of your heart.

Early on in the ministry of Jesus, when He preached in the Temple of King Herod, He revealed that His body was the Temple of God. (The Second Temple was rebuilt 70 years after the first Temple of King Solomon was destroyed by the Babylonians in 586 B.C.) Jesus told the Jews on that day that if they destroyed this Temple, He would raise it up in three days. When Jesus made this statement, He was alluding to the Temple of His body. The Jews thought He was referring to the Second Temple that King Herod had expanded for over forty-six years. Jesus was referring to Himself being crucified and buried before being risen in three days. The religious leaders of Jesus' day had no idea that the Temple they were worshiping God in was a representation of the body of Jesus.

John 2:13-22 (KJV)

*13 And the Jews' passover was at hand, and Jesus went up to Jerusalem, 14 And found in the **temple** those that sold oxen and sheep and doves, and the changers of money sitting: 15 And when he had made a scourge of small cords, he drove them all out of the **temple**, and the sheep, and the oxen; and poured out the changers' money, and overthrew the tables; 16 And said unto them that sold doves, Take these things hence; make not my Father's house an house of merchandise. 17 And his disciples remembered that it was written, The zeal of thine house hath eaten me up. 18 Then answered the Jews and said unto him, What sign shewest thou unto us, seeing that thou doest these things? 19 Jesus answered and said unto them, **Destroy this temple, and in three days I will raise it up. 20 Then said the Jews, Forty and six years was this temple in building, and wilt thou rear it up in three days? 21 But he spake of the temple of his body.** 22 When therefore he was risen from the dead, his disciples remembered that he had said this unto them; and they believed the scripture, and the word which Jesus had said.*

When Jesus rose from the dead, He sprinkled His blood on the hearts of His believers and gave them the Holy Spirit to dwell on the inside of their bodies. When this happened, the believer became **THE HOLY TEMPLE OF GOD**. The believer's body became God's dwelling place, and a physical Temple on the Earth was no longer needed. God was now dwelling on the inside of His children in the Temple of their bodies, making them sons of God.

The mystery of the *Secret Place* is now unlocked with the knowledge of us being the Temple of God. With this prophetic insight, we can see why the Law of Moses was written. The Law of Moses was written to help us understand what was going to happen inside the New Testament believers' bodies. *This Astounding Revelation Changes Everything!*

The *Secret Place* is the Holy of Holies, and the Holy Place is found within your own body's Temple. As you read, the priest could not enter the Holy Place (Inner Court) unless they first sacrificed at the Brazen Altar and washed in the Brazen Laver. You also cannot enter your own Holy of Holies or Holy Place unless your sin is atoned for and you have cleansed yourself with the washing of the water by the Word. You must adhere to the Laws of God if you want to enter your *Secret Place* inside the Temple of your body.

It is revealed in the Book of Revelations that God has made us kings and priests in the New Covenant.

Revelation 1:5-6 (KJV)
*5 And from Jesus Christ, who is the faithful witness, and the first begotten of the dead, and the prince of the kings of the earth. Unto him that loved us, and washed us from our sins in his own blood, 6 **And hath made us kings and priests unto God and his Father;** to him be glory and dominion for ever and ever. Amen.*

Revelation 5:9-10 (KJV)
*9 And they sung a new song, saying, Thou art worthy to take the book, and to open the seals thereof: for thou wast slain, and hast redeemed us to God by thy blood out of every kindred, and tongue, and people, and nation; 10 **And hast made us unto our God kings and priests:** and we shall reign on the earth.*

The Apostle Peter said that we are a holy and royal priesthood.

1 Peter 2:5 (KJV)

*5 Ye also, as lively stones, are built up a spiritual house, an **holy priesthood**, to offer up spiritual sacrifices, acceptable to God by Jesus Christ.*

1 Peter 2:9 (KJV)

*9 But ye are a chosen generation, a **royal priesthood**, an holy nation, a peculiar people; that ye should shew forth the praises of him who hath called you out of darkness into his marvellous light:*

God has made you the priest of your own Temple, and Jesus is your High Priest. If you want to enter into the Holy Place and the Holy of Holies of your own body, which is the *Secret Place*, you must acknowledge there are Laws, rules, and guidelines that must be obeyed. If you violate any of these Laws, rules, and guidelines, you cannot dwell in the *Secret Place*, and certain violations of God's laws could even cost you your life. The *Secret Place* is very sacred, and once you know what God expects of His New Testament priests to dwell there, your life will never be the same. Jesus died so we could enter into an *Everlasting New Covenant* as His loyal disciples and fellowship with God Himself as priests in the Temple of our own body.

When Jesus died, the Veil in the Temple was torn in two, which meant that the Holy Place (Inner Court) and the Holy of Holies became one Holy Place. This means that as New Testament priests, we can now access the Ark of the Covenant, located in our Holy of Holies, not just Jesus, our High Priest. In the Old Covenant, the High Priest could only go into the Holy of Holies once a year, so the Levitical priests had no access to the Holy of Holies. New Testament priestly believers can now access God in the *Secret Place* of the Holy Temple of their body.

Hebrews 9:6-8 (KJV)

*6 Now when these things were thus ordained, **the priests went always into the first tabernacle, accomplishing the service of God.** 7 But into the second went the high priest alone once every year, not without blood, which he offered for himself, and for the errors of the people: 8 The Holy Ghost this signifying, that the way into the holiest of all was not yet made manifest, while as the first tabernacle was yet standing:*

The *Secret Place* and your body being a Temple of the Holy Spirit was so valuable to God that He sent His Only Begotten Son to die for us so our bodies could become the Holy Temple of God. We can now enter into this Holy Covenant, where we have full access to God Himself through the portal of our own body. Once you comprehend what is at stake in the revelation of the *Secret Place*, you must diligently study and learn everything you can to maintain this privileged access. Old Testament priests and High Priests studied the Law of Moses regularly to learn how not to violate any of the Laws of God concerning His Tabernacle, which later was replaced by the Temple of King Solomon.

Joshua, the servant of Moses, was fully aware of the importance of the Tabernacle. Joshua stayed in the Tabernacle, even when Moses returned to the camp. We must be like Joshua, remain in the *Secret Place*, and never leave this Holy Place.

Exodus 33:11 (KJV)

*11 And the Lord spake unto Moses face to face, as a man speaketh unto his friend. And he turned again into the camp: **but his servant***

Joshua, the son of Nun, a young man, departed not out of the tabernacle.

God has sent me on a mission to help His people become aware of the spiritual importance of the *Secret Place*. I am also called to teach His people the guidelines, rules, and laws that govern the *Secret Place*. The rest of this book is full of vital and valuable secrets you need to know about the **Secret Place of the Most High.** Understanding these secrets will help you gain revelational insight so you can never lose access to the *Secret Place*. Prepare to learn how to have the most beautiful and intimate relationship with your Maker you could ever imagine. **WHATEVER THE COST, IT IS WORTH IT!**

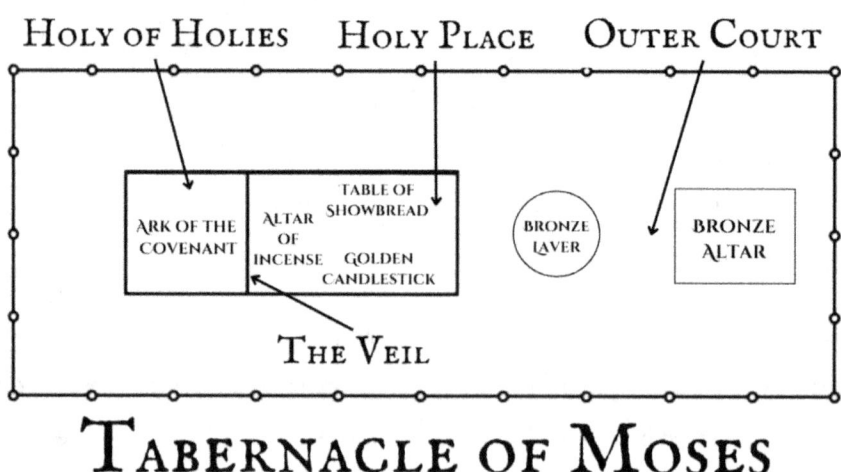

HOLY OF HOLIES   HOLY PLACE   OUTER COURT

ARK OF THE COVENANT — ALTAR OF INCENSE — TABLE OF SHOWBREAD — GOLDEN CANDLESTICK — BRONZE LAVER — BRONZE ALTAR

THE VEIL

TABERNACLE OF MOSES

CHAPTER
THREE

ARK OF THE
COVENANT

The *Ark of the Covenant* in the Old Testament is the only holy artifact placed in the Holy of Holies, which is the *Secret Place*. The Holy of Holies is the heart of the *Secret Place* found in the Tabernacle of Moses and the Temple that King Solomon built. The believer's body becomes the Temple of God in the New Covenant. We have the astonishing privilege of housing in the Temple of our bodies what the *Ark of the Covenant* represents, which is the Holy Spirit. In this chapter, I will go into more detail about the mysteries of the *Ark of the Covenant* to fully understand the *Secret Place*.

The *Ark of the Covenant* was a box or chest made of acacia wood and overlaid with pure gold. The *Ark of the Covenant* was also called the *Ark of the Testimony*. Testimony was a term used to describe the Ten Commandments written on tablets of stone by the finger of God. The Ten Commandments were made up of the Five Commandments on how humankind should behave towards God and the other Five Commandments on how people should treat each other. A covenant is a verbal binding agreement in which there are blessings if kept and curses if broken. The Ten Commandments were audibly spoken by God from Mount Sinai so that all of the children of Israel could hear and obey them. This event was so dreadful to the children of Israel that they feared they would die, and they asked Moses to speak to them instead of God.

Exodus 20:1-19 (KJV)
1 And God spake all these words, saying, 2 I am the LORD thy God, which have brought thee out of the land of Egypt, out of the house of bondage. 3 Thou shalt have no other gods before me. 4 Thou shalt not make unto thee any graven image, or any likeness of any thing that is in heaven above, or that is in the earth beneath, or that

is in the water under the earth: 5 Thou shalt not bow down thyself to them, nor serve them: for I the LORD thy God am a jealous God, visiting the iniquity of the fathers upon the children unto the third and fourth generation of them that hate me; 6 And shewing mercy unto thousands of them that love me, and keep my commandments. 7 Thou shalt not take the name of the LORD thy God in vain; for the LORD will not hold him guiltless that taketh his name in vain. 8 Remember the sabbath day, to keep it holy. 9 Six days shalt thou labour, and do all thy work: 10 But the seventh day is the sabbath of the LORD thy God: in it thou shalt not do any work, thou, nor thy son, nor thy daughter, thy manservant, nor thy maidservant, nor thy cattle, nor thy stranger that is within thy gates: 11 For in six days the LORD made heaven and earth, the sea, and all that in them is, and rested the seventh day: wherefore the LORD blessed the sabbath day, and hallowed it. 12 Honour thy father and thy mother: that thy days may be long upon the land which the LORD thy God giveth thee. 13 Thou shalt not kill. 14 Thou shalt not commit adultery. 15 Thou shalt not steal. 16 Thou shalt not bear false witness against thy neighbour. 17 Thou shalt not covet thy neighbour's house, thou shalt not covet thy neighbour's wife, nor his manservant, nor his maidservant, nor his ox, nor his ass, nor any thing that is thy neighbour's. 18 And all the people saw the thunderings, and the lightnings, and the noise of the trumpet, and the mountain smoking: and when the people saw it, they removed, and stood afar off. 19 And they said unto Moses, Speak thou with us, and we will hear: but let not God speak with us, lest we die.

After this historical event of God speaking from Heaven, Moses went up to Mount Sinai for forty days and forty nights. During this time, God wrote the Ten Commandments on two tables of stone and called them the Two Tables of Testimony. The word Testimony means witness. The stone tablets were a witness of the Ten Commandments that God commanded the children of Israel to obey when He spoke to them from Mount Sinai.

Exodus 31:18 (KJV)

*18 And he gave unto Moses, when he had made an end of communing with him upon mount Sinai, **two tables of testimony, tables of stone, written with the finger of God.***

Exodus 32:15-16 (KJV)

*15 And Moses turned, and went down from the mount, and the **two tables of the testimony** were in his hand: the tables were written on both their sides; on the one side and on the other were they written. 16 **And the tables were the work of God**, and **the writing was the writing of God, graven upon the tables.***

God also called these two tablets of stone the Tables of the Covenant. This is why the *Ark* that contained the Ten Commandment is called the *Ark of the Covenant.* The Covenant has everything to do with the Ten Commandments.

Deuteronomy 9:11 (KJV)

*11 And it came to pass at the end of forty days and forty nights, **that the LORD gave me the two tables of stone**, even the **tables of the covenant.***

Hebrews 9:3-5 (KJV)

*3 And after the second veil, the tabernacle which is called the Holiest of all; 4 Which had the golden censer, and the **ark of the covenant** overlaid round about with gold, wherein was the golden pot that had manna, and Aaron's rod that budded, and **the tables of the covenant**; 5 And over it the cherubims of glory shadowing the mercyseat; of which we cannot now speak particularly.*

Moses broke the first set of the Ten Commandments written on stone when he came down from the Mountain of God and saw the children of Israel worshiping a golden calf.

Exodus 32:19 (KJV)

*19 And it came to pass, as soon as he came nigh unto the camp, that he saw the calf, and the dancing: **and Moses' anger waxed hot, and he cast the tables out of his hands, and brake them beneath the mount.***

God commanded Moses to make two more tables of stone because he broke the first set, and God rewrote the Ten Commandments on these two new tablets. These two new stone tablets were placed inside the *Ark of the Covenant.*

Deuteronomy 10:1-5 (KJV)

*1 At that time the LORD said unto me, **Hew thee two tables of stone like unto the first**, and come up unto me into the mount, and make thee an **ark** of wood. 2 **And I will write on the tables the words that were in the first tables which thou brakest, and thou shalt put them in the ark.** 3 And I made an **ark** of shittim wood, **and hewed two tables of stone like unto the first**, and went up into the mount, **having the two tables in mine hand. 4 And he wrote on the***

tables, according to the first writing, the ten commandments,
which the LORD spake unto you in the mount out of the midst of
the fire in the day of the assembly: and the LORD gave them unto
me. 5 And I turned myself and came down from the mount, and
put the tables in the ark which I had made; and there they be, as the
LORD commanded me.

Later, Aaron's rod that budded was placed inside the *Ark of the Covenant* along with a golden pot that had manna in it. Aaron's rod that budded represented God's chosen leadership. A group of priests stood up against Moses and Aaron, and God made a test that whoever's rod budded by the morning was His chosen leadership. Aaron's rod supernaturally budded because God ordained him as His chosen leader. The manna represents the Word of God and God's supernatural provision. Manna was an angelic-like food that appeared each morning except on the Sabbath Day, so the children of Israel had food to eat while they wandered in the wilderness.

Hebrews 9:3-4 (KJV)
3 And after the second veil, the tabernacle which is called the
Holiest of all; 4 Which had the golden censer, and the ark of the
covenant overlaid round about with gold, wherein was the golden
pot that had manna, and Aaron's rod that budded, and the tables of
the covenant;

The Mercy Seat was placed on top of the *Ark of the Covenant* and represented the Throne of God. The Mercy Seat was made of pure gold and had two Cherubims crafted from gold with their wings spread and their faces were looking one to another toward the Mercy Seat. God said He would commune from the top of the Mercy Seat, which meant He would speak from above the Mercy Seat. The word commune also means to answer. God would speak to His people above the *Ark of the Covenant* and answer prayers when talking to Him in the *Secret Place* (Holy of Holies). If you want God to hear and answer your prayers, you must be in Covenant with Him.

> *Exodus 25:21-22 (KJV)*
>
> *21 And thou shalt put the **mercy seat** above upon the **ark**; and in the **ark** thou shalt put the testimony that I shall give thee. 22 And there I will meet with thee, and **I will commune with thee from above the mercy seat**, from between the two cherubims which are upon the **ark of the testimony**, of all things which I will give thee in commandment unto the children of Israel.*

Cherubims are high-ranking angels whom God commissioned to protect and guard the *Secret Place*, where the Throne of God is located. The two Cherubims on the Mercy Seat were continually to look after God's Throne (Ezekiel 10:1), the Covenant, and the *Secret Place*.

> *Exodus 25:17-20 (KJV)*
>
> *17 And thou shalt make a mercy seat of pure gold: two cubits and a half shall be the length thereof, and a cubit and a half the breadth thereof. 18 And thou shalt make **two cherubims of gold**, of beaten work shalt thou make them, in the two ends of the mercy seat. 19 And make **one cherub** on the one end, and the other **cherub** on the other end: even of the mercy seat shall ye make the **cherubims** on the two ends thereof. 20 And **the cherubims shall stretch forth their wings on high, covering the mercy seat with their wings,** and their faces shall look one to another; **toward the mercy seat shall the faces of the cherubims be.***

God instructed Moses to fill the Tabernacle with Cherubim imagery and have images of Cherubims woven into the Veil that separated the Holy of Holies from the Holy Place (Inner Court). He was also commanded to have images of Cherubims placed on the ten curtains that surrounded the inside of the Tabernacle. King Solomon also decorated the Second Temple with images of Cherubims. King Solomon was also instructed to mold two Cherubims of gold to be placed in the Holy of Holies overseeing the **Ark of the Covenant**. God commissioned Cherubims to guard the Garden of Eden so Adam and Eve couldn't eat from the Tree of Life once they were kicked out because of their disobedience. The Garden of Eden was the first *Secret Place* where God fellowshipped and spoke with Adam and Eve daily.

Genesis 3:24 (KJV)

*24 So he drove out the man; and he placed at the east of the garden of Eden **Cherubims**, and a flaming sword which turned every way, **to keep the way of the tree of life.***

Moses heard the voice of God speaking to him from the Mercy Seat whenever he went into the Holy of Holies.

Numbers 7:89 (KJV)

*89 And when Moses was gone into the tabernacle of the congregation to speak with him, **then he heard the voice of one speaking unto him from off the mercy seat that was upon the ark of testimony,** from between the two cherubims: **and he spake unto him.***

God also promised to appear in a cloud upon the Mercy Seat.

Leviticus 16:2c (KJV)

2 ...for I will appear in the cloud upon the mercy seat.

A cloud covered the Tabernacle when Moses finished setting it up, and it was filled with the glory of the Lord. The cloud of the Lord was on the Tabernacle by day, and fire was on it by night. The cloud that covered the Tabernacle was the same cloud that led the children of Israel by day and a fire by night when they came out of Egypt (Exodus 13:21-22).

Exodus 40:33-38 (KJV)

*33 And he reared up the court round about the tabernacle and the altar, and set up the hanging of the court gate. So Moses finished the work. 34 **Then a cloud covered the tent of the congregation, and the glory of the Lord filled the tabernacle.** 35 And Moses was not able to enter into the tent of the congregation, because the cloud abode thereon, and **the glory of the Lord filled the tabernacle.** 36 And when the **cloud** was taken up from over the tabernacle, the children of Israel went onward in all their journeys: 37 But if the **cloud** were not taken up, then they journeyed not till the day that it was taken up. 38 **For the cloud of the Lord was upon the tabernacle by day, and fire was on it by night,** in the sight of all the house of Israel, throughout all their journeys.*

God supernaturally used the *Ark of the Covenant* to part the Jordan River when Joshua and the children of Israel were first entering the Promised Land.

Joshua 3:1-17 (KJV)

*1 And Joshua rose early in the morning; and they removed from Shittim, and came to Jordan, he and all the children of Israel, and lodged there before they passed over. 2 And it came to pass after three days, that the officers went through the host; 3 And they commanded the people, saying, **When ye see the ark of the covenant of the Lord your God, and the priests the Levites bearing*** *it*, then ye shall remove from your place, and go after it. *4 Yet there shall be a space between you and it, about two thousand cubits by measure: come not near unto it, that ye may know the way by which ye must go: for ye have not passed this way heretofore. 5 And Joshua said unto the people, Sanctify yourselves: for to morrow the Lord will do wonders among you. 6 And Joshua spake unto the priests, saying,* **Take up the ark of the covenant, and pass over before the people.** *And they took up the* **ark of the covenant,** *and went before the people. 7 And the Lord said unto Joshua, This day will I begin to magnify thee in the sight of all Israel, that they may know that, as I was with Moses, so I will be with thee. 8 And thou shalt command the priests that bear the* **ark of the covenant,** *saying, When ye are come to the brink of the water of Jordan, ye shall stand still in Jordan. 9 And Joshua said unto the children of Israel, Come hither, and hear the words of the Lord your God. 10 And Joshua said, Hereby ye shall know that the living God is among you, and that he will without fail drive out from before you the Canaanites, and the Hittites, and the Hivites, and the Perizzites, and the Girgashites, and the Amorites, and the Jebusites. 11 Behold, the* **ark of the covenant** *of the Lord of all the earth passeth over before you into Jordan. 12 Now therefore take you twelve men out of the tribes of Israel, out of every tribe a man. 13 And it shall come to pass, as soon as the soles of the feet of the priests that bear the* **ark of the Lord,** *the Lord of all the earth, shall rest in the waters of Jordan, that the waters of Jordan shall be cut off from the waters that come down from above; and they shall stand upon an heap. 14 And it came to pass, when the people removed from their tents, to pass over Jordan, and the priests bearing the* **ark of the covenant**

Vince Baker

*before the people; 15 And as they that bare the **ark** were come unto Jordan, and the feet of the priests that bare the **ark** were dipped in the brim of the water, (for Jordan overfloweth all his banks all the time of harvest,) 16 That the waters which came down from above stood and rose up upon an heap very far from the city Adam, that is beside Zaretan: and those that came down toward the sea of the plain, even the salt sea, failed, and were cut off: and the people passed over right against Jericho. 17 And the priests that bare the **ark of the covenant of the Lord** stood firm on dry ground in the midst of Jordan, and all the Israelites passed over on dry ground, until all the people were passed clean over Jordan.*

God instructed Joshua to march the ***Ark of the Covenant*** around the walls of Jericho when they went to war with the people of that city. The ***Ark of the Covenant*** was used to help them in battle. When the ***Ark of the Covenant*** was brought into war, it was a declaration that the children of Israel had a Covenantal right with God to take the Promised Land from it's sinful inhabitants. When the ***Ark of the Covenant*** was marched around the city walls of Jericho for six days and seven times on the seventh day, God was revealing that the people dwelling in Jericho were going to be destroyed for breaking His Ten Commandments.

Joshua 6:1-16 (KJV)

*1 Now Jericho was straitly shut up because of the children of Israel: none went out, and none came in. 2 And the Lord said unto Joshua, See, I have given into thine hand Jericho, and the king thereof, and the mighty men of valour. 3 And ye shall compass the city, all ye men of war, and go round about the city once. Thus shalt thou do six days. 4 And seven priests shall bear before the **ark** seven trumpets of rams' horns: and the seventh day ye shall compass the* *city seven times, and the priests shall blow with the trumpets. 5 And it shall come to pass, that when they make a long blast with the ram's horn, and when ye hear the sound of the trumpet, all the people shall shout with a great shout; and the wall of the city shall fall down flat, and the people shall ascend up every man straight before him. 6 And Joshua the son of Nun called the priests, and said unto them, Take up the* **ark of the covenant**, *and let seven priests bear seven trumpets of rams' horns before the* **ark of the Lord**. *7 And he said unto the people, Pass on, and compass the city, and let him that is armed pass on before the* **ark of the Lord**. *8 And it came to pass, when Joshua had spoken unto the people, that the seven priests bearing the seven trumpets of rams' horns passed on before the Lord, and blew with the trumpets: and the* **ark of the covenant** *of the Lord followed them. 9 And the armed men went before the priests that blew with the trumpets, and the rereward came after the* **ark**, *the priests going on, and blowing with the trumpets. 10 And Joshua had commanded the people, saying, Ye shall not shout, nor make any noise with your voice, neither shall any word proceed out of your mouth, until the day I bid you shout; then shall ye shout. 11 So the* **ark of the Lord** *compassed the city, going about it once: and they came into the camp, and lodged in the camp. 12 And Joshua rose early in the morning, and the priests took up the* **ark of the Lord**. *13 And seven priests bearing seven trumpets of rams' horns before the* **ark of the Lord** *went on continually, and blew with the trumpets: and the armed men went before them; but the rereward came after the* **ark of the Lord**, *the priests going on, and blowing with the trumpets. 14 And the second day they compassed the city once, and returned into the camp: so they did six days. 15*

And it came to pass on the seventh day, that they rose early about the dawning of the day, and compassed the city after the same manner seven times: only on that day they compassed the city seven times. 16 And it came to pass at the seventh time, when the priests blew with the trumpets, Joshua said unto the people, Shout; for the Lord hath given you the city.

Joshua 6:20-21 (KJV)

20 So the people shouted when the priests blew with the trumpets: and it came to pass, when the people heard the sound of the trumpet, and the people shouted with a great shout, that the wall fell down flat, so that the people went up into the city, every man straight before him, and they took the city. 21 And they utterly destroyed all that was in the city, both man and woman, young and old, and ox, and sheep, and ass, with the edge of the sword.

After Joshua started conquering the Promised Land, God led him to set up the Tabernacle of Moses in a location called Shiloh.

Joshua 18:1 (KJV)

*1 And the whole congregation of the children of Israel assembled together at **Shiloh**, and set up the **tabernacle of the congregation** there. And the land was subdued before them.*

The **Ark of the Covenant** rested in the Tabernacle of Moses until it was stolen by the Philistines around 450 years after the Israelites entered the Promised Land. The Philistines, however, had to return the **Ark of the Covenant** to the children of Israel because the Hand of God was judging them, and many of the Philistines were dying. Later, King David brought the **Ark of the Covenant** into the Holy City of Jerusalem and placed the **Ark** in a

Tabernacle (Tent). This Tent was called the Tabernacle of David. In the next chapter, I will reveal the spiritual significance of the *Ark of the Covenant* and the Tabernacle of David.

God commanded King Solomon, the son of King David, to build a Temple to house the *Ark of the Covenant* and all of the other Holy artifacts found in the Tabernacle of Moses. When King Solomon finished building the Temple and the *Ark of the Covenant* was placed in the Holy of Holies, the glory of the Lord filled the Temple. This experience was so overwhelming and powerful that priests could not stand to minister.

1 Kings 8:1-13 (KJV)
*1 Then Solomon assembled the elders of Israel, and all the heads of the tribes, the chief of the fathers of the children of Israel, unto king Solomon in Jerusalem, that they might bring up the **ark of the covenant** of the Lord out of the city of David, which is Zion. 2 And all the men of Israel assembled themselves unto king Solomon at the feast in the month Ethanim, which is the seventh month. 3 And all the elders of Israel came, and the priests took up the **ark**. 4 And they brought up the **ark of the Lord**, and the tabernacle of the congregation, and all the holy vessels that were in the tabernacle, even those did the priests and the Levites bring up. 5 And king Solomon, and all the congregation of Israel, that were assembled unto him, were with him before the **ark**, sacrificing sheep and oxen, that could not be told nor numbered for multitude. 6 And the priests brought in the **ark of the covenant** of the Lord unto his place, into the oracle of the house, to the most holy place, even under the wings of the cherubims. 7 For the cherubims spread forth their two wings over the place of the **ark**, and the cherubims*

*covered the ark and the staves thereof above. 8 And they drew out the staves, that the ends of the staves were seen out in the holy place before the oracle, and they were not seen without: and there they are unto this day. 9 **There was nothing in the ark save the two tables of stone**, which Moses put there at Horeb, when the Lord made a covenant with the children of Israel, when they came out of the land of Egypt. 10 And it came to pass, when the priests were come out of the holy place, that **the cloud filled the house of the Lord, 11 So that the priests could not stand to minister because of the cloud: for the glory of the Lord had filled the house of the Lord**. 12 Then spake Solomon, The Lord said that he would dwell in the thick darkness. 13 I have surely built thee an house to dwell in, a settled place for thee to abide in for ever.*

Now that we know some of the history of the *Ark of the Covenant* and how God instructed Moses to set up the Tabernacle, which later became the Temple of King Solomon, let's explore how this applies to the *Secret Place*. God built the Tabernacle of Moses and the Temple of King Solomon to show the importance of our Covenant with God. The *Secret Place* has everything to do with keeping God's Covenant. This is why the **Ark of the Covenant** contains the Ten Commandments and is in the Holy of Holies. The Ten Commandments were at the heart of the Old Covenant that God made with the children of Israel. To access the *Secret Place* and dwell there, one must enter and keep the Covenant of God. You cannot have a special relationship with God without keeping His Covenant.

The Ten Commandments written on the two tablets came into existence because God spoke them, and they were etched into stone by the finger of God. The Ten Commandments testify that God desires to speak to His children daily and have them hear His voice. When you dwell in the *Secret Place*, God will have much to say about His Covenant and Commandments. You know God is talking to you if you hear Him speak about keeping His Covenant.

> ### Deuteronomy 4:11-13 (KJV)
> *11 And ye came near and stood under the mountain; and the mountain burned with fire unto the midst of heaven, with darkness, clouds, and thick darkness. 12 **And the LORD spake unto you out of the midst of the fire: ye heard the voice of the words, but saw no similitude; only ye heard a voice. 13 And he declared unto you his covenant, which he commanded you to perform, even ten commandments; and he wrote them upon two tables of stone.***

Since the fall of Adam and Eve, God had never spoken out of Heaven as He did on that memorable day on Mount Sinai.

> ### Deuteronomy 4:32-33 (KJV)
> *32 For ask now of the days that are past, which were before thee, since the day that God created man upon the earth, and ask from the one side of heaven unto the other, whether there hath been any such thing as this great thing is, or hath been heard like it? 33 **Did ever people hear the voice of God speaking out of the midst of the fire, as thou hast heard, and live?***

The day God spoke the Ten Commandments from Heaven was so critically important that He had what He spoke engraved on tables of stone. He then placed these tablets of stone in the *Ark of the Covenant* and placed the *Ark* in the heart of the Tabernacle of Moses. God revealed what was extremely important to Him and what should also be extremely important to us. God showed that you cannot walk in a close relationship with Him and dwell in His *Secret Place* unless you keep His Covenant by obeying His Commands.

The most valuable aspect of the *Secret Place* is being in a Covenant with God, and this is what the *Ark of the Covenant* represents.

Historically, the children of Israel disobeyed God by not keeping the Covenant that He made through Moses by sinning against His Commands. Jesus came to the Earth to make a New Covenant because the children of Israel broke the first Covenant God made with them.

> *Jeremiah 31:31-34 (KJV)*
>
> *31 Behold, the days come, saith the LORD, that I will make a **new covenant** with the house of Israel, and with the house of Judah: 32 Not according to the covenant that I made with their fathers in the day that I took them by the hand to bring them out of the land of Egypt; which my covenant they brake, although I was an husband unto them, saith the LORD: 33 But this shall be the **covenant** that I will make with the house of Israel; After those days, saith the LORD, I will put my law in their inward parts, and write it in their hearts; and will be their God, and they shall be my people. 34 And they shall teach no more every man his neighbour, and every man his brother, saying, Know the LORD: for they shall all know me, from the least of them unto the greatest of them, saith the LORD: for I will forgive their iniquity, and I will remember their sin no more.*

The New Covenant is all about the Laws of God being written in our inward parts and hearts. The Laws that were engraved on the tables of stone in the Old Covenant were now going to be etched in the tables of the New Testament believer's heart by the Spirit of God.

2 Corinthians 3:3 (KJV)

*3 Forasmuch as ye are manifestly declared to be the epistle of Christ ministered by us, written not with ink, **but with the Spirit of the living God; not in tables of stone, but in fleshy tables of the heart.***

To fully comprehend the New Covenant and the Laws of God being written on our hearts, we must go to the Book of Hebrews. The author of the Book of Hebrews declared that the Old Covenant is decaying, waxing old, and ready to vanish.

Hebrews 8:13 (KJV)

*13 In that he saith, **A new covenant, he hath made the first old. Now that which decayeth and waxeth old is ready to vanish away.***

Hebrews Chapter 10 reveals a profound revelation of what the Laws of God being written on our hearts and minds represent.

Hebrews 10:15-22 (KJV)

*15 Whereof the Holy Ghost also is a witness to us: for after that he had said before, 16 **This is the covenant that I will make with them after those days,** saith the Lord, **I will put my laws into their hearts, and in their minds will I write them;** 17 And their sins and iniquities will I remember no more. 18 Now where remission of these is, there is no more offering for sin. 19 Having therefore, brethren, boldness to enter into the holiest by the blood of Jesus, 20 By a new and living way, which he hath consecrated for us, through the veil, that is to say, his flesh; 21 And having an high priest over the house of God; 22 Let us draw near with a true heart in full assurance of faith, **having our hearts sprinkled from an evil conscience, and our bodies washed with pure water.***

Hebrews 10:22 reveals that when we draw near to God in the *Secret Place*, our evil conscience is sprinkled with the blood of Jesus. Our bodies are also washed with pure water. The Laws of God written on the tables of your heart has everything to do with your conscience. Jesus died so His blood could be sprinkled on your evil conscience. The blood of Jesus cleanses your evil conscience.

Once Jesus cleanses someone's conscience with His blood, their body becomes a Temple of the Holy Spirit.

> *1 Corinthians 6:19-20 (KJV)*
> *19 What?* ***know ye not that your body is the temple of the Holy Ghost which is in you,*** *which ye have of God, and ye are not your own? 20 For ye are bought with a price: therefore glorify God in your body, and in your spirit, which are God's.*

The ***Ark of the Covenant*** in the Old Testament represented the Holy Spirit. Through the New Covenant, the Holy Spirit now rests in the heart of the Holy of Holies within the Temple of the New Testament believer. Jesus died so we could become Temples of the Holy Spirit.

> *1 Corinthians 3:16-17 (KJV)*
> *16* ***Know ye not that ye are the temple of God,*** *and that the Spirit of God dwelleth in you? 17 If any man defile* ***the temple of God,*** *him shall God destroy; for* ***the temple of God*** *is holy,* ***which temple ye are.***

The Holy Spirit writes the Laws of God on our hearts, and our newly cleansed conscience helps us to do what is right in the sight of the Lord. Those who walk and live with a pure conscience can now dwell in the *Secret Place*. Our bodies being washed with pure water involves obeying all the Commands of

Christ. The Words of Jesus are usually highlighted in red letters in most Bibles, signifying their utmost importance. So, we can conclude from these Scriptures that when someone walks with a pure conscience while obeying all the Words of Christ, they are in the New Covenant with God and are dwelling in the *Secret Place of the Most High*.

In the Great Commission, Jesus commanded His disciples to teach all nations to observe all things that He Commanded.

> *Matthew 28:18-20 (KJV)*
> *18 And Jesus came and spake unto them, saying, All power is given unto me in heaven and in earth. 19 Go ye therefore, and teach all nations, baptizing them in the name of the Father, and of the Son, and of the Holy Ghost: 20 **Teaching them to observe all things whatsoever I have commanded you**: and, lo, I am with you alway, even unto the end of the world. Amen.*

To be a disciple of Christ, you must continue in His Word. The word continue means to live, remain, dwell, and abide.

> *John 8:31-32 (KJV)*
> *31 Then said Jesus to those Jews which believed on him, **If ye continue in my word, then are ye my disciples indeed**; 32 And ye shall know the truth, and the truth shall make you free.*

This is what the Bible has to say about your conscience.

Titus 1:15 (KJV)

*15 Unto the pure all things are pure: but unto them that are defiled and unbelieving is nothing pure; but **even their mind and conscience is defiled**.*

Romans 2:14-16 (KJV)

*14 For when the Gentiles, which have not the law, do by nature the things contained in the law, these, having not the law, are a law unto themselves: 15 Which shew the work of **the law written in their hearts, their conscience also bearing witness, and their thoughts the mean while accusing or else excusing one another;)** 16 In the day when God shall judge the secrets of men by Jesus Christ according to my gospel.*

Your conscience is like a mechanism in your heart that tells you beforehand if you are about to break a moral code of God's Laws. Your conscience will accuse you at the highest level if you disobey it. The Holy Spirit is not your conscience but works with your conscience to help guide you into doing what is right before the Lord. A new believer may not know the whole Word of God, but through the blood of Jesus, they will have a cleansed conscience and can know right from wrong.

If you are going to dwell in the *Secret Place* of your own Temple, you must adhere to all of the inward Laws of God written on the tables of your heart by obeying your conscience. You are also required to obey all that Jesus Commanded in His Word, which is transcribed in the four Gospels. Obeying your conscience and keeping all of the Words of Christ is how we dwell in the *Secret Place*. The fastest way to get removed from the *Secret Place* is to disobey any of the Words of Christ, sin against your conscience, walk in the flesh, or grieve the Holy Spirit in disobedience to His voice.

A person dwelling in the *Secret Place of the Most High* bears the fruit of the Holy Spirit and puts the works of the flesh to death daily.

> *Galatians 5:16-25 (KJV)*
> *16 **This I say then, Walk in the Spirit, and ye shall not fulfil the lust of the flesh.** 17 For the flesh lusteth against the Spirit, and the Spirit against the flesh: and these are contrary the one to the other: so that ye cannot do the things that ye would. 18 **But if ye be led of the Spirit, ye are not under the law.** 19 Now the works of the flesh are manifest, which are these; Adultery, fornication, uncleanness, lasciviousness, 20 Idolatry, witchcraft, hatred, variance, emulations, wrath, strife, seditions, heresies, 21 Envyings, murders, drunkenness, revellings, and such like: of the which I tell you before, as I have also told you in time past, that they which do such things shall not inherit the kingdom of God. 22 But the fruit of the Spirit is love, joy, peace, longsuffering, gentleness, goodness, faith, 23 Meekness, temperance: against such there is no law. 24 And they that are Christ's have crucified the flesh with the affections and lusts. 25 If we live in the Spirit, let us also walk in the Spirit.*

A believer whom the Holy Spirit leads in the Temple of their body is no longer under the Old Testament Law but is under the New Testament Law of the Spirit.

> *Romans 8:1-4 (KJV)*
> *1 There is therefore now no condemnation to them which are in Christ Jesus, who walk not after the flesh, but after the Spirit. 2 **For***

the law of the Spirit of life in Christ Jesus hath made me free from the law of sin and death. 3 For what the law could not do, in that it was weak through the flesh, God sending his own Son in the likeness of sinful flesh, and for sin, condemned sin in the flesh: 4 **That the righteousness of the law might be fulfilled in us, who walk not after the flesh, but after the Spirit.**

God has granted us the privilege of being Temples of the Holy Spirit and the opportunity to dwell with Him in the *Secret Place*. However, the *Secret Place* has to be respected by obeying all of the Words of Christ, keeping our conscience pure, and putting to death all the works of the flesh by the power of the Holy Spirit. This is how we continually keep a Covenant with God.

Even though God did away with the Old Covenant, it doesn't mean He did away with His Commands. Jesus expanded on the Laws of God written on the tables of stone during the time of Moses and took them to a greater level. In the Ten Commandments, God commanded that we are not to commit adultery, but Jesus commanded us not to even lust after a woman. Jesus taught that if a man lusted after a woman in his heart, he was committing adultery with her in his heart. *Thou Shalt Not Commit Adultery was* one of the Laws etched into stone that was placed in the **Ark of the Covenant**.

> *Matthew 5:27-28 (KJV)*
> *27 Ye have heard that it was said by them of old time,* **Thou shalt not commit adultery:** *28 But I say unto you, That whosoever looketh on a woman to lust after her hath committed adultery with her already in his heart.*

Jesus also took the Command of thou shalt not kill to an even deeper level in the heart. *Thou Shalt Not Kill* was another Law etched into stone and placed in the *Ark of the Covenant.*

Matthew 5:21-22 (KJV)
21 Ye have heard that it was said by them of old time, Thou shalt not kill; and whosoever shall kill shall be in danger of the judgment:
22 But I say unto you, That whosoever is angry with his brother without a cause shall be in danger of the judgment: and whosoever shall say to his brother, Raca, shall be in danger of the council: but whosoever shall say, Thou fool, shall be in danger of hell fire.

God placed the Ten Commandments in the *Ark of the Covenant* to reveal what is important to Him and what it means to keep Covenant with Him. Jesus taught the highest of all laws is the *Golden Rule* of doing unto others as you would want done unto yourself. God revealed to me by His Spirit that He will not allow anyone into the Holy of Holies *(Secret Place)* if they don't live by the *Golden Rule.*

Matthew 7:12 (KJV)
12 Therefore all things whatsoever ye would that men should do to you, do ye even so to them: for this is the law and the prophets.

The *Secret Place* is a Holy Temple filled with unconditional love, selflessness, purity, holiness, godliness, humility, and caring for others. How can you say you love God, whom you don't see if you can't love your brother or sister, who you do see? We reveal the love of God by doing unto others what we would want done to ourselves.

1 John 4:19-21 (KJV)

*19 We love him, because he first loved us. 20 If a man say, I love God, and hateth his brother, he is a liar: **for he that loveth not his brother whom he hath seen, how can he love God whom he hath not seen?** 21 And this commandment have we from him, That he who loveth God love his brother also.*

In the *Secret Place*, loving God and loving others is the highest Law of the Spirit.

Matthew 22:35-40 (KJV)

*35 Then one of them, which was a lawyer, asked him a question, tempting him, and saying, 36 Master, which is the great commandment in the law? 37 **Jesus said unto him, Thou shalt love the Lord thy God with all thy heart, and with all thy soul, and with all thy mind.** 38 This is the first and great commandment. 39 And the second is like unto it, **Thou shalt love thy neighbour as thyself.** 40 On these two commandments hang all the law and the prophets.*

Jesus gave us a New Commandment to love one another as He loved us. This means we are to imitate and practice how Jesus loved people and not follow our own interpretation of love. We must walk in the same love that Jesus had for others: **Unconditional Divine Love.** We can only learn about the Divine Love of Christ by the Holy Spirit teaching us from the Word of God.

John 13:34 (KJV)

*34 **A new commandment I give unto you, That ye love one another; as I have loved you, that ye also love one another.***

I have learned these secrets while dwelling in the *Secret Place* for many years. If you are serious about walking in the *Secret Place*, you must be careful to obey all the Words of Christ and love others. Anyone who gets close to God would never do any harm to anyone. They will also be very forgiving of the mistakes of others, knowing that God forgave them. This is how we truly know God and stay close to His heart. This is also how we obey the engraved Words of God's Laws written on our hearts with the pen of the Holy Spirit. *God is a God of love!*

1 John 4:7-8 (KJV)
7 Beloved, let us love one another: for love is of God; and every one that loveth is born of God, and knoweth God. 8 He that loveth not knoweth not God; for God is love.

God desires to bring you into His *Secret Place* and reveal the secrets of His Covenant to you. He who has ears to hear, let him hear.

Psalms 25:14 (KJV)
14 The secret of the LORD is with them that fear him; and he will shew them his covenant.

In the heart of the Temple is the Holy of Holies, and in the Holy of Holies, you will find the **Ark of the Covenant**. The **Ark of the Covenant** represents the Holy Spirit. Inside the **Ark of the Covenant**, you will find the Ten Commandments that command us to love God and others. The Ten Commandments are the Laws of the Old Covenant, which Jesus later expanded upon. In His teachings, Jesus took these Ten Commandments to a higher level when He walked on this Earth. In the New Covenant, the Holy Spirit writes the Laws of God on oFur hearts as the power of the blood of Jesus cleanses our conscience. It is imperative to dwell in the *Secret Place;* we must obey all of the Words of Christ and keep our conscience clean if we want our bodies to remain a Temple of the Holy Spirit.

People died and were heavily punished for not recognizing the sacredness of the *Ark of the Covenant* throughout history. The *Ark of the Covenant* represents our Covenant relationship with the Lord, and God takes the New Covenant more passionately, fiercely, and seriously than we may ever know. People were also highly favored and blessed when they obeyed the laws that governed the *Ark of the Covenant.* God gave us by His Spirit the *Ark of the Covenant* as a prophetic symbol to reveal in the Scriptures how to walk closely with Him and what it means to dwell in the *Secret Place of the Most High.*

In conclusion, we can see that our bodies were made Temples of the Holy Spirit in the New Testament. The *Ark of the Covenant* from the Old Testament represented the Holy Spirit and the redemptive plan of God in New Testament believers. Understanding what is in the heart of the Temple gives you a profound knowledge of who God is, what pleases Him, and what He is looking for. Love is at the center of God's heart and what is most important to Him. The *Ark of the Covenant* reveals that God is a God of love, and we keep God's Holy Covenant by walking in the Spirit and the love of God. Anyone who dwells in the *Secret Place* of the Holy of Holies of their own Temple will not only love God with all of their heart, but they will also love others.

Arise, O Lord, into thy rest; thou, and the ark of thy strength.

Psalm 132:8 (KJV)

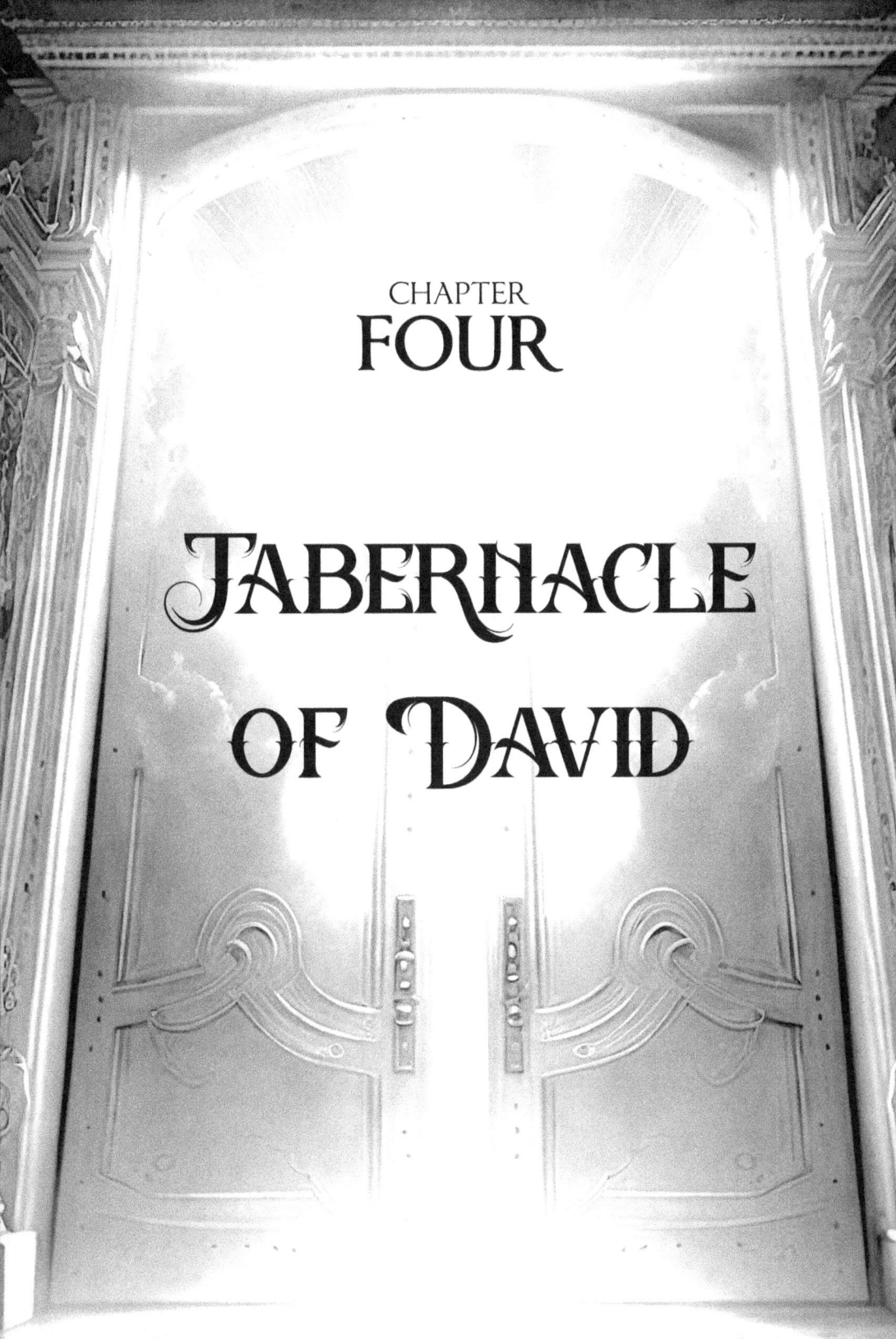

CHAPTER
FOUR

TABERNACLE
OF DAVID

The *Tabernacle of David* played a vital role in the historical importance of the *Ark of the Covenant*. The *Tabernacle of David* was a temporary resting place for the *Ark of the Covenant* before it was placed in the Holy of Holies in King Solomon's Temple. The *Tabernacle of David* only came about because the Philistines stole the *Ark of the Covenant* during a war with Israel, and it was never relocated into the Tabernacle of Moses. However, the *Tabernacle of David* was still in God's plan for what it would represent in future events after the death of Jesus Christ. In this chapter, I will reveal the hidden mysteries of the *Tabernacle of David* and how it plays a key role in the life of New Testament believers dwelling in the *Secret Place*.

The Tabernacle of Moses and the *Tabernacle of David* were both tents, but the *Tabernacle of David* differed from the Tabernacle of Moses. The Tabernacle of Moses was a tent comprising of the *Outer Court*, the *Inner Court*, and the *Holy of Holies*. The Tabernacle of Moses housed all of God's holy relics: *Bronze Altar, Bronze Laver, Table of Shewbread, Golden Candlestick, Altar of Incense*, and the *Ark of the Covenant*. The *Ark of the Covenant*, however, was the only holy relic residing in the *Tabernacle of David*, and this is what made it different from the Tabernacle of Moses.

To understand how the *Tabernacle of David* came about, we have to study the Biblical history of what happened to the *Ark of the Covenant* before David became the King of Israel. When Joshua, the servant of Moses, started conquering the Promised Land, he placed the Tabernacle of Moses in an area in the Promised Land called Shiloh. Shiloh is near the Jordan River in northeastern Israel. The Tabernacle of Moses was also named the Tabernacle of the Congregation.

Joshua 18:1 (KJV)

1 And the whole congregation of the children of Israel assembled together at Shiloh, and set up the tabernacle of the congregation there. And the land was subdued before them.

The Israelites entered the Promised Land around 1572 BC. It was about 1082 BC (Over 450 Years Later) when a prominent prophet named Samuel lived in Shiloh near the Tabernacle of Moses. When Samuel was a little boy, many of the children of Israel had fallen away from the Lord. Samuel was given as a gift to the Lord by his mother, Hannah, and was raised by the High Priest Eli. Hannah was barren and vowed to the Lord that if He gave her a child, she would dedicate him to the Lord all the days of his life.

The High Priest Eli had two sons, Hophni and Phinehas, who were also priests of the Lord, but they did evil before the Lord. They were violating the children of Israel's sacrifices to the Lord and having sexual relationships with the women who came to the Lord's Tabernacle.

1 Samuel 2:12-17 (KJV)

12 Now the sons of Eli were sons of Belial; they knew not the Lord. 13 And the priest's custom with the people was, that, when any man offered sacrifice, the priest's servant came, while the flesh was in seething, with a fleshhook of three teeth in his hand; 14 And he struck it into the pan, or kettle, or caldron, or pot; all that the fleshhook brought up the priest took for himself. So they did in Shiloh unto all the Israelites that came thither. 15 Also before they burnt the fat, the priest's servant came, and said to the man that sacrificed, Give flesh to roast for the priest; for he will not have sodden flesh of thee, but raw. 16 And if any man said unto him, Let them not fail to burn the fat presently, and then take as much as thy soul desireth; then he would answer him, Nay; but thou shalt give it me now: and if not, I will take it by force. 17 **Wherefore the sin of the young men was very great before the Lord: for men abhorred the offering of the Lord.**

1 Samuel 2:22-25 (KJV)
22 **Now Eli was very old, and heard all that his sons did unto all Israel; and how they lay with the women that assembled at the door of the tabernacle of the congregation.** *23 And he said unto them, Why do ye such things?* **for I hear of your evil dealings by all this people.** *24 Nay, my sons; for it is no good report that I hear: ye make the Lord's people to transgress. 25 If one man sin against another, the judge shall judge him: but if a man sin against the Lord, who shall intreat for him?* **Notwithstanding they hearkened not unto the voice of their father, because the Lord would slay them.**

Eli, the High Priest, warned his two sons but didn't do anything to stop them from perverting the priestly office of the Lord. Because Eli didn't do anything to prevent his two sons from causing the children of Israel to sin, God sent a prophet to prophesy a judgment on Eli and his two sons. The prophet told Eli that he was honoring his sons above the Lord. He prophesied that his family line would be cut off from being priests, and he would see an enemy in the habitation of the Lord. He also prophesied that his two sons, Hophni and Phinehas, would die in one day.

Soon after this prophecy, the children of Israel went to war with the Philistines. The Philistines were the arch-enemies of the children of Israel. When the battle lines were set, the Israelites brought the *Ark of the Covenant* into their camp, assuming God would help them win the war if the *Ark of the Covenant* were with them. Hophni and Phinehas were two of the priests who brought the *Ark of the Covenant* to the battlefield. However, the children of Israel had broken the Holy Covenant of God, and Hophni and Phinehas were not doing what was right in the sight of the Lord, so God was not with them.

The Philistines were afraid of the *Ark of the Covenant* at first, but when the battle began, they found out that God was not helping the Israelites. Because God was not helping the Israelites, the Philistines won the war, stole the *Ark of the Covenant*, and killed Eli's two sons, Hophni and Phinehas. When news of the *Ark of the Covenant* was stolen became known to Eli, he fell from his seat backward, broke his neck, and died.

> *1 Samuel 4:17-18 (KJV)*
>
> *17 And the messenger answered and said, Israel is fled before the Philistines, and there hath been also a great slaughter among the people, and **thy two sons also, Hophni and Phinehas, are dead, and the ark of God is taken.** 18 And it came to pass, **when he made mention of the ark of God,** that **he fell from off the seat backward by the side of the gate, and his neck brake, and he died:** for he was an old man, and heavy. And he had judged Israel forty years.*

When Eli's daughter-in-law heard about her husband Phinehas dying and the *Ark of the Covenant* being in the hands of the Philistines, she cried out while giving birth and named her child Ichabod. Ichabod means without glory, or where is the glory? She gave her son this name on her deathbed to indicate that the glory had departed from Israel because the *Ark of the Covenant* was taken. After she gave birth to Ichabod, she died.

1 Samuel 4:19-22 (KJV)

*19 And his daughter in law, Phinehas' wife, was with child, near to be delivered: **and when she heard the tidings that the ark of God was taken**, and that her father in law and her husband were dead, she bowed herself and travailed; for her pains came upon her. 20 And about the time of her death the women that stood by her said unto her, Fear not; for thou hast born a son. But she answered not, neither did she regard it. 21 And she named the child **Ichabod**, saying, **The glory is departed from Israel: because the ark of God was taken**, and because of her father in law and her husband. 22 And she said, **The glory is departed from Israel: for the ark of God is taken.***

The Philistines took the *Ark of the Covenant* and placed it in the house of their god, dagon. When they woke up in the morning, the idol of their god, dagon, was on his face. They put him back up, and the next day, he had fallen down again, and both the head and palms of dagon were cut off. The hand of the Lord was also against any of the Philistine cities that the *Ark of the Covenant* came into. The Philistines were getting judged with hemorrhoids, which could also be tumors, and there was also a plague of mice running through their cities. Those judged with hemorrhoids were dying, and the Hand of God was heavy against them.

1 Samuel 5:11-12 (KJV)

*11 So they sent and gathered together all the lords of the Philistines, and said, **Send away the ark of the God of Israel, and let it go again to his own place, that it slay us not, and our people: for there was a deadly destruction throughout all the city; the hand of God was very heavy there.** 12 And the men that died not were smitten with the emerods: and the cry of the city went up to heaven.*

So, the Philistines returned the *Ark of the Covenant* to the children of Israel on a new cart with five golden hemorrhoids and five golden mice with jewels of gold for a trespass offering. The *Ark of the Covenant* (also known as the *Ark of the Lord*) came to Bethshemesh in the Land of Israel. However, the people of Bethshemesh sinned against the Lord by looking into the *Ark of the Covenant*, and God killed 53,310 men. Because of this great slaughter, the men of Bethshemesh sent messengers to the inhabitants of Kirjathjearim to retrieve the *Ark of the Covenant.*

> *1 Samuel 6:19-21 (KJV)*
> *19 **And he smote the men of Bethshemesh, because they had looked into the ark of the Lord, even he smote of the people fifty thousand and threescore and ten men:** and the people lamented, because the Lord had smitten many of the people with a great slaughter. 20 And the men of Bethshemesh said, Who is able to stand before this holy Lord God? and to whom shall he go up from us? 21 **And they sent messengers to the inhabitants of Kirjathjearim**, saying, The Philistines have brought again the **ark of the Lord**; come ye down, and **fetch it up to you.***

When David became the King, he attempted to bring the *Ark of the Covenant* into the Holy City of Jerusalem about 20 years later. King David's first attempt to bring the *Ark of the Covenant* to Jerusalem ended tragically when they transported it the wrong way. According to the Law of Moses, the *Ark of the Covenant* was supposed to be transported on the shoulders of four priests. A man named Uzzah died by wrongfully touching the *Ark of the Covenant* when the oxen stumbled as they attempted to transport the *Ark of the Covenant* to Jerusalem. Because of this tragedy, King David sent the *Ark of the Covenant* to the house of a man named Obededom the Gittite. The *Ark of the Covenant* remained there for three months, and during this time, God blessed Obededom.

2 Samuel 6:10-11 (KJV)

10 So David would not remove the ark of the Lord unto him into the city of David: but David carried it aside into the house of Obededom the Gittite. 11 And the ark of the Lord continued in the house of Obededom the Gittite three months: and the Lord blessed Obededom, and all his household.

Once King David saw that God was blessing Obededom because of the *Ark of the Covenant,* he quickly learned how to transport the *Ark of the Covenant* correctly according to the Law of Moses. He then brought the *Ark of the Covenant* into the Holy City of Jerusalem. King David then made a *Tabernacle (Tent)* and placed the *Ark of the Covenant* in this Tent. This Tent became known as the *Tabernacle of David.*

2 Samuel 6:17 (KJV)

17 And they brought in the ark of the Lord, and set it in his place, in the midst of the tabernacle that David had pitched for it: and David offered burnt offerings and peace offerings before the Lord.

King David had the revelation that God would bless him if he honored what the *Ark of the Covenant* stood for. The *Ark of the Covenant* represented God's Holy Covenant with all Israel. King David's relationship with the Lord was intertwined with the *Ark of the Covenant* all the days he lived as the King of Israel. As long as King David obeyed the Laws of God's Holy Covenant, he was blessed in battle, in his finances and health.

The Tabernacle of Moses was set up in a place called Gibeon after the destruction of Shiloh. The *Ark of the Covenant* was never again placed in the Tabernacle of Moses. The *Ark of the Covenant* was always intended to dwell in the Holy of Holies in the Tabernacle of Moses, so the *Tabernacle of David* was a hidden mystery in the plan of God. We will see this hidden mystery later as I reveal more profound revelations about the *Ark of the Covenant* and the *Tabernacle of David*.

While King David was living in Jerusalem with the *Tabernacle (Tent)* he had set up for the *Ark of the Covenant*, he had a Divine thought. King David had the wonderful idea of building a Temple where the *Ark of the Covenant* could rest in the Holy of Holies and not just a temporary Tent. King David was the only person in the history of the children of Israel who had the original thought to build a Temple for the Lord. God never asked anyone to build Him a Temple.

King David loved the Lord with all of his heart and recognized the spiritual value of the *Ark of the Covenant*. He also understood the *Ark of the Covenant* needed to be reconnected with the other Holy Artifacts from the Tabernacle of Moses in the Temple. The *Tabernacle of David* was only meant to be a temporary place for the *Ark of the Covenant* to rest, but God's will was still being accomplished. The *Tabernacle of David* was only established during the time of King David, and the *Ark of the Covenant* never left Jerusalem during his reign.

> *2 Samuel 7:1-7 (KJV)*
>
> *1 And it came to pass, when the king sat in his house, and the Lord had given him rest round about from all his enemies; 2 That the king said unto Nathan the prophet, **See now, I dwell in an house of cedar, but the ark of God dwelleth within curtains.** 3 And Nathan said to the king, Go, do all that is in thine heart; for the Lord is with thee. 4 And it came to pass that night, that the word of the Lord came unto Nathan, saying, 5 Go and tell my servant David, **Thus saith the Lord, Shalt thou build me an house for me to dwell in?** 6 Whereas I have not dwelt in any house since the time that I brought up the children of Israel out of Egypt, even to this day, **but have walked in a tent and in a tabernacle.** 7 In all the places wherein I*

have walked with all the children of Israel spake I a word with any

of the tribes of Israel, whom I commanded to feed my people Israel,

saying, **Why build ye not me an house of cedar?**

King David, however, was not allowed by the Lord to build a Temple because God said he had shed too much blood and made great wars. God prophesied to King David that he would have a son named Solomon, who would build Him a Temple.

1 Chronicles 22:7-9 (KJV)

7 And David said to Solomon, My son, as for me, it was in my mind to build an house unto the name of the Lord my God: 8 But the word of the Lord came to me, saying, **Thou hast shed blood abundantly, and hast made great wars: thou shalt not build an house unto my name, because thou hast shed much blood upon the earth in my sight.** *9 Behold, a son shall be born to thee, who shall be a man of rest; and I will give him rest from all his enemies round about: for his name shall be* **Solomon***, and I will give peace and quietness unto Israel in his days.*

King Solomon fulfilled this prophecy and finished building the Temple of the Lord around 957 B.C. When King Solomon placed the *Ark of the Covenant* in the Holy of Holies with the other artifacts taken from the Tabernacle of Moses, God's glory filled the newly built Temple (2 Chronicles 5:5-14). The children of Israel entered a time of great prosperity and peace under the reign of King Solomon once the Temple was finished.

Now that we know the history of the *Tabernacle of David* and the *Ark of the Covenant*, let's explore their prophetic implications. There are many Divine mysteries surrounding the *Tabernacle of David* and the *Ark of the Covenant* that we need to know today. God's hidden mystery regarding the *Tabernacle of David* wouldn't be revealed until the Book of Acts.

Numerous Biblical teachers have reduced the *Tabernacle of David* to just a revelation about God's worship; however, God's plan goes much deeper than just worship. King David instituted worship around the *Tabernacle* when the *Ark of the Covenant* was in Jerusalem, which is important. But I will reveal an even deeper secret than just the worship of God.

In the Book of Acts, a council of early Church leaders assembled to answer the question of whether the newly saved Gentiles should keep the Law of Moses and be circumcised. This dispute arose because God had also poured out the Holy Spirit with the evidence of speaking in tongues on the Gentiles on the Day of Pentecost as He did with the believing Jews. Many Gentiles were getting saved and filled with the Holy Spirit, and some Jewish Christian leaders believed they needed to keep the Law of Moses and be circumcised.

This debate caused no small stir, leading to a council of Church leaders coming together in Jerusalem to discuss this matter. The Church elders concluded with a confirmation from the Holy Spirit that the Gentiles didn't need to be circumcised and keep the Law of Moses. At the Council of Jerusalem, James, one of the chief spokespeople for the early Church, pointed to an ancient prophecy found in the Book of Amos concerning the *Tabernacle of David.* This prophecy was used to confirm their decision on the matter of the Gentiles keeping the Law of Moses and being circumcised. I will reveal more details about their decision later in this chapter.

> *Amos 9:11-12 (KJV)*
> *11 In that day will I raise up the Tabernacle of David that is fallen, and close up the breaches thereof; and I will raise up his ruins, and I will build it as in the days of old: 12 That they may possess the*

remnant of Edom, and of all the heathen, which are called by my name, saith the Lord that doeth this.

This prophecy is incredibly significant and profound. Why didn't God say He would raise up the Tabernacle of Moses or the Temple of King Solomon? This means there must be a profound mystery surrounding the *Tabernacle of David* beyond the revelation of the Tabernacle of Moses and the Temple that King Solomon had built. When studying the Word of God, it is critical to ask the right questions. Divine questions will always lead you to Divine answers! Remember, the *Tabernacle of David* has everything to do with the *Ark of the Covenant.*

The *Ark of the Covenant* is only mentioned by name twice in the New Testament. The first time the *Ark of the Covenant* is mentioned in the New Testament, it says they can't speak about it now particularly.

Hebrews 9:3-5 (KJV)

*3 And after the second veil, the tabernacle which is called the Holiest of all; 4 Which had the golden censer, and the **ark of the covenant** overlaid round about with gold, wherein was the golden pot that had manna, and Aaron's rod that budded, and the tables of the covenant; 5 And over it the cherubims of glory shadowing the mercyseat; **of which we cannot now speak particularly.***

The next time the *Ark of the Covenant* is mentioned is in the Book of Revelations, where it is seen in the Temple of God in Heaven.

Revelation 11:19 (KJV)

*19 And the temple of God was opened in heaven, and there was seen in his temple the **ark of his testament:** and there were lightnings, and voices, and thunderings, and an earthquake, and great hail.*

You must know what you are looking for to find the *Ark of the Covenant* anywhere else in the New Testament. God's mysteries are always buried deep in the Word of God but hidden in plain sight. I have spent years asking God to open the eyes of my understanding to comprehend the Scriptures. Without the Lord's help, we would all be in the dark regarding the more profound secret revelations of God found in His precious Word.

> *Luke 24:45 (KJV)*
> *45 Then opened he their understanding, that they might understand the scriptures,*

Several years ago, I asked why Jesus had never mentioned the *Ark of the Covenant* in the history of the four Gospels (Matthew, Mark, Luke, and John). It puzzled me that the Son of God didn't have anything on written record in the Word of God about this sacred artifact. I let the question go because I didn't have an answer. Then, one day, after I confessed the Word of God, the Holy Spirit fell on me, and I went into a vision. In the vision, I saw four men carrying the *Ark of the Covenant* onto the platform of a large modern Church. As I experienced the vision, the Holy Spirit said to me, wherever you read *Ark of the Covenant* in the Old Testament, think Holy Spirit, and wherever you read Holy Spirit in the New Testament, think *Ark of the Covenant*. Put the two together, and you will know Me.

After this experience, I went and studied the *Ark of the Covenant* everywhere I could in the Old Testament, and I studied everywhere I could find the Holy Spirit in the New Testament. This study took me a very long time, but the revelations I gained were life-changing. I found a hidden place in the New Testament where the *Ark of the Covenant* was mentioned, but you have to know what you are looking for. God also taught me a new way to study the Scriptures. From that point on, the Holy Spirit led me to research subjects everywhere, from Genesis to Revelation. I have currently done over four hundred studies that have dramatically changed my life.

We must study the Book of Acts to tie in the mystery of the *Tabernacle of David* and how the *Ark of the Covenant* relates to the New Testament believer. A few historical events in the Book of Acts changed everything for the New Testament church, which is connected to the *Ark of the Covenant* and the *Tabernacle of David.* These events led to the Council of Church leaders being assembled in Jerusalem, which I mentioned earlier concerning whether the Gentiles should keep the Law of Moses and be circumcised.

The first historical event in the Book of Acts was the Day of Pentecost. The Holy Spirit was poured out on the New Testament Christians that day, because they were now the Temple of God. The believers were filled with the Holy Spirit and spoke in other tongues as the Holy Spirit came upon them. Wind and fire were also experienced on this Great Day of Pentecost.

> *Acts 2:1-4 (KJV)*
> *1 And when the **day of Pentecost** was fully come, they were all with one accord in one place. 2 And suddenly there came a sound from heaven as of a rushing mighty wind, and it filled all the house where they were sitting. 3 And there appeared unto them cloven tongues like as of fire, and it sat upon each of them. 4 And they were all filled with the Holy Ghost, and began to speak with other tongues, as the Spirit gave them utterance.*

The precious Holy Spirit could now come back into believers of Christ. When Jesus died on the Cross and was resurrected from the dead, the Holy Spirit, who was lost from the fall of Adam, could now return inside someone who was born again. Jesus also referred to the Holy Spirit as the Comforter.

John 16:7 (KJV)

7 Nevertheless I tell you the truth; It is expedient for you that I go away: for if I go not away, the Comforter will not come unto you; but if I depart, I will send him unto you.

Now, Christians' bodies become Temples of the Holy Spirit. The *Passion of Christ* restored believers in Him to God the Father, and the Holy Spirit could now reside in the believer's body. Believers in Christ were now made priests of their own Temple. So, you have to ask yourself, if we are now Temples of the living God, what does the *Ark of the Covenant* represent? Great question!

To answer this question, we need to examine the next historical event in the Book of Acts to get closer to gaining a greater knowledge of the mystery of the *Ark of the Covenant.* The following historical event is when God sent the Apostle Peter to preach the Gospel to the Gentiles. Up to this point, the atoning work of Christ on the Cross was only for the Jews. God was now offering salvation to the Gentiles.

A Gentile named Cornelius, a Roman Centurion, had seen a vision and was commanded by an angel to send for Peter. The Apostle Peter also saw a vision from God and was sent by the Holy Spirit to go to Cornelius' house in Caesarea. Remember, at this time, it was unlawful for a Jew to go into a Gentile's house. However, Peter's vision from God addressed this issue.

When Peter arrived on the scene and started preaching in the house of Cornelius, the Holy Spirit fell on the Gentiles as He did with the first Jewish believers on the Day of Pentecost. Let's pick up this story when Peter starts preaching to Cornelius, his family, and near friends who were with him in his house.

Acts 10:34-48 (KJV)

*34 Then Peter opened his mouth, and said, Of a truth I perceive that God is no respecter of persons: 35 But in every nation he that feareth him, and worketh righteousness, is accepted with him. 36 The word which God sent unto the children of Israel, preaching peace by Jesus Christ: (he is Lord of all:) 37 That word, I say, ye know, which was published throughout all Judaea, and began from Galilee, after the baptism which John preached; 38 How God anointed Jesus of Nazareth with the Holy Ghost and with power: who went about doing good, and healing all that were oppressed of the devil; for God was with him. 39 And we are witnesses of all things which he did both in the land of the Jews, and in Jerusalem; whom they slew and hanged on a tree: 40 Him God raised up the third day, and shewed him openly; 41 Not to all the people, but unto witnesses chosen before God, even to us, who did eat and drink with him after he rose from the dead. 42 And he commanded us to preach unto the people, and to testify that it is he which was ordained of God to be the Judge of quick and dead. 43 To him give all the prophets witness, that through his name whosoever believeth in him shall receive remission of sins. 44 **While Peter yet spake these words, the Holy Ghost fell on all them which heard the word.** 45 And they of the circumcision which believed were astonished, as many as came with Peter, because that **on the Gentiles also was poured out the gift of the Holy Ghost. 46 For they heard them speak with tongues, and magnify God.** Then answered Peter, 47 **Can any man forbid water, that these should not be baptized, which have received the Holy Ghost as well as we?** 48 And he commanded them to be baptized in the name of the Lord. Then prayed they him to tarry certain days.*

The Gentiles received the same Holy Spirit as the Jewish Christians did on the Day of Pentecost. This historical event shook the Jewish Christian community. Because there was so much controversy about this event, the Apostles and Church leaders called for a meeting in Jerusalem to discuss what to do. Many of the religious Jewish Christians were demanding that the Christian Gentiles keep the whole Law of Moses and be circumcised.

At this meeting, the early Church leaders determined by the Holy Spirit that the Gentiles should not have to keep the whole Law of Moses and be circumcised. I mentioned this Church Council of Jerusalem earlier when talking about the *Tabernacle of David*. Now let's see how this story and prophecy tie in with the *Tabernacle of David* and the *Ark of the Covenant.*

> *Acts 15:13-21 (KJV)*
>
> *13 And after they had held their peace, James answered, saying, Men and brethren, hearken unto me: 14 Simeon hath declared how God at the first did visit the Gentiles, to take out of them a people for his name. 15 **And to this agree the words of the prophets; as it is written, 16 After this I will return, and will build again the tabernacle of David, which is fallen down; and I will build again the ruins thereof, and I will set it up: 17 That the residue of men might seek after the Lord, and all the Gentiles, upon whom my name is called, saith the Lord, who doeth all these things.** 18 Known unto God are all his works from the beginning of the world. 19 Wherefore my sentence is, that we trouble not them, which from among the Gentiles are turned to God: 20 But that we write unto them, that they abstain from pollutions of idols, and from fornication, and from things strangled, and from blood. 21 For Moses of old time hath in every city them that preach him, being read in the synagogues every sabbath day.*

The *Ark of the Covenant* was the only holy artifact in the *Tabernacle of David*. So, when you are talking about the *Tabernacle of David* you are talking about the *Ark of the Covenant*. When James mentions this prophecy from the Book of Amos, he reveals that the *Ark of the Covenant* found in the *Tabernacle of David* refers to the Holy Spirit. Amos prophesied about the *Tabernacle of David* because it was only during the time of King David that people could get close to the *Ark of the Covenant* when it was in the Tent that King David had erected. The Gentiles and all believers could now access the Holy Spirit, represented by the *Ark of the Covenant*, after the resurrection of Jesus Christ. The *Ark of the Covenant* of the Old Testament was symbolic of the Holy Spirit, which symbolized the Holy Spirit dwelling in the Temple of the New Testament believer's body.

As we have seen in many of the Biblical stories I mentioned from the Old Testament, the *Ark of the Covenant* was removed from the Holy of Holies during certain times of travel or warfare. When the *Ark of the Covenant* was removed from the Holy of Holies, it was accessible to anyone who came near it. God revealed that the *Tabernacle of David* was a future revelation of believers being able to access the Holy Spirit within the *Secret Place* of their own body's Temple.

To say this plainly, God could use anyone with a *Secret Place* relationship with Him, like Peter, to allow the *Ark of the Covenant*, which is the Holy Spirit, to be accessed by people in need to receive blessings from God. This is what the Scriptures call the **ANOINTING!**

When the Apostle Peter preached the Gospel to the Gentiles, the Holy Spirit within him was now on him, and the Gentiles had access to the Holy Spirit through him. The Apostle Peter's body became the *Tabernacle of David* when operating in the Anointing, where the Gentiles could access the Holy

Spirit through him. The reason God uses the *Tabernacle of David* as symbolic of the Holy Spirit being poured out is that when the *Ark of the Covenant* was in the *Tabernacle of David*, everyone had access to the *Ark of the Lord*. No one could access the *Ark of the Covenant*, or the Holy Spirit when hidden in the Holy of Holies of the Temple or the Tabernacle of Moses.

Psalm 91 talks about dwelling in the *Secret Place of the Most High* and abiding under the shadow of the Almighty. It is recorded in the Book of Acts that Peter's shadow was healing people. The Apostle Peter was dwelling in the *Secret Place*, and people were accessing God's shadow through his shadow and getting healed.

Acts 5:15 (KJV)
*15 Insomuch that they brought forth the sick into the streets, and laid them on beds and couches, that at the least **the shadow of Peter** passing by might **overshadow** some of them.*

Psalm 91:1 (KJV)
*1 He that dwelleth in the **secret place of the most High** shall abide under **the shadow of the Almighty**.*

Peter and the other Apostles developed a *Secret Place* relationship with God during their time with Jesus. When the religious leaders of the day saw the boldness of Peter and John, they knew they had been with Jesus.

Acts 4:13 (KJV)
*13 Now when they saw the boldness of Peter and John, and perceived that they were unlearned and ignorant men, they marvelled; and **they took knowledge of them, that they had been with Jesus**.*

The Book of Acts displays what can happen when New Testament believers dwell in the *Secret Place* of their own Temple and develop a secret relationship with God. They obey His Commands and keep their hearts clean through a pure conscience. New Testament believers obey all the Commands of Christ, and God the Father and Jesus manifest to them personally in the *Secret Place.*

> *John 14:21-24 (KJV)*
> *21 He that hath my commandments, and keepeth them, he it is that loveth me: and he that loveth me shall be loved of my Father, and I will love him, and will manifest myself to him. 22 Judas saith unto him, not Iscariot, Lord, how is it that thou wilt manifest thyself unto us, and not unto the world? 23 Jesus answered and said unto him, If a man love me, he will keep my words: and my Father will love him, and we will come unto him, and make our abode with him. 24 He that loveth me not keepeth not my sayings: and the word which ye hear is not mine, but the Father's which sent me.*

When you obey the Words of Christ, Jesus gives you the Holy Spirit, who is the Comforter, to Abide with you forever.

> *John 14:15-18 (KJV)*
> *15 If ye love me, keep my commandments. 16 And I will pray the Father, and he shall give you another Comforter, that he may abide with you for ever; 17 Even the Spirit of truth; whom the world cannot receive, because it seeth him not, neither knoweth him: but ye know him; for he dwelleth with you, and shall be in you. 18 I will not leave you comfortless: I will come to you.*

Jesus dwelled in the *Secret Place* in His private walk with the Father and the Holy Spirit. When Jesus was sent into the world, He became a *Tabernacle of David*, and people started accessing the Spirit of God through Him. All the miracles you read in the Gospels came about because Jesus was dwelling in the *Secret Place of the Most High.* Jesus taught His disciples how to dwell in the *Secret Place.* When they learned from the Master how to have a deep personal and secret walk with God, they were sent out as *Tabernacles of David* and produced the same results as their beloved Messiah. When you see a genuine anointing on someone, you know they dwell in the *Secret Place.*

The Old Testament is overflowing with stories of saints who learned how to have a personal and private walk with God. The Law of Moses was a shadow of the good things to come and revealed how to have a *Secret Place* relationship with God. God wants to use you to bless the world as a *Tabernacle of David*, but first, you must enter the *Secret Place* of your own Temple through the New Covenant. Learn everything you can about the New Covenant because everything you seek in the Ark of the Covenant from the Old Testament is found in the Holy of Holies of your body.

The Tabernacle of Moses, the *Tabernacle of David*, the Temple of King Solomon, the Second Temple, and the Ark of Covenant were all shadows of the good things to come in the New Covenant. We are the Temple of the Holy Spirit and have a Covenant with God through the Holy Spirit. The Ark of the Covenant was a shadow of the Holy Spirit to come. This is why Jeremiah prophesied that the Ark of the Covenant wouldn't be remembered or visited anymore. It was only a shadow of the good things to come found in Christ, the New Covenant, and the Holy Spirit.

Jeremiah 3:16 (KJV)

16 And it shall come to pass, when ye be multiplied and increased in the land, in those days, saith the Lord, they shall say no more, The ark of the covenant of the Lord: neither shall it come to mind: neither shall they remember it; neither shall they visit it; neither shall that be done any more.

In conclusion, the *Tabernacle of David* reveals the mystery of God manifesting the Anointing of the Holy Spirit through a believer dwelling in the *Secret Place*. The Spirit of God can manifest His glory, and people in need can access God through an anointed man or woman of God. The *Ark of the Covenant* represents the Holy Spirit, and the *Tabernacle of David* represents the ability of people to access the Holy Spirit through the anointing on a minister of the Gospel. The *Tabernacle of David* was symbolically used to reveal God's plan of using His children to allow the Holy Spirit *(Ark of the Covenant)* to minister through them. Understanding this revelation will help you grow in your walk with God; by knowing this, you can walk in a greater anointing. Blessed be the God and Father of our Lord Jesus Christ, who has revealed the mystery of the *Tabernacle of David.*

TABERNACLE OF DAVID

CHAPTER
FIVE

SECOND

TEMPLE

L ocated in the heart of Jerusalem, the Temple of King Solomon played an important role in Jewish history. The Temple was the central location where the ancient Israelites gathered to worship the Lord through sacrifices according to the Old Covenant pattern shown to Moses. When the Babylonians destroyed the Temple, it had a devastating effect on all of Israel. The First Temple that King Solomon built was destroyed because the people of God had broken God's Covenant. However, God had another plan to rebuild the Temple, which was called the Second Temple. In this chapter, I will teach the importance of the Second Temple, what it represents, and how it ties into the *Secret Place.*

After King Solomon dedicated the First Temple, God appeared to him in a dream with a warning for all Israel. In this warning, God said He would cast this Temple out of His sight and make it a byword among all people if they turned away from following Him. God warned the children of Israel to keep His Commandments and not serve and worship other gods.

> *1 Kings 9:6-9 (KJV)*
>
> *6 But if ye shall at all turn from following me, ye or your children, and will not keep my commandments and my statutes which I have set before you, but go and serve other gods, and worship them: 7* **Then will I cut off Israel out of the land which I have given them; and this house, which I have hallowed for my name, will I cast out of my sight; and Israel shall be a proverb and a byword among all people: 8 And at this house, which is high, every one that passeth by it shall be astonished, and shall hiss; and they shall say, Why hath the Lord done thus unto this land, and to this house?** *9 And they shall answer, Because they forsook the Lord their God, who brought forth their fathers out of the land of Egypt, and have taken*

hold upon other gods, and have worshipped them, and served
them: therefore hath the Lord brought upon them all this evil.

The Babylonians destroyed the First Temple that King Solomon built in 586 B.C. because the children of Israel had fallen away from the Lord and were serving other gods. Moses had warned the Israelites if they broke God's Laws and worshipped other gods, they would be punished and sent to other nations.

Deuteronomy 28:64 (KJV)
64 And the Lord shall scatter thee among all people, from the one
end of the earth even unto the other; and there thou shalt serve
other gods, which neither thou nor thy fathers have known, even
wood and stone.

During the destruction of the First Temple by the Babylonians, a prophet named Jeremiah prophesied that God's people would serve the King of Babylon for seventy years. At the end of the seventy years, God prophesied that He would punish the King of Babylon.

Jeremiah 25:11-12 (KJV)
11 And this whole land shall be a desolation, and an astonishment;
***and these nations shall serve the king of Babylon seventy years.** 12*
*And it shall come to pass, **when seventy years are accomplished,***
that I will punish the king of Babylon, and that nation, saith the
Lord, for their iniquity, and the land of the Chaldeans, and will
make it perpetual desolations.

Jeremiah also prophesied that after the 70 years were completed, God would visit Israel and cause them to return to the Promised Land.

Jeremiah 29:10-14 (KJV)

*10 For thus saith the Lord, That after seventy years be accomplished at Babylon I will visit you, and perform my good word toward you, in causing you to return to this place. 11 For I know the thoughts that I think toward you, saith the Lord, thoughts of peace, and not of evil, to give you an expected end. 12 Then shall ye call upon me, and ye shall go and pray unto me, and I will hearken unto you. 13 And ye shall seek me, and find me, when ye shall search for me with all your heart. 14 **And I will be found of you, saith the Lord: and I will turn away your captivity, and I will gather you from all the nations, and from all the places whither I have driven you, saith the Lord; and I will bring you again into the place whence I caused you to be carried away captive.***

The Babylonians were judged by God when the Persian King "Cyrus the Great" conquered Babylon in 539 B.C. King Cyrus allowed the Jews to return to the land of Israel and rebuild the Temple of God. King Cyrus decreed that the Lord had charged him to build Him a House (Temple) in Jerusalem.

2 Chronicles 36:22-23 (KJV)

*22 Now in the first year of Cyrus king of Persia, that the word of the Lord spoken by the mouth of Jeremiah might be accomplished, the Lord stirred up the spirit of Cyrus king of Persia, that he made a proclamation throughout all his kingdom, and put it also in writing, saying, 23 **Thus saith Cyrus king of Persia, All the kingdoms of the earth hath the Lord God of heaven given me; and he hath charged me to build him an house in Jerusalem, which is in Judah.** Who is there among you of all his people? The Lord his God be with him, and let him go up.*

The rebuilding of the Second Temple was completed in 515 B.C. When the foundation of the Second Temple was laid, some of God's people who had seen the First Temple that King Solomon had built wept. They wept because the Second Temple's foundation paled in comparison to the First Temple that King Solomon built (Ezra 3:10-13). The Lord, however, prophesied through the Prophet Haggai that the glory of the latter house would be greater than the former house.

Haggai 2:9 (KJV)
9 The glory of this latter house shall be greater than of the former, saith the Lord of hosts: and in this place will I give peace, saith the Lord of hosts.

Neither the First nor the Second Temple was God's original plan. The First Temple was King David's dream for a place that could house the Ark of the Covenant. King David didn't like that he dwelt in a house of Cedar while the Ark of the Covenant dwelt under a Tabernacle (Tent). However, God commanded King David to have his son Solomon build the First Temple because King David had shed too much blood on the Earth in His sight (1 Chronicles 22:7-10).

Later, God commanded King Cyrus to build the Second Temple around the destruction of the First Temple. The Tabernacle of David was also not part of God's original plan. The Ark of the Covenant only ended up in the Tabernacle of David because the Philistines stole it due to the disobedience of God's people. God's original plan for the Ark of the Covenant was to dwell in the Tabernacle of Moses.

When the Ark of the Covenant was placed in the First Temple King Solomon had built, the glory of God filled the Temple. So, how could the Second

Temple be filled with more glory without housing the Ark of the Covenant as prophesied by the Prophet Haggai? Historians teach that the Ark of the Covenant was hidden from the Babylonians when they came to destroy Jerusalem, the First Temple, and steal all her wealth.

After the destruction of the First Temple, the Ark of the Covenant was never mentioned in the Scriptures as being placed in the Second Temple built by King Cyrus. It is also not recorded anywhere in the Word of God that God's glory filled the Second Temple as He did with the First Temple that King Solomon had built when the Ark of the Covenant was placed in the Holy of Holies. Everything revealed in the Scriptures points to the fact that the Ark of the Covenant disappeared around the time of the destruction of the First Temple.

The Ark of the Covenant was never found in the Second Temple that Jesus visited, which King Herod had expanded. We know this to be true because there was no historical evidence of the Ark of the Covenant being mentioned when the Romans destroyed the Second Temple in 70 A.D. The Romans would have recorded that they found the Ark of the Covenant while they were destroying Jerusalem and the Second Temple.

A great historical mystery surrounds the whereabouts of the Ark of the Covenant after the destruction of the First Temple. We may never know what happened to the Ark of the Covenant. Don't forget that Jeremiah prophesied that the Ark of the Covenant would no longer come to mind, be remembered, or be visited. Jeremiah, who was alive during the destruction of the First Temple, was given prophetic insight into the mystery of what would happen to the Ark of the Covenant.

Jeremiah 3:16 (KJV)

*16 And it shall come to pass, when ye be multiplied and increased in the land, **in those days, saith the Lord, they shall say no more, The ark of the covenant of the Lord: neither shall it come to mind: neither shall they remember it; neither shall they visit it; neither shall that be done any more.***

The crucial questions that must be asked are: "What do the First and Second Temples represent?" "Why is the Ark of the Covenant not found in the Second Temple?" and "Why is the Second Temple prophesied to have more glory than the first without the Ark of the Covenant being placed in it?" Everything found in God's Word and everything not found in God's Word is significant. God has a Divine purpose in everything He does and reveals in the Scriptures. There are notable prophetic implications to God's Holy Tabernacles, Temples, and the Ark of the Covenant.

The First Temple represented the Old Covenant, and the Second Temple represented the New Covenant. In the Old Covenant, the children of God would visit the Temple in Jerusalem. In the New Covenant, the children of God *BECOME* God's Holy Temple. No Ark of the Covenant is found in the Second Temple because there is no physical Ark of the Covenant found in the Temple of the New Testament believers' bodies. The Ark of the Covenant represents the Holy Spirit and our New Covenant with God. The New Temples of the New Covenant have more glory than the Old Testament Temple that King Solomon built because they are filled with the Holy Spirit. The Old Testament was written as a shadow of the good things to come and to reveal the hidden mysteries found in New Covenant believers.

Hebrews 8:4-5 (KJV)

*4 For if he were on earth, he should not be a priest, seeing that there are priests that offer gifts according to the law: 5 **Who serve unto the example and shadow of heavenly things, as Moses was admonished of God when he was about to make the tabernacle: for, See, saith he, that thou make all things according to the pattern shewed to thee in the mount.***

Hebrews 10:1 (KJV)

*1 **For the law having a shadow of good things to come, and not the very image of the things,** can never with those sacrifices which they offered year by year continually make the comers thereunto perfect.*

New Testament believers have now become the Temple of God, where the Spirit of God resides. The New Covenant we have through the Holy Spirit represents the Ark of the Covenant found in the Old Testament. Only through faith in the death, burial, and resurrection of Jesus can our bodies become Temples of the Holy Spirit.

1 Corinthians 6:19 (KJV)

*19 **What? know ye not that your body is the temple of the Holy Ghost which is in you, which ye have of God, and ye are not your own?***

On the Day of Pentecost, the Holy Spirit filled the believers with the glory of God. The glory of God that filled the Tabernacle of Moses and King Solomon's Temple cannot be compared to the glory found in the New Testament saints. The Old Testament glory was only a shadow of what God now does in New Testament believers. New Testament believers' bodies are destined to be changed and filled with God's glory now and in the coming age. The glory of the Old Testament passed away, but the glory of the New Testament will never pass away. *It is more glorious to be filled with the Holy Spirit than to visit a Temple in the city of Jerusalem where God's glory used to reside.*

> *2 Corinthians 3:8-11 (KJV)*
> *8 How shall not the ministration of the spirit be rather glorious? 9 For if the ministration of condemnation be glory, **much more doth the ministration of righteousness exceed in glory.** 10 For even that which was made glorious had no glory in this respect, **by reason of the glory that excelleth.** 11 For if that which is done away was glorious, **much more that which remaineth is glorious.***

Your study of the Scriptures comes alive once you grasp these truths. Everything you read about having to do with the Tabernacles and Temples in the Old Testament will now make sense in how it applies to what God is doing in the Temple of your body. This prophetic insight helps you realize the amazing privilege God has given us to be a Holy Temple where His glorious Holy Spirit resides and where we can dwell in the *Secret Place of the Most High.*

The actual Ark of the Covenant is no longer needed, just as we no longer need a physical Temple of God to visit on the earth. You can visit with God, and God can commune with you from inside the Temple of your own body. As you keep your Covenant with God by obeying all the Words of Christ, keeping your conscience pure, dying to the works of the flesh, and being led by the Holy Spirit, you can access God within yourself. This revelation changes everything. This is the **GREAT** secret to the *Secret Place*!

Dwelling in the *Secret Place* has everything to do with accessing God within the Temple of your own body and keeping your Temple clean from all defilement. As a Temple of God, you must glorify God in your body, and you are now joined to the Lord by the Holy Spirit.

> *1 Corinthians 6:17-20 (KJV)*
>
> *17 But he that is joined unto the Lord is one spirit. 18 Flee fornication. Every sin that a man doeth is without the body; but he that committeth fornication sinneth against his own body. 19 **What? know ye not that your body is the temple of the Holy Ghost which is in you, which ye have of God,** and ye are not your own? 20 **For ye are bought with a price: therefore glorify God in your body, and in your spirit, which are God's.***

The Bible warns us that if we defile the Temple of God, which is our body, God will destroy us. After accepting Christ into your heart, you cannot underestimate how important your body is to God and what you do with it. Once you become a born-again believer, your body is no longer your own. The Holy of Holies within the Temple of your body becomes the *Secret Place* where you meet with God. Your body becomes the sacred location where God dwells within you and communes with you. You have to keep your body holy because God is **HOLY**.

> *1 Corinthians 3:16-17 (KJV)*
>
> *16 **Know ye not that ye are the temple of God, and that the Spirit of God dwelleth in you? 17 If any man defile the temple of God, him shall God destroy; for the temple of God is holy, which temple ye are.***

Temple Wealth

The Prophet Haggai had much to say about the wealth and provision of God's people during the reconstruction of the Second Temple. These prophetic words are highly critical for the New Testament Church to be aware of. God revealed to the Prophet Haggai that God's people were cursed because they were not taking care of the House of the Lord. God said these people have sown much and bring in little. He also said that they earn wages and put it in bags with holes.

> *Haggai 1:5-9 (KJV)*
> *5 Now therefore thus saith the Lord of hosts; Consider your ways.*
> *6 **Ye have sown much, and bring in little;** ye eat, but ye have not enough; ye drink, but ye are not filled with drink; ye clothe you, but there is none warm; and **he that earneth wages earneth wages to put it into a bag with holes.** 7 Thus saith the Lord of hosts; Consider your ways. 8 Go up to the mountain, and bring wood, and build the house; and I will take pleasure in it, and I will be glorified, saith the Lord. 9 **Ye looked for much, and, lo it came to little; and when ye brought it home, I did blow upon it. Why? saith the Lord of hosts. Because of mine house that is waste, and ye run every man unto his own house.***

During this time, God also called for a drought upon the land, the mountains, the corn, the new wine, the oil, and more.

> *Haggai 1:10-11 (KJV)*
> *10 Therefore the heaven over you is stayed from dew, and the earth is stayed from her fruit. 11 And I called for a drought upon the land, and upon the mountains, and upon the corn, and upon the new*

wine, and upon the oil, and upon that which the ground bringeth forth, and upon men, and upon cattle, and upon all the labour of the hands.

The people of God repented and rebuilt the Lord's Second Temple. When they started to rebuild the Second Temple, God began to bless the works of their hands. They earned their income through harvesting crops, and God began to bless their harvests.

Haggai 2:15-19 (KJV)
15 And now, I pray you, consider from this day and upward, from before a stone was laid upon a stone in the temple of the Lord: 16 Since those days were, when one came to an heap of twenty measures, there were but ten: when one came to the pressfat for to draw out fifty vessels out of the press, there were but twenty. 17 I smote you with blasting and with mildew and with hail in all the labours of your hands; yet ye turned not to me, saith the Lord. 18 Consider now from this day and upward, from the four and twentieth day of the ninth month, even from the day that the foundation of the Lord's temple was laid, consider it. 19 Is the seed yet in the barn? yea, as yet the vine, and the fig tree, and the pomegranate, and the olive tree, hath not brought forth: from this day will I bless you.

The Lord is genuinely concerned and cares about the financial well-being of His people. When we tend to His Temple, which is our bodies, God promises to bless us financially. This financial blessing can come in supernatural provision or great wealth. God prophesied through the Prophet Haggai that all the gold and silver are His. When God fills His Temple with glory, He also provides abundantly for His people and gives them peace.

Haggai 2:6-9 (KJV)
*6 For thus saith the Lord of hosts; Yet once, it is a little while, and I will shake the heavens, and the earth, and the sea, and the dry land; 7 And I will shake all nations, and the desire of all nations shall come: **and I will fill this house with glory, saith the Lord of hosts. 8 The silver is mine, and the gold is mine, saith the Lord of hosts.** 9 The glory of this latter house shall be greater than of the former, saith the Lord of hosts: and in this place will I give peace, saith the Lord of hosts.*

Throughout Biblical history, God blessed everyone who was connected to His Tabernacles and Temples with wealth. When the children of Israel came out of Egypt, they came out with great wealth. The Egyptians gave them silver and gold as they were leaving Egypt. Some of this silver and gold was used to create the Holy artifacts found in the Tabernacle of Moses.

Psalm 105:37-38 (KJV)
*37 **He brought them forth also with silver and gold:** and there was not one feeble person among their tribes. 38 Egypt was glad when they departed: for the fear of them fell upon them.*

King David was so wealthy that it is estimated that he gave around twenty billion dollars to construct the First Temple. God blessed King David with wealth because he set his affection to build a Temple for the Lord. During this time, Israel's chief fathers and princes also donated their wealth to build the Lord's House.

1 Chronicles 29:2-5 (KJV)

2 Now I have prepared with all my might for the house of my God the gold for things to be made of gold, and the silver for things of silver, and the brass for things of brass, the iron for things of iron, and wood for things of wood; onyx stones, and stones to be set, glistering stones, and of divers colours, and all manner of precious stones, and marble stones in abundance. 3 Moreover, because I have set my affection to the house of my God, I have of mine own proper good, of gold and silver, which I have given to the house of my God, over and above all that I have prepared for the holy house. 4 Even three thousand talents of gold, of the gold of Ophir, and seven thousand talents of refined silver, to overlay the walls of the houses withal: 5 The gold for things of gold, and the silver for things of silver, and for all manner of work to be made by the hands of artificers. And who then is willing to consecrate his service this day unto the Lord?

An amazing Biblical fact is that King Solomon, who built the First Temple of God, became one of the wealthiest men in history ever to live. King Solomon was estimated to have a net worth of 2.1 trillion dollars. God made King Solomon uniquely rich, even so much so that other nations of the earth were bringing him wealth yearly. Many people traveled from afar to hear the wisdom of King Solomon and bring him gifts.

1 Kings 10:23-25 (KJV)

23 So king Solomon exceeded all the kings of the earth for riches and for wisdom. 24 And all the earth sought to Solomon, to hear his wisdom, which God had put in his heart. 25 And they brought every man his present, vessels of silver, and vessels of gold, and garments, and armour, and spices, horses, and mules, a rate year by year.

King Solomon was so wealthy that silver became like stones during his reign.

1 Kings 10:27 (KJV)
27 And the king made silver to be in Jerusalem as stones, and cedars made he to be as the sycomore trees that are in the vale, for abundance.

God promised to establish His Covenant if the children of Isreal remembered the Lord their God. The establishing of His Covenant would be to give them the power to get wealth. A big part of God establishing His Covenant is giving His faithful children the power to get wealth.

Deuteronomy 8:18 (KJV)
18 But thou shalt remember the Lord thy God: for it is he that giveth thee power to get wealth, that he may establish his covenant which he sware unto thy fathers, as it is this day.

God financially blessed everyone involved in building the Second Temple. God's plan has always been to financially bless anyone associated with building His Tabernacles and Temples. Now, you might ask how this applies to the New Testament believers. Does God still financially bless His New Testament church? To find this answer, we must turn to the Book of Acts.

On the Day of Pentecost, the Holy Spirit filled all believers in the upper room. It was official: New Testament believers became the Temple of the Holy Spirit on this Holy Feast Day. Now, it is important to note that in the same chapter where the Holy Spirit filled believers for the first time, it mentions

God's provision (Acts 2). Multiple Scriptures in the Book of Acts point to God blessing His people financially. Believers were selling their possessions and goods and giving to people in need. God was providing for all of the needs of His people during this time.

> *Acts 2:44-46 (KJV)*
> *44 And all that believed were together, and had all things common;*
> *45 And sold their possessions and goods, and parted them to all men, as every man had need. 46 And they, **continuing daily with one accord in the temple,** and breaking bread from house to house, did eat their meat with gladness and singleness of heart,*

During the Book of Acts, no one in the Church lacked because Christians sold their lands and houses to provide for their fellow believers in need. The money from these sales was laid at the Apostles' feet, and distribution was made for the believers living in Jerusalem at that time.

> *Acts 4:34-37 (KJV)*
> *34 **Neither was there any among them that lacked: for as many as were possessors of lands or houses sold them, and brought the prices of the things that were sold, 35 And laid them down at the apostles' feet: and distribution was made unto every man according as he had need.** 36 And Joses, who by the apostles was surnamed Barnabas, (which is, being interpreted, The son of consolation,) a Levite, and of the country of Cyprus, 37 **Having land, sold it, and brought the money, and laid it at the apostles' feet.***

Selling their possessions and giving all the proceeds to the Church became a big part of New Testament ministry, and the Apostles had to assign men of God to take over the distribution.

Acts 6:1-6 (KJV)

*1 And in those days, when the number of the disciples was multiplied, there arose a murmuring of the Grecians against the Hebrews, because their widows were neglected in the daily ministration. 2 Then the twelve called the multitude of the disciples unto them, and said, It is not reason that we should leave the word of God, and serve tables. 3 **Wherefore, brethren, look ye out among you seven men of honest report, full of the Holy Ghost and wisdom, whom we may appoint over this business.** 4 But we will give ourselves continually to prayer, and to the ministry of the word. 5 And the saying pleased the whole multitude: and they chose Stephen, a man full of faith and of the Holy Ghost, and Philip, and Prochorus, and Nicanor, and Timon, and Parmenas, and Nicolas a proselyte of Antioch: 6 Whom they set before the apostles: and when they had prayed, they laid their hands on them.*

The revelation to sell your goods and give to people experiencing poverty came from Jesus Himself. The Apostles did not invent this idea. Jesus had been teaching people to seek God and His Kingdom first and that God would take care of all their needs.

Matthew 6:33 (KJV)
*33 **But seek ye first the kingdom of God, and his righteousness; and all these things shall be added unto you.***

The power of the *Secret Place* is that if you put God and His Kingdom first, God Himself will provide for you. In the *Secret Place*, you make God more important than money. In return, God provides for all of your needs, just like

He provides for the birds of the air and clothes the lilies of the field better than King Solomon in all of his glory.

Matthew 6:24-30 (KJV)

24 No man can serve two masters: for either he will hate the one, and love the other; or else he will hold to the one, and despise the other. Ye cannot serve God and mammon. 25 Therefore I say unto you, Take no thought for your life, what ye shall eat, or what ye shall drink; nor yet for your body, what ye shall put on. Is not the life more than meat, and the body than raiment? 26 Behold the fowls of the air: for they sow not, neither do they reap, nor gather into barns; yet your heavenly Father feedeth them. Are ye not much better than they? 27 Which of you by taking thought can add one cubit unto his stature? 28 And why take ye thought for raiment? Consider the lilies of the field, how they grow; they toil not, neither do they spin: 29 And yet I say unto you, That even Solomon in all his glory was not arrayed like one of these. 30 Wherefore, if God so clothe the grass of the field, which to day is, and to morrow is cast into the oven, shall he not much more clothe you, O ye of little faith?

One day, a rich man came to Jesus and asked Him what he must do to be saved. Let's look at the answer Jesus gave him.

Mark 10:17-22 (KJV)

17 And when he was gone forth into the way, there came one running, and kneeled to him, and asked him, Good Master, what shall I do that I may inherit eternal life? 18 And Jesus said unto him, Why callest thou me good? there is none good but one, that is, God.

*19 Thou knowest the commandments, Do not commit adultery, Do not kill, Do not steal, Do not bear false witness, Defraud not, Honour thy father and mother. 20 And he answered and said unto him, Master, all these have I observed from my youth. 21 **Then Jesus beholding him loved him, and said unto him, One thing thou lackest: go thy way, sell whatsoever thou hast, and give to the poor, and thou shalt have treasure in heaven: and come, take up the cross, and follow me. 22 And he was sad at that saying, and went away grieved: for he had great possessions.***

This rich man was grieved at the answer Jesus gave him. The rich man could have thought to himself; I thought God wanted me to be blessed according to the Blessings of Father Abraham. This rich man had no idea that Jesus was offering him entrance into the *Secret Place*. If this rich man had taken Jesus up on His offer, he could have been able to walk with the Lord during His brief time on this earth. He could have entered the *Secret Place* with Jesus Himself and learned the mysteries of the Kingdom of God.

It is unfortunate to see when people choose wealth over the *Secret Place*. Jesus doesn't command or make an offer for everyone to sell everything they have, but if He asks you to do this, He has a *High Calling* on your life. If you sell everything you have, make sure the Lord is leading you. The main point is that to dwell in the *Secret Place of the Most High*, you must put God first above riches in your heart.

There is another hidden mystery to those who choose the *Secret Place* over wealth. If you are not careful, you may miss great mysteries in the Word of God. Right after Jesus spoke to this rich man who rejected His offer, Jesus taught His disciples more about riches. Jesus taught that the issue had to do with trusting in riches. Jesus also painted a picture of a camel going through the eye of a needle. In Biblical times, a camel had to be stripped of everything and placed on its knees to go through a doorway in the gate of a city called the needle to enter at night after the city gate was closed.

Mark 10:24-27 (KJV)

*24 And the disciples were astonished at his words. But Jesus answereth again, and saith unto them, **Children, how hard is it for them that trust in riches to enter into the kingdom of God! 25 It is easier for a camel to go through the eye of a needle, than for a rich man to enter into the kingdom of God.** 26 And they were astonished out of measure, saying among themselves, Who then can be saved? 27 And Jesus looking upon them saith, With men it is impossible, but not with God: for with God all things are possible.*

The Apostle Peter declared to the Lord that he and all of the Apostles had left all to follow Him. These twelve men had left their families and professions to follow their Messiah. At this point, Jesus made some very profound statements concerning wealth.

Mark 10:28-31 (KJV)

*28 **Then Peter began to say unto him, Lo, we have left all, and have followed thee.** 29 And Jesus answered and said, Verily I say unto you, There is no man that hath left house, or brethren, or sisters, or father, or mother, or wife, or children, or lands, for my sake, and the gospel's, 30 **But he shall receive an hundredfold now in this time, houses, and brethren, and sisters, and mothers, and children,***

125

and lands, with persecutions; and in the world to come eternal life.

31 But many that are first shall be last; and the last first.

Jesus revealed to His disciples that those who left everything for Him would receive new family members, houses, and lands a hundredfold in this lifetime. This truth has a thought-provoking revelation in it. When we give up everything for Jesus, He will give it back to us and more. But we must make Jesus our Lord and Master. Money cannot have a hold on you if you want to dwell in the *Secret Place*. Once Jesus is your Lord and Master, you can be trusted with wealth. You can have wealth as long as wealth doesn't have you.

I gave up a three-bedroom home and everything in it when I was younger and went into full-time ministry at the leading of the Lord. During this time, I lived entirely by faith with no income from a job. In this season, God challenged me to the depths of my being, but I saw numerous miracles of provision. I also couldn't possess anything of value as God was dealing with my heart. As the years passed, I completely died to covetousness and greed. I learned to put God and His Kingdom first. Jesus is my Lord and Master. Now, I can have things because they don't have me. I am thankful for what God taught me during those early years of living by faith.

If you want to enter the *Secret Place*, the issues of money, fortune, and the things of this world must be dealt with within your heart. You will find in the *Secret Place* that God is more than enough. Living in a wonderful relationship with your Creator in the *Secret Place* makes you content. The things of this world lose their allure. Once you get lost in the *Secret Place* with God, you can be faithful to manage substantial amounts of wealth. The disciples left everything and were granted the opportunity of a lifetime to oversee one of the most significant moves of God and all of the wealth that came with it. *The rich man lost out!*

The Lord revealed to me that believers and church leadership must deal correctly with money if there is to be a genuine revival. Serving money more than God can hinder God's move. Therefore, Church leaders must govern money and the giving of the saints correctly for the move of God to keep going. When God starts moving through the anointing, God's people will want to give. God watches how ministers and His people respond when this giving is released.

In conclusion, we can see great Divine mysteries found in the Tabernacles, the Temples of God, and the Ark of the Covenant. The *Secret Place* is located within the body of the New Believer, but they can only access this *Secret Place* if they put God above money. You can be trusted with great wealth once you dwell in the *Secret Place*. God has always intended to bless His people, but not at the expense of them setting their hearts on riches. We must seek God and His Kingdom first and forsake all that this world has to offer. Once you enter the *Secret Place*, you will find that God is your provider, and He is more than enough. Now is the time to take up the call of God and forsake all to dwell with God in the *Secret Place*.

SECOND TEMPLE

CHAPTER
SIX

Knowing
God

The *Secret Place* has everything to do with knowing God. Anyone dwelling in the *Secret Place of the Most High* will have a special, intimate, and heartfelt relationship with the Lord. Getting to know the Lord is the highest attainment one can reach in this life. The Bible has a lot to say about who knows God and who doesn't know Him. Just because someone knows all about God doesn't mean they know Him personally. Many people may say they know the Lord, but they prove otherwise in their actions. Only those who know the Lord can dwell in the *Secret Place* and enter Heaven. In this chapter, I will reveal what it means to genuinely know the Lord.

The Prophet Jeremiah prophesied that in the New Covenant, God's people would know Him for themselves without anyone teaching them to know Him. God said that all would know Him from the least to the greatest in this New Covenant. This is a wonderful revelation to meditate on!

Jeremiah 31:31-34 (KJV)

*31 Behold, the days come, saith the Lord, that I will make a **new covenant** with the house of Israel, and with the house of Judah: 32 Not according to the covenant that I made with their fathers in the day that I took them by the hand to bring them out of the land of Egypt; which my covenant they brake, although I was an husband unto them, saith the Lord: 33 But this shall be the **covenant** that I will make with the house of Israel; After those days, saith the Lord, I will put my law in their inward parts, and write it in their hearts; and will be their God, and they shall be my people. 34 **And they shall teach no more every man his neighbour, and every man his brother, saying, Know the Lord: for they shall all know me, from the least of them unto the greatest of them, saith***

the Lord: *for I will forgive their iniquity, and I will remember their sin no more.*

The word *know* in Hebrew, means to *know* relationally and experientially rather than mere intellectual awareness. The word *know* signifies that you *know* the deepest secret thoughts of God, because you are close to His heart. One example of the word *know* has to do with an intimate relationship with a husband and wife. Intimacy is the highest form of knowing someone, which can only be cultivated through Covenant, friendship, trust, honesty, loyalty, selflessness, respect, and unconditional love.

The *Secret Place* is where a New Covenant believer enters a private loving relationship with God and shows Him how much they love Him by complete obedience to the Words of Christ. God, in return, reveals Himself to you through the Word of God and prayer as you spend alone time with Him in the *Secret Place*. You will come to really know the Lord personally by the secrets He reveals to you about Himself through the Scriptures and private times of prayer.

There is a manifested difference between someone who loves God in the *Secret Place* and someone who thinks they know God. The best way to describe this is by saying various Christians say they love God but show by their actions that they are not in the *Secret Place*. These Christians are near the things of God, near the *Secret Place*, but not *IN* the *Secret Place*. This is called Outer Court Christianity. What I mean by Outer Court Christianity is they confess Christ as their Lord, but in their actions, sinful lifestyle, how they treat other people, and lack of wisdom they prove they are not in the *Secret Place* and don't know the Lord. They may even preach, do miracles, and serve God's people. Jesus had a lot to say about these so-called believers.

Matthew 7:21-23 (KJV)

*21 Not every one that saith unto me, Lord, Lord, shall enter into the kingdom of heaven; but he that doeth the will of my Father which is in heaven. 22 **Many will say to me in that day, Lord, Lord, have we not prophesied in thy name? and in thy name have cast out devils? and in thy name done many wonderful works?** 23 And then will I profess unto them, I never knew you: depart from me, ye that work iniquity.*

The last most grieving and fearful thing you want to hear from the mouth of Christ is, *"I never knew you: depart from Me you that work iniquity."* Some Christians have read this verse and feared to prophesy, cast out devils, and do wonderful works in fear of Jesus telling them to depart from Him. This verse, however, is not talking about Christ not knowing someone because they operated in the gifts of the Spirit, but rather someone working iniquity. Iniquity was the defining factor of Christ not knowing them, and it wasn't the working of miracles.

The word iniquity means lawlessness or the violation of the Law. This person is wicked and disobedient to the Commands of Christ. They also violate their own moral code of the Laws of God written on their heart and don't keep their conscience clean. This type of person is selfish and doesn't do to others what they would want done unto themselves.

Matthew 7:12 (KJV)

*12 **Therefore all things whatsoever ye would that men should do to you, do ye even so to them:** for this is the law and the prophets.*

The Scriptures warn us not to sin willfully against our conscience. Willful sin means the person knows in their conscience if something is right or wrong, and they deliberately go against the truth of the moral code that God wrote in their heart and sin against God. This is what the Bible calls searing your conscience with a hot iron (1 Timothy 4:2). Any person who lives this way does not know God and is not living in the *Secret Place.*

Hebrews 10:26-31 (KJV)

26 For if we sin wilfully after that we have received the knowledge of the truth, there remaineth no more sacrifice for sins, 27 But a certain fearful looking for of judgment and fiery indignation, which shall devour the adversaries. 28 He that despised Moses' law died without mercy under two or three witnesses: 29 Of how much sorer punishment, suppose ye, shall he be thought worthy, who hath trodden under foot the Son of God, and hath counted the blood of the covenant, wherewith he was sanctified, an unholy thing, and hath done despite unto the Spirit of grace? 30 For we know him that hath said, Vengeance belongeth unto me, I will recompense, saith the Lord. And again, The Lord shall judge his people. 31 It is a fearful thing to fall into the hands of the living God.

Anyone dwelling in the *Secret Place of the Most High* obeys all the Words of Christ and watches over their conscience like an army guarding gold. This faithful believer won't tolerate a cheap message of greasy grace that says they can do whatever they want since Christ died for them. Instead, they say because Christ died for me and my sins, I will be careful never to sin against my Maker. The grace of God taught them to deny ungodliness and worldly lusts. The grace of God also taught them how to live soberly, righteously, and godly in this present world.

Titus 2:11-12 (KJV)

*11 For **the grace of God that bringeth salvation** hath appeared to all men, 12 **Teaching us that, denying ungodliness and worldly lusts, we should live soberly, righteously, and godly,** in this present world;*

The closer you get to the Lord, the more you realize how you treat others matters to Him. Anyone living in the *Secret Place* will have had many conversations with God about how they treat Him and others. Sinning against others is sinning against God. If you say you know God, you will keep His Commandments and treat others with love and respect.

1 John 2:3-6 (KJV)

*3 **And hereby we do know that we know him, if we keep his commandments. 4 He that saith, I know him, and keepeth not his commandments, is a liar,** and the truth is not in him. 5 **But whoso keepeth his word, in him verily is the love of God perfected: hereby know we that we are in him.** 6 He that saith he abideth in him ought himself also so to walk, even as he walked.*

Jesus came to this Earth, died, was buried, and rose again to take away our sins. Anyone who continues living in sin does not know God or why Jesus came to the earth. There is no sin in the *Secret Place*. Anyone living in the *Secret Place* is living a holy life according to the teachings of Jesus. Someone continuing in sin has not seen or known the Lord. Anyone *Abiding* in the *Secret Place of the Most High* sinneth not and immediately repents if they do sin.

1 John 3:4-6 (KJV)

*4 Whosoever **committeth sin** transgresseth also the law: for sin is the transgression of the law. 5 **And ye know that he was manifested to take away our sins; and in him is no sin.** 6 **Whosoever abideth in him sinneth not: whosoever sinneth hath not seen him, neither known him.***

God defines love as obedience to His Commands and not just by feelings or insincere words. Some people might think they love God because they worship and sing love songs to Him. Singing worship songs is great and can be wonderful if sung from the heart of someone keeping Christ's Commands. Jesus said that people draw near to Him with their mouths, but their hearts are far from Him. This type of person is a hypocrite and worships God in vain.

Matthew 15:7-9 (KJV)

*7 Ye hypocrites, well did Esaias prophesy of you, saying, 8 **This people draweth nigh unto me with their mouth, and honoureth me with their lips; but their heart is far from me.** 9 But **in vain they do worship me,** teaching for doctrines the commandments of men.*

My purpose in writing this chapter is not to beat anyone up but to help people come to the revelation that if they want to know God, they must obey all of the Commands of Christ, treat others the way they want to be treated, and keep their conscience clean. If you are reading this book about the *Secret Place*, you are serious about your walk with Christ. I am sent to help people not be deceived by false doctrines of demons. False doctrines of demons will keep you away from really knowing God in the *Secret Place*. I am speaking the wisdom of God by the Spirit of the Lord to all who want to go deeper in their walk with the Lord.

The Apostle Paul said he counted everything but loss for the excellency of the knowledge of Christ Jesus, his Lord. He counted everything but dung that he might win Christ and know Him.

> *Philippians 3:7-11 (KJV)*
> *7 But what things were gain to me, those I counted loss for Christ. 8 Yea doubtless, and I count all things but loss for the excellency of the knowledge of Christ Jesus my Lord: for whom I have suffered the loss of all things, and do count them but dung, that I may win Christ, 9 And be found in him, not having mine own righteousness, which is of the law, but that which is through the faith of Christ, the righteousness which is of God by faith: 10 That I may know him, and the power of his resurrection, and the fellowship of his sufferings, being made conformable unto his death; 11 If by any means I might attain unto the resurrection of the dead.*

The night before Jesus went to the Cross, He declared that *Eternal Life* was to know Him and the Father who sent Him. *Eternal Life* is knowing God by obeying the Words of Christ. This is how one enters the *Secret Place* and *Eternal Life.*

> *John 17:1-3 (KJV)*
> *1 These words spake Jesus, and lifted up his eyes to heaven, and said, Father, the hour is come; glorify thy Son, that thy Son also may glorify thee: 2 As thou hast given him power over all flesh, that he should give eternal life to as many as thou hast given him. 3 And*

this is life eternal, that they might know thee the only true God, and Jesus Christ, whom thou hast sent.

On the same night, Jesus said there would be those who would kill His disciples, thinking that they were doing God's service. Throughout Church history, real men and women of God have been killed by religious leaders and their followers, thinking they were doing God's service. Jesus prophesied that they would do this because they have not known the Father nor Him.

John 16:1-4 (KJV)

*1 These things have I spoken unto you, that ye should not be offended. 2 **They shall put you out of the synagogues: yea, the time cometh, that whosoever killeth you will think that he doeth God service. 3 And these things will they do unto you, because they have not known the Father, nor me.** 4 But these things have I told you, that when the time shall come, ye may remember that I told you of them. And these things I said not unto you at the beginning, because I was with you.*

Some of the worst attacks you may face will come from people who say they know God but, in works, deny Him. These false Christians are not dwelling in the *Secret Place.*

Titus 1:16 (KJV)

*16 **They profess that they know God; but in works they deny him, being abominable, and disobedient, and unto every good work reprobate.***

I know this is a heavy chapter, but there are too many warnings in the Holy Scriptures about this issue for me to remain criminally silent. Anyone who names the name of Christ must depart from iniquity, and the Lord knows them that are His.

2 Timothy 2:19 (KJV)
*19 Nevertheless the foundation of God standeth sure, having this seal, **The Lord knoweth them that are his. And, let every one that nameth the name of Christ depart from iniquity.***

Anyone dwelling in the *Secret Place* or wanting to enter the *Secret Place* of their own Holy of Holies in their body will love what I am writing about. You will love it because you know it is the **TRUTH**. You desire the truth and no longer want to be lied to. It is only the truth of Christ that will make you free.

John 8:31-32 (KJV)
*31 Then said Jesus to those Jews which believed on him, **If ye continue in my word, then are ye my disciples indeed; 32 And ye shall know the truth, and the truth shall make you free.***

I have been revealing the truth of God's Word, and one of those truths is that the Ark of the Covenant represents the Holy Spirit. An integral aspect of knowing God is knowing the Holy Spirit, who dwells in the Temple of your body. Now, I will share what the Bible says about how we should treat the Holy Spirit. Jesus said someone could speak a word against Him, and it could be forgiven, but if someone spoke against the Holy Spirit, it would never be forgiven. Jesus made this proclamation after the Pharisees said He was casting out devils by beelzebub (the prince of the devils) and not by the Holy Spirit (Matthew 12:24).

Matthew 12:31-32 (KJV)

31 Wherefore I say unto you, All manner of sin and blasphemy shall be forgiven unto men: **but the blasphemy against the Holy Ghost shall not be forgiven unto men.** *32 And whosoever speaketh a word against the Son of man, it shall be forgiven him:* **but whosoever speaketh against the Holy Ghost, it shall not be forgiven him, neither in this world, neither in the world to come.**

Dwelling in the *Secret Place of the Most High* means you are committed to being sensitive to the Holy Spirit. The Scriptures warn us what not to do when walking with the Holy Spirit. These warnings must be taught and respected so that you can enter your Temple's Holy of Holies *(Secret Place)* and stay close to God. After the death of our Lord and Saviour, the Holy Spirit was given to comfort us, lead us, bring to our remembrance the Words that Jesus taught, teach us truth, and prepare us for the afterlife.

Remember, the Ark of the Covenant represents the Holy Spirit, and the Ark of the Covenant is the only Holy artifact found in the Holy of Holies. The Ark of the Covenant is also the most significant artifact in the Tabernacle of Moses, the Temple of King Solomon, and the Tabernacle of David. Therefore, the Holy Spirit should be respected in the New Testament as the Ark of the Covenant was revered in the Old Covenant.

If you say you know the Lord and are dwelling in the *Secret Place*, there are seven things you should never do to the Holy Spirit. Anyone who declares they know God is careful in how they treat God's precious Holy Spirit.

WE SHOULD NEVER:

1. Strive with the Holy Spirit

2. Grieve the Holy Spirit

3. Quench the Holy Spirit

4. Rebel Against & Vex the Holy Spirit

5. Resist the Holy Spirit

6. Do Despite to the Spirit of Grace

7. Blaspheme the Holy Spirit

OFFENSES AGAINST THE HOLY SPIRIT

1. STRIVING WITH THE HOLY SPIRIT

To strive means being in contention and struggling in opposition to another. This word paints a picture of someone contending with the Holy Spirit, who is more powerful than them. Anyone dwelling in the *Secret Place* will never struggle, quarrel, argue, and fight with the Holy Spirit.

> *Genesis 6:3 (KJV)*
> *3 And the Lord said, **My spirit shall not always strive with man**, for that he also is flesh: yet his days shall be an hundred and twenty years.*

2. GRIEVING THE HOLY SPIRIT

The Bible teaches that the Holy Spirit can be grieved by how we treat God and others. The word grieve means to afflict with sorrow, make them mourn, be in inward grief, and cause pain. The Holy Spirit grieves when we treat God and others unjustly. The Holy Spirit can also be grieved if you allow corrupt communication to proceed out of your mouth.

Ephesians 4:29-32 (KJV)

*29 Let no corrupt communication proceed out of your mouth, but that which is good to the use of edifying, that it may minister grace unto the hearers. 30 **And grieve not the holy Spirit of God, whereby ye are sealed unto the day of redemption.** 31 Let all bitterness, and wrath, and anger, and clamour, and evil speaking, be put away from you, with all malice: 32 And be ye kind one to another, tenderhearted, forgiving one another, even as God for Christ's sake hath forgiven you.*

3. QUENCHING THE HOLY SPIRIT

Quench means extinguishing a fire, quieting one, or repressing passion and emotion. The Holy Spirit is quenched when someone prevents Him from exerting His full influence. Someone quenches the Holy Spirit in another person when they despise the gift of prophecy in them. You must be careful never to shut down the Holy Spirit when He is speaking through another person. The Holy Spirit, who is like a fire, is also quenched when someone tries to keep a person from being on fire for God.

1 Thessalonians 5:19-23 (KJV)

*19 **Quench not the Spirit.** 20 **Despise not prophesyings.** 21 Prove all things; hold fast that which is good. 22 Abstain from all appearance of evil. 23 And the very God of peace sanctify you wholly; and I pray God your whole spirit and soul and body be preserved blameless unto the coming of our Lord Jesus Christ.*

4. REBELLING & VEXING THE HOLY SPIRIT

To rebel means resisting the authority of one in control over you. Rebelling is when you are disobedient to the Voice and leading of the Holy Spirit and provoke Him to anger. To vex the Holy Spirit means to hurt, displease, cause emotional pain, and make Him angry. God will become your enemy and fight against you if you rebel and vex the Holy Spirit.

Isaiah 63:10 (KJV)

10 But they rebelled, and vexed his holy Spirit: therefore he was turned to be their enemy, and he fought against them.

5. RESISTING THE HOLY SPIRIT

To resist the Holy Spirit means to stand firm against and oppose Him. Someone stiff-necked and uncircumcised in heart sets themselves against the Holy Spirit. Some resist and close their ears to the Holy Spirit when they reject what He has revealed by ignoring what He has said. A stiff-necked person is stubborn and refuses to bow in submission to the Holy Spirit. Uncircumcised in heart and ears is a metaphor that reveals a person with a hard heart who won't listen to and obey the Holy Spirit.

Acts 7:51 (KJV)

51 Ye stiffnecked and uncircumcised in heart and ears, ye do always resist the Holy Ghost: as your fathers did, so do ye.

6. DESPITE AGAINST THE SPIRIT OF GRACE

A person who does despite against the Holy Spirit is defiant with contempt. A willful sin against your conscience is doing despite to the Spirit of Grace. A person sins willfully when they know the truth and still sins, knowing full well that what they are doing is wrong. The Scriptures call this doing despite to the Spirit of Grace and counting the Blood of the Covenant as an unholy thing.

Hebrews 10:26-31 (KJV)

*26 **For if we sin wilfully after that we have received the knowledge of the truth**, there remaineth no more sacrifice for sins, 27 But a certain fearful looking for of judgment and fiery indignation, which shall devour the adversaries. 28 He that despised Moses' law died without mercy under two or three witnesses: 29 **Of how much sorer punishment, suppose ye, shall he be thought worthy, who hath trodden under foot the Son of God, and hath counted the blood of the covenant, wherewith he was sanctified, an unholy thing, and hath done despite unto the Spirit of grace?** 30 For we know him that hath said, Vengeance belongeth unto me, I will recompense, saith the Lord. And again, The Lord shall judge his people. 31 It is a fearful thing to fall into the hands of the living God.*

7. BLASPHEME AGAINST THE HOLY SPIRIT

Blasphemy of the Holy Spirit is the worst of all things a person can do against the Holy Spirit. There is no forgiveness for the one who blasphemes the Holy Spirit. Jesus taught that blasphemy of the Holy Spirit is when someone calls the work of the Holy Spirit the work of the devil. Jesus said the Pharisees blasphemed the Holy Spirit when they said He was casting out devils by the prince of devils (beelzebub). The Father and the Son are very protective of the Holy Spirit, and we should be also.

Matthew 12:22-32 (KJV)

*22 Then was brought unto him one possessed with a devil, blind, and dumb: and he healed him, insomuch that the blind and dumb both spake and saw. 23 And all the people were amazed, and said, Is not this the son of David? 24 **But when the Pharisees heard it,*** *they said, This fellow doth not cast out devils, but by Beelzebub the prince of the devils. 25 And Jesus knew their thoughts, and said unto them, Every kingdom divided against itself is brought to desolation; and every city or house divided against itself shall not stand: 26 And if Satan cast out Satan, he is divided against himself; how shall then his kingdom stand? 27 And if I by Beelzebub cast out devils, by whom do your children cast them out? therefore they shall be your judges. 28 But if I cast out devils by the Spirit of God, then the kingdom of God is come unto you. 29 Or else how can one enter into a strong man's house, and spoil his goods, except he first bind the strong man? and then he will spoil his house. 30 He that is not with me is against me; and he that gathereth not with me scattereth abroad. 31 Wherefore I say unto you, **All manner of sin and blasphemy shall be forgiven unto men: but the blasphemy against the Holy Ghost shall not be forgiven unto men.** 32 And whosoever speaketh a word against the Son of man, it shall be forgiven him: but whosoever speaketh against the Holy Ghost, it shall not be forgiven him, neither in this world, neither in the world to come.*

The Scriptures teach us that God is known by His judgments. God reveals Himself by what He likes and doesn't like when He executes a judgment. The Lord makes Himself known among us when He brings judgment.

Psalm 9:16 (KJV)
*16 **The Lord is known by the judgment which he executeth**: the wicked is snared in the work of his own hands. Higgaion. Selah.*

Ezekiel 35:11 (KJV)

*11 Therefore, as I live, saith the Lord God, I will even do according to thine anger, and according to thine envy which thou hast used out of thy hatred against them; **and I will make myself known among them, when I have judged thee.***

I am teaching what God likes and doesn't like, as revealed in His Word. I highly advise anyone reading this book to search the Scriptures to see if my words are true. If you want to dwell in the *Secret Place of the Most High* and get close to God, you must learn what He approves and disapproves of. If you want to be close to the Holy Spirit and have the Ark of the Covenant in your life, you must know how to treat Him. God wants you to know Him, and He wants to get to know you, but it has to be on His terms.

The Prophet Jeremiah prophesied that men should not glory in their own wisdom, might, or riches. If we are to glory, we are to glory in that we understand and know God. I want to know God and do what pleases Him. Knowing God means that you understand that He exercises lovingkindness, judgment, and righteousness in the earth. These are the things the Lord delights in.

Jeremiah 9:23-24 (KJV)

23 Thus saith the Lord, Let not the wise man glory in his wisdom, neither let the mighty man glory in his might, let not the rich man glory in his riches: 24 But let him that glorieth glory in this, that he understandeth and knoweth me, that I am the Lord which exercise lovingkindness, judgment, and righteousness, in the earth: for in these things I delight, saith the Lord.

God wants to reveal His ways to you and not just His acts. Many people want to see the miracles of God, but God desires to teach you His ways, thoughts, and judgments.

> *Psalm 103:7-8 (KJV)*
> *7 He made known his ways unto Moses, his acts unto the children of Israel. 8 The Lord is merciful and gracious, slow to anger, and plenteous in mercy.*

Another way to know if someone knows the Lord is how they treat the poor and needy. Someone dwelling in the *Secret Place* will be very generous to those in need around them. Through the Prophet Jeremiah, God said that Josiah, the King of Israel, knew God because he judged the cause of the poor and needy.

> *Jeremiah 22:16 (KJV)*
> *16 He judged the cause of the poor and needy; then it was well with him: was not this to know me? saith the Lord.*

Jesus spoke a challenging parable before He left Earth about His return and who He would be coming back for. This parable is called the *Parable of the Ten Virgins*. Jesus described five virgins as wise, having oil in their lamps, waiting, and ready for His return. Jesus revealed the other five virgins to be foolish and didn't prepare by not having enough oil. When it came time for His return, the five foolish virgins didn't have enough oil for their lamps to meet the Bridegroom. They asked the five wise virgins for some of their oil, but they refused to give them any, fearing they would not have enough. So, the five foolish virgins left to get oil, and while they were gone, Christ returned as the Bridegroom. The five foolish virgins were not taken but left behind.

At the end of this insightful parable, Jesus revealed why the five foolish virgins were not ready. Jesus said to them, I know you not. Being prepared for the return of Christ has everything to do with knowing Him. Knowing Him was the secret to the five wise virgins having oil for their lamps. Those dwelling in the *Secret Place* know God and are prepared for His return because they daily prove they know Him in how they think, speak, and act. When you dwell in the *Secret Place* you are living prepared and are always ready to meet the Lord when He returns.

Matthew 25:1-13 (KJV)

*1 Then shall the kingdom of heaven be likened unto ten virgins, which took their lamps, and went forth to meet the bridegroom. 2 And five of them were wise, and five were foolish. 3 They that were foolish took their lamps, and took no oil with them: 4 But the wise took oil in their vessels with their lamps. 5 While the bridegroom tarried, they all slumbered and slept. 6 And at midnight there was a cry made, Behold, the bridegroom cometh; go ye out to meet him. 7 Then all those virgins arose, and trimmed their lamps. 8 And the foolish said unto the wise, Give us of your oil; for our lamps are gone out. 9 But the wise answered, saying, Not so; lest there be not enough for us and you: but go ye rather to them that sell, and buy for yourselves. 10 And while they went to buy, the bridegroom came; and they that were ready went in with him to the marriage: and the door was shut. 11 **Afterward came also the other virgins, saying, Lord, Lord, open to us. 12 But he answered and said, Verily I say unto you, I know you not.** 13 Watch therefore, for ye know neither the day nor the hour wherein the Son of man cometh.*

We live in a day and age where crowds of people say they know God, but do they? The Scriptures reveal what it means to know God. I have gone into great detail and revealed many Scriptures in this chapter to help you better understand what it means to truly know God. God wants you to know Him and has invited you into the *Secret Place*, but it must be entirely on His conditions. It's His *Secret Place*, and He makes the rules.

The Scriptures teach that the people that do know their God shall be strong and do exploits.

> *Daniel 11:32b (KJV)*
> *32...but the people that do know their God shall be strong, and do exploits.*

God wants us to discern between the righteous and the wicked, between him that serves God and him that doesn't serve Him. God records in a book of remembrance those who fear Him and think upon His name. Those who fear Him often speak one to another about the Lord.

> *Malachi 3:16-18 (KJV)*
> *16 Then they that feared the Lord spake often one to another: and the Lord hearkened, and heard it, and a book of remembrance was written before him for them that feared the Lord, and that thought upon his name. 17 And they shall be mine, saith the Lord of hosts, in that day when I make up my jewels; and I will spare them, as a man spareth his own son that serveth him. 18 Then shall ye return, and discern between the righteous and the wicked, between him that serveth God and him that serveth him not.*

SECRET PLACE CONVERSATIONS

A strong relationship with the Lord is based on how much you pray to Him and how much He talks with you. You can only know the Lord based on your private conversations with Him as you obey His Word. The closer you are to the Lord in the *Secret Place,* the deeper your conversations with Him will be. God has many things to teach and communicate with us as we draw near to Him. The *Secret Place* is where the Lord can share His most intimate thoughts with you.

When Jesus was on this Earth, He said that He preached in parables to the multitudes, but to His closest disciples, He revealed the mysteries of the Kingdom of Heaven.

> *Matthew 13:10-11 (KJV)*
> *10 And the disciples came, and said unto him,* **Why speakest thou unto them in parables? 11 He answered and said unto them, Because it is given unto you to know the mysteries of the kingdom of heaven, but to them it is not given.**

Jesus said He spoke to the multitudes in parables because they don't see, hear, or understand. He revealed that they were responsible for not hearing, seeing, and understanding. Jesus said these types of people's hearts waxed gross, which means they hardened their hearts, making themselves spiritually blind.

> *Matthew 13:13-15 (KJV)*
> *13 Therefore speak I to them in parables: because they seeing see not; and hearing they hear not, neither do they understand. 14 And in them is fulfilled the prophecy of Esaias, which saith, By hearing*

*ye shall hear, and shall not understand; and seeing ye shall see, and shall not perceive: 15 **For this people's heart is waxed gross, and their ears are dull of hearing, and their eyes they have closed; lest at any time they should see with their eyes and hear with their ears, and should understand with their heart,** and should be converted, and I should heal them.*

In this same passage of Scripture, Jesus said to His disciples that their eyes and ears were blessed for hearing and seeing what God was revealing to them. The close disciples of Christ who had left everything to follow Him were shown revelations that prophets and righteous men desired to hear and see.

Matthew 13:16-17 (KJV)
*16 **But blessed are your eyes, for they see: and your ears, for they hear.** 17 **For verily I say unto you, That many prophets and righteous men have desired to see those things which ye see, and have not seen them; and to hear those things which ye hear, and have not heard them.***

Jesus revealed that God wants to have deeper conversations with His people, but some are not ready to hear what He has to say. God's conversation with someone dwelling in the *Secret Place* is much different than that of a person not near Him. The responsibility, however, lies on us as to what level we hear from God. God is looking for those who will spiritually mature to the point they can hear all God wants to say to them.

God revealed in the building of the Tabernacle of Moses the revelation of how to hear from the Lord. The level of conversations God can have with you is based upon where you are found in His Holy Temple. The layout of the Temple is a representation of our walk with the Lord and how He communicates with His people. The mystery of knowing the Lord can be discovered as we draw close to the Lord through the different spiritual locations found in His Tabernacle.

A person not dwelling in God's Tabernacle will only hear God speak in parables. This person is living in sin, has a hard heart, and shuts their spiritual ears and eyes so they cannot hear or see what God is saying. This type of person is not living in the Covenant of God. God doesn't have any deep conversations with this type of person because they are not prepared to hear what He has to say.

A person living in *the Outer Court* of the Temple, where the **Bronze Altar** and **Bronze Laver** can be found, will start to hear God speak to them about their sins. The **Bronze Altar** is where sacrifice is made for sin and the **Bronze Laver** is where you clean yourself with the washing of the Word of God. God speaks to a person dwelling in the *Outer Court* directly about their sin and tells them they must repent. God will use preachers like John the Baptist to get people right with Him and to be baptized in water while they confess their sins. Baptism in water represents the washing of the water of the Word in the **Bronze Laver.**

> *Mark 1:4-5 (KJV)*
> *4 John did baptize in the wilderness, and preach the baptism of* **repentance for the remission of sins.** *5 And there went out unto him all the land of Judaea, and they of Jerusalem,* **and were all** **baptized of him in the river of Jordan, confessing their sins.**

Those who hear God's message of holiness and repent of their sins are made ready to enter the *Inner Court.* The *Inner Court* of the Tabernacle of Moses is also called the *Holy Place,* where the *Table of Shewbread, Golden Candlestick,* and *Altar of Incense* are located. When believers dwell in the *Inner Court,* they will hear God reveal His revelations, and their eyes will be opened to spiritual truth. The bread on the *Table of Shewbread* represents God's Word, and the *Golden Candlestick's* light represents the illumination of God and Who He is. They are also in a position to offer up prayers that will be heard from God like the smoke rising off of the *Altar of Incense* before the *Ark of the Covenant.* The *Holy Place (Inner Court)* is where God speaks to you about the mysteries of His Kingdom and illuminates to you His profound truths. These truths prepare you to commune with Him in the *Holy of Holies,* where the *Ark of the Covenant* resides.

Once believers receive the light of God's Word and their eyes and ears are opened to see the light of the knowledge of the Glory of God found in the face of Jesus Christ, they are ready to enter the *Holy of Holies.*

> *2 Corinthians 4:6 (KJV)*
> *6 For God, who commanded the light to shine out of darkness, hath shined in our hearts, to give the light of the knowledge of the glory of God in the face of Jesus Christ.*

A believer who has repented of their sins and received the light of knowledge of God's Word is ready to enter the *Holy of Holies.* The *Holy of Holies* is the *Secret Place* where God can commune with you as a part of His family and a friend. *Secret Place Conversations* are found here, and sometimes the Presence of God is so wonderful you don't even want to talk. In this sacred place, God will begin to share His secrets with you and show you more about His Covenant.

Psalm 25:14 (KJV)

14 The secret of the Lord is with them that fear him; and he will shew them his covenant.

This is where Moses was dwelling as he was taught the deeper thoughts of God as he spent time in the *Secret Place*. God spoke to Moses face to face as a man speaks to his friend.

Exodus 33:11a (KJV)

11 And the Lord spake unto Moses face to face, as a man speaketh unto his friend...

We know that Moses was dwelling in the *Holy of Holies (Secret Place)*, communing with God, who hovered above the Mercy Seat on the Ark of the Covenant.

Exodus 25:22 (KJV)

22 And there I will meet with thee, and I will commune with thee from above the mercy seat, from between the two cherubims which are upon the ark of the testimony, of all things which I will give thee in commandment unto the children of Israel.

When you dwell in the *Holy of Holies,* which is the *Secret Place*, you and God can share your innermost thoughts. God shared with Moses what happened in the Garden of Eden as Moses was led to write the Book of Genesis. Moses was also given the layout of the Tabernacle, and he was given the Old Testament Law. As you dwell in the *Secret Place,* God can reveal His most profound secrets to you because He trusts you. The *Secret Place* is a place of intimacy, love, respect and friendship. Some things can occur in your

Secret Place relationship with God that you may be unable to talk about because they are so private.

All the revelations found in the books I have written have come from spending time in the *Secret Place*. This book also emerged from my time with God in the *Holy of Holies*. Many of the miracles that have occurred in my life came from God speaking to me and telling me what to do. As I listened and obeyed, God performed miracles and saved my life from destruction. I don't know where I would be today if I didn't have alone time with God in the *Secret Place*. God has changed my life as I listened to Him as a Father instructs a son. I love the Lord with all my heart, mind, soul, and strength. He is my all and all.

Here is a recap of the levels of conversations people have with God:

WITHOUT THE TABERNACLE (TEMPLE)
God will speak to you in parables in hopes of you drawing closer to Him. Parables are intended to draw your interest, so you will want God to speak to you more.

OUTER COURT
God will speak to you about your sin(s) in hopes you will repent and stay clean by the washing of the water of His Word. Your sins are dealt with on the **Bronze Altar,** and you clean yourself at the **Bronze Laver.** God only talks to you in the *Outer Court* about your sins and speaks to you about cleaning your life up and getting right with Him.

INNER COURT (HOLY PLACE)
When God speaks to you in the *Holy Place,* He will open your eyes and ears to the mysteries of the Kingdom of Heaven. You are permitted to eat the Holy Bread from the **Table of Showbread**, representing the Word of God. The **Golden Candlestick**, which

represents God's light, illuminates your spiritual eyes to see the mysteries of God. There is no natural light in the *Holy Place.* You are also able to offer up prayers to God like the smoke rising from the **Altar of Incense.** Your prayers come before God as a sweet-smelling aroma.

HOLY OF HOLIES

The *Holy of Holies* is the *Secret Place* where you commune with God in the most intimate way. God speaks to you like a Father to a child and as a friend. God hovers above the **Ark of the Covenant** in your *Holy of Holies* and allows you to partake of His glory. In this place, you are changed into the very image of Christ. The conversations that take place here with God are so private that many of them cannot be repeated. The *Secret Place* is also where God will tell you what to do so He can perform miracles through you.

Secret Place Conversations is the great mystery revealed in the Tabernacle of Moses. Many people don't want God to speak to them. We can see this truth in the Old Testament when the children of Israel asked that God would not speak to them anymore but wanted Moses to speak to them.

Exodus 20:19 (KJV)
19 And they said unto Moses, Speak thou with us, and we will hear: but let not God speak with us, lest we die.

The Bible teaches us that we are not to harden our hearts when God speaks to us. The children of Israel hardened their hearts when God spoke to them and were not allowed to enter His Rest (Promised Land).

Hebrews 3:7-11 (KJV)

7 Wherefore (as the Holy Ghost saith, To day if ye will hear his voice, 8 Harden not your hearts, as in the provocation, in the day of temptation in the wilderness: 9 When your fathers tempted me, proved me, and saw my works forty years. 10 Wherefore I was grieved with that generation, and said, They do alway err in their heart; and they have not known my ways. 11 So I sware in my wrath, They shall not enter into my rest.)

We need to be like Elijah, who heard the still small voice of God.

1 Kings 19:11-12 (KJV)

11 And he said, Go forth, and stand upon the mount before the Lord. And, behold, the Lord passed by, and a great and strong wind rent the mountains, and brake in pieces the rocks before the Lord; but the Lord was not in the wind: and after the wind an earthquake; but the Lord was not in the earthquake: 12 And after the earthquake a fire; but the Lord was not in the fire: and after the fire a still small voice.

We also need to be like the Prophet Samuel, who was commanded by the High Priest Eli to say to the Lord, speak for thy servant heareth.

1 Samuel 3:9-10 (KJV)

9 Therefore Eli said unto Samuel, Go, lie down: and it shall be, if he call thee, that thou shalt say, Speak, Lord; for thy servant heareth. So Samuel went and lay down in his place. 10 And the Lord came, and stood, and called as at other times, Samuel, Samuel. Then Samuel answered, Speak; for thy servant heareth.

When the Apostle Paul went to the third Heaven, he said he heard unspeakable words which were not lawful for a man to utter. He was hearing *Secret Place Conversations* that were not to be repeated.

> *2 Corinthians 12:4 (KJV)*
> *4 How that he was caught up into paradise, and heard unspeakable words, which it is not lawful for a man to utter.*

Jesus performed miracles by seeing in the *Secret Place* what the Father was doing.

> *John 5:19-20 (KJV)*
> *19 Then answered Jesus and said unto them, Verily, verily, I say unto you, The Son can do nothing of himself, but what he seeth the Father do: for what things soever he doeth, these also doeth the Son likewise. 20 For the Father loveth the Son, and sheweth him all things that himself doeth: and he will shew him greater works than these, that ye may marvel.*

In conclusion, God is looking for someone He can get to know in the *Secret Place*. You can only know the Lord and dwell in the *Secret Place* by obeying the Commands of Christ and hearing His Voice. Knowing the Lord has everything to do with hearing His Voice and receiving revelations about His Kingdom. There are many mysteries that God wants to reveal to His children, but they are only found in the *Secret Place*. Now is the time to draw near to God and hear everything He has to say so we can know Him and be prepared to meet Him when He returns.

CHAPTER
SEVEN

MAKING
VOWS

Our generation, for the most part, has not understood the importance of making vows to God. Vows, however, played a key role in the Old Testament and throughout Church history. Famous Biblical characters such as Jacob, Samson, and the Prophet Samuel made vows to God. Their vow was a secret to the anointing on their lives and what God did through them. In this chapter, I will reveal the power of making vows to God, how they can affect your life, and their role in the *Secret Place*.

A vow to God is a solemn promise spoken out loud to perform a duty to the Lord or to abstain from performing a particular thing. People usually made vows to the Lord to gain an anointing, blessing, or an answer to prayer. Sometimes, parents make a vow when dedicating their child to the Lord. This is the case of Samson and the Prophet Samuel. They vowed to keep specific requirements; if kept, they would be separated unto the Lord with a powerful anointing. People also sometimes make vows when going through difficult situations or need an answer to a prayer. Once a vow was made, it had to be fulfilled by the one who made it, and it was a sin if they did not keep their vow. The Lord takes vows very seriously.

Vows are entirely voluntary, but once made, the person who made the vow is bound to keep it. The golden question that must be asked is why someone would feel compelled to make a vow to the Lord if they didn't have to. The answer to this question is the vow becomes a sacrifice to the Lord. The person who makes a vow to the Lord wants to offer a sacrifice by not doing or doing something in their life. The vow requests God to answer a prayer, bless them in some way, or grant a special anointing on their life. When God hears the vow, He is more inclined to listen to their prayer, bless them, or grant them with a powerful anointing. The person making the vow to the Lord becomes bound to Him in the vow. God binds Himself to honor their vow as long as the vow is kept.

Numbers 30:1-2 (KJV)

1 And Moses spake unto the heads of the tribes concerning the children of Israel, saying, This is the thing which the LORD hath commanded. 2 If a man vow a vow unto the LORD, or swear an oath to bind his soul with a bond; he shall not break his word, he shall do according to all that proceedeth out of his mouth.

Jacob was the first person recorded in the Holy Scriptures to make a vow to the Lord. Jacob was the grandson of Abraham, and he loved the birthright. The Abrahamic Blessing was to be carried down through Abraham's bloodline as a Covenant with God. Jacob highly coveted the birthright so much that he made his older brother Esau sell it to him for a meal when Esau was hungry (Genesis 25:29-34; Hebrews 12:16). Later, Jacob also deceived his dad, Isaac, by pretending to be Esau, the firstborn son, so that he would pronounce the Abrahamic Blessing over him instead of his brother. Jacob was able to deceive his father, Isaac, because he was old and couldn't see.

After Jacob received the Abrahamic Blessing from his father Isaac, he left the Promised Land to marry a wife from the land of Padanaram. On the way to Padanaram, Jacob fell asleep and had a dream from God. In the dream, he saw a ladder set up on the Earth, and the top of it reached Heaven. In this dream, Jacob saw angels ascending and descending on it. The Lord stood above the ladder and spoke to Jacob about the Abrahamic Blessing. God promised Jacob that He would be with him wherever he went and bring him back to the Promised Land.

When Jacob awoke from the dream, he said, surely the Lord is in this place, and I knew it not. He called that place Bethel; "The House of God" (The Gate of Heaven). Then Jacob made a vow to the Lord. Jacob vowed that if God would be with him, keep him the way he is going, give him bread to eat, clothes to put on and return him to his father's house in peace, then God would be his God, and he would give Him a tenth of all that God gave him. A tithe is an offering to the Lord of ten percent of whatever God blesses you with. Jacob was the first person in the Bible to make a vow like this to the Lord. Jacob's vow had everything to do with the Abrahamic Covenant Blessing. Jacob was not required to make this vow because God had already promised to bless him, so this vow he made was a sacrifice to the Lord.

Genesis 28:20-22 (KJV)
*20 **And Jacob vowed a vow,** saying, If God will be with me, and will keep me in this way that I go, and will give me bread to eat, and raiment to put on, 21 So that I come again to my father's house in peace; then shall the Lord be my God: 22 And this stone, which I have set for a pillar, shall be God's house: and of all that thou shalt give me I will surely give the tenth unto thee.*

A number of years later, when Jacob was being sent back to the Promised Land by God, Jacob was reminded of his vow in a dream by the angel of God.

Genesis 31:11-13 (KJV)
*11 And the angel of God spake unto me in a dream, saying, Jacob: And I said, Here am I. 12 And he said, Lift up now thine eyes, and see, all the rams which leap upon the cattle are ringstraked, speckled, and grisled: for I have seen all that Laban doeth unto thee. 13 **I am the God of Bethel, where thou anointedst the pillar, and where thou vowedst a vow unto me:** now arise, get thee out from this land, and return unto the land of thy kindred.*

Another famous historical Biblical figure who had a vow on his life was the Israelite Judge named Samson. The angel of the Lord appeared to his barren mother and prophesied to her that she would give birth to a son. With this prophetic word, the angel of the Lord warned his mother, Manoah, that her son was to have no razor cut his hair his whole life and he was to be a Nazarite unto God from the womb. Being a Nazarite was about the vow of a Nazarite that Moses wrote about in the Law. This prophetic word, spoken by the angel of the Lord, also foretold that Samson would begin to deliver Israel out of the hands of the Philistines. The Philistines had been oppressing the Israelites for the last forty years because God was judging the children of Israel for doing evil in His sight.

> *Judges 13:3-5 (KJV)*
>
> *3 And the angel of the Lord appeared unto the woman, and said unto her, Behold now, thou art barren, and bearest not: but thou shalt conceive, and bear a son. 4 Now therefore beware, I pray thee, and drink not wine nor strong drink, and eat not any unclean thing: 5 For, lo, thou shalt conceive, and bear a son;* **and no razor shall come on his head: for the child shall be a Nazarite unto God from the womb:** *and he shall begin to deliver Israel out of the hand of the Philistines.*

The Nazarite Vow that Samson kept with its requirements can be found in Numbers Chapter 6.

> *Numbers 6:1-8 (KJV)*
>
> *1 And the Lord spake unto Moses, saying, 2 Speak unto the children of Israel, and say unto them,* **When either man or woman shall separate themselves to vow a vow of a Nazarite,** *to separate themselves unto the Lord: 3 He shall separate himself from wine and strong drink, and shall drink no vinegar of wine, or vinegar of strong drink, neither shall he drink any liquor of grapes, nor eat*

moist grapes, or dried. 4 All the days of his separation shall he eat nothing that is made of the vine tree, from the kernels even to the husk. 5 All the days of the vow of his separation there shall no razor come upon his head: until the days be fulfilled, in the which he separateth himself unto the Lord, he shall be holy, and shall let the locks of the hair of his head grow. 6 All the days that he separateth himself unto the Lord he shall come at no dead body. 7 He shall not make himself unclean for his father, or for his mother, for his brother, or for his sister, when they die: because the consecration of his God is upon his head. 8 All the days of his separation he is holy unto the Lord.

When Samson came of age, the Spirit of the Lord came upon him and empowered him with supernatural strength in obedience to the keeping of the Nazarite Vow. With this supernatural anointing of strength, Samson could defeat the Philistines single-handedly in battle. He also did numerous other exploits, such as slaying a lion with his bare hands, catching three hundred foxes and using them to burn down the Philistine's crops, carrying off the gates of a city around nine miles away, and many more feats of strength did Samson exhibit.

Samson's Nazarite Vow was broken when his hair was cut off by Deliah's trickery. Deliah was a Philistine woman with whom Samson fell in love, and she kept enticing Samson to tell her the secret of his strength. After finally wearing him down, she found out about his Nazarite Vow and had someone cut off his hair as he slept on her lap. When his hair was cut off, his vow was broken, and he lost his supernatural strength. The Philistines then captured him and poked out his eyes. He was then bound by fetters of brass and forced to grind in a prison house.

This story warns everyone who vows to the Lord to keep their vow. In the end, when Samson's hair started to grow back, his strength returned with one final feat to pull down the pillars of a house, killing himself and many Philistines. In his death, he killed more Philistines than he had killed in his life.

The Prophet Samuel was another Biblical figure with a vow on his life. His mother, Hannah, was barren and sought the Lord for a child. While praying for a child, she made a vow to God that if He granted her request, she vowed to dedicate her child to Him all the days of his life, and no razor would come on his head (Nazarite Vow). God granted her request, and she gave birth to Samuel. The name Samuel means God Heard.

> *1 Samuel 1:10-11 (KJV)*
> *10 And she was in bitterness of soul, and prayed unto the Lord, and wept sore. 11 **And she vowed a vow, and said, O Lord of hosts, if thou wilt indeed look on the affliction of thine handmaid, and remember me, and not forget thine handmaid, but wilt give unto thine handmaid a man child, then I will give him unto the Lord all the days of his life, and there shall no razor come upon his head.***

Samuel became one of the most powerful prophets in Israel. He was also a Priest of the Lord and a Judge of Israel. Prophet Samuel was the last Judge of Israel and was used by God to anoint the first king of Israel. He was also used to anoint David as the next King because of the disobedience of the first King of Israel, Saul. Samuel kept the Nazarite Vow all the days of his life, unlike Samson, and because of it, God anointed him mightily.

Making vows to God can be used to receive answers to prayers and unleash a high level of God's anointing. I am teaching the truth about making vows to the Lord in the *Secret Place* because God wants to restore the power of vows to our generation. I also understand by the Spirit of the Lord that anyone who enters the *Secret Place* will have vowed vows to the Lord. We are not called to the Old Testament Law of Moses, but I believe certain vows should be confessed and kept for those who want to dwell in the *Secret Place of the Most High.*

A friend of mine was battling cancer, and in the middle of her fight, she made a vow to God. She vowed that if God healed her, she would only listen to Christian music. She said this vow would be a sacrifice unto the Lord if He healed her. The Lord healed her, and she joyfully keeps her vow to God. Anyone who rides in her car gets to listen to Christian music with her because of her vow. She uses her vow and how God healed her as a testimony to minister to other people.

When you enter the New Covenant, you confess a *Covenant Vow* to make Jesus your Lord and your husband. The church is the Bride of Christ.

> *Revelation 21:9 (KJV)*
> *9 And there came unto me one of the seven angels which had the seven vials full of the seven last plagues, and talked with me, saying,* **Come hither, I will shew thee the bride, the Lamb's wife.**

The only way to get saved is by believing in your heart that God raised Jesus from the dead and confessing that Jesus is Lord. The word confess means publicly agreeing, verbally acknowledging openly, and promising as in a covenant.

Romans 10:9 (KJV)

*9 That if thou shalt **confess** with thy mouth the Lord Jesus, and shalt believe in thine heart that God hath raised him from the dead, thou shalt be saved.*

When someone confesses Jesus as their Lord, they are cutting a covenant with their mouth that He is also their Bridegroom, and they will obey Him in all things, the same way a wife would submit to her husband.

Ephesians 5:22-27 (KJV)

*22 Wives, submit yourselves unto your own husbands, as unto the Lord. 23 **For the husband is the head of the wife, even as Christ is the head of the church**: and he is the saviour of the body. 24 **Therefore as the church is subject unto Christ, so let the wives be to their own husbands in every thing.** 25 Husbands, love your wives, even as Christ also loved the church, and gave himself for it; 26 That he might sanctify and cleanse it with the washing of water by the word, 27 That he might present it to himself a glorious church, not having spot, or wrinkle, or any such thing; but that it should be holy and without blemish.*

The *Secret Place* is an intimate place of relationship with the Lord where you are in a Marriage Covenant with Him. In this Divine Marriage Covenant, you are to make vows to the Lord, just like a wife makes vows to her husband. God has also made Covenant vows to us. This is the great mystery of the *Secret Place*; we are married to the Lord. The *Secret Place* is an intimate place between us and our Lord, just like the private room of a husband and wife.

I have learned valuable lessons throughout the decades of spending time in the *Secret Place* with the Lord. God has intimate secrets to share with us if we take the time to seek Him in the *Secret Place*. There are some things the Lord will show you in the *Secret Place* that you cannot share with other people. Not everyone is ready for the more profound things of the Spirit. A deeper commitment to the Lord must be made in every revelation God shows you. The Lord revealed the mystery of vows that He wants us to make in our *Covenant Relationship* with Him.

There are at least forty vows from the Word of God that believers married to the Lord who desire to dwell in the *Secret Place* should make and keep. I will list these vows along with the Scriptures where they are found. You can study these vows for yourself in the Word of God. Some of these vows may challenge you, but if you are serious about the *Secret Place*, you wouldn't be afraid to make them. Anyone who doesn't want to make any vows to the Lord is revealing a lack of commitment. God is fully committed to us to the point of the death of His Son, Jesus. I admonish you to look over the following vows that God has revealed to me from the Word of God and understand that when you get close to the Lord in the *Secret Place*, you must keep these holy vows.

NEW COVENANT MARRIAGE VOWS

1. I VOW THAT JESUS IS MY LORD, AND I WILL DO WHAT HE SAYS

Romans 10:9 (KJV)
9 That if thou shalt confess with thy mouth the Lord Jesus, and shalt believe in thine heart that God hath raised him from the dead, thou shalt be saved.

Luke 6:46 (KJV)
46 And why call ye me, Lord, Lord, and do not the things which I say?

2. I Vow to Observe and Obey all the Words of Christ

Matthew 28:19-20 (KJV)

19 Go ye therefore, and teach all nations, baptizing them in the name of the Father, and of the Son, and of the Holy Ghost: 20 Teaching them to observe all things whatsoever I have commanded you: and, lo, I am with you always, even unto the end of the world. Amen.

3. I Vow to Love God by Keeping His Commandments

1 John 5:2 (KJV)

2 By this we know that we love the children of God, when we love God, and keep his commandments.

4. I Vow to Walk and Live in the Truth

1 John 2:27 (KJV)

27 But the anointing which ye have received of him abideth in you, and ye need not that any man teach you: but as the same anointing teacheth you of all things, and is truth, and is no lie, and even as it hath taught you, ye shall abide in him.

5. I Vow to Watch the Words that I Speak

Matthew 12:36-37 (KJV)

36 But I say unto you, That every idle word that men shall speak, they shall give account thereof in the day of judgment. 37 For by thy words thou shalt be justified, and by thy words thou shalt be condemned.

Ephesians 4:29 (KJV)

29 Let no corrupt communication proceed out of your mouth, but that which is good to the use of edifying, that it may minister grace unto the hearers.

6. I Vow to keep my Conscience Pure

Titus 1:15 (KJV)

15 Unto the pure all things are pure: but unto them that are defiled and unbelieving is nothing pure; but even their mind and conscience is defiled.

Hebrews 10:22 (KJV)

22 Let us draw near with a true heart in full assurance of faith, having our hearts sprinkled from an evil conscience, and our bodies washed with pure water.

7. I Vow to Be Led by the Holy Spirit

Romans 8:14 (KJV)

14 For as many as are led by the Spirit of God, they are the sons of God.

8. I Vow to Walk in the Spirit

Galatians 5:16-21 (KJV)

16 This I say then, Walk in the Spirit, and ye shall not fulfil the lust of the flesh. 17 For the flesh lusteth against the Spirit, and the Spirit against the flesh: and these are contrary the one to the other: so that ye cannot do the things that ye would. 18 But if ye be led of the Spirit, ye are not under the law. 19 Now the works of the flesh are manifest, which are these; Adultery, fornication, uncleanness, lasciviousness, *20 Idolatry, witchcraft, hatred, variance, emulations, wrath, strife, seditions, heresies, 21 Envyings, murders, drunkenness, revellings, and such like: of the which I tell you before, as I have also told you in time past, that they which do such things shall not inherit the kingdom of God.*

9. I Vow to Bear the Fruit of the Spirit

Galatians 5:22-25 (KJV)

22 But the fruit of the Spirit is love, joy, peace, longsuffering, gentleness, goodness, faith, 23 Meekness, temperance: against such there is no law. 24 And they that are Christ's have crucified the flesh with the affections and lusts. 25 If we live in the Spirit, let us also walk in the Spirit.

10. I Vow to Not Defile the Temple of My Body

1 Corinthians 3:16-17 (KJV)

16 Know ye not that ye are the temple of God, and that the Spirit of God dwelleth in you? 17 If any man defile the temple of God, him shall God destroy; for the temple of God is holy, which temple ye are.

11. I Vow to Love God with all My Heart, Soul, Mind, and Strength

Mark 12:29-30 (KJV)

29 And Jesus answered him, The first of all the commandments is, Hear, O Israel; The Lord our God is one Lord: 30 And thou shalt love the Lord thy God with all thy heart, and with all thy soul, and with all thy mind, and with all thy strength: this is the first commandment.

12. I Vow to Love My Neighbor as Myself

Matthew 22:39 (KJV)
39 And the second is like unto it, Thou shalt love thy neighbour as thyself.

13. I Vow to Live By the Golden Rule

Matthew 7:12 (KJV)
12 Therefore all things whatsoever ye would that men should do to you, do ye even so to them: for this is the law and the prophets.

14. I Vow to Have No other gods Before the Lord

Exodus 20:3 (KJV)
3 Thou shalt have no other gods before me.

15. I Vow to Worship the Lord, and Him Only will I Serve

Matthew 4:10 (KJV)
10 Then saith Jesus unto him, Get thee hence, Satan: for it is written, Thou shalt worship the Lord thy God, and him only shalt thou serve.

16. I Vow to Deny Myself and Take Up My Cross Daily

Luke 9:23 (KJV)
23 And he said to them all, If any man will come after me, let him deny himself, and take up his cross daily, and follow me. 24 For whosoever will save his life shall lose it: but whosoever will lose his life for my sake, the same shall save it.

17. I Vow to Seek First the Kingdom of God and His Righteousness

Matthew 6:33 (KJV)

33 But seek ye first the kingdom of God, and his righteousness; and all these things shall be added unto you.

18. I Vow to Forgive Everyone from the Heart

Matthew 6:14-15 (KJV)

14 For if ye forgive men their trespasses, your heavenly Father will also forgive you: 15 But if ye forgive not men their trespasses, neither will your Father forgive your trespasses.

Matthew 18:35 (KJV)

*35 So likewise shall my heavenly Father do also unto you, **if ye from your hearts forgive not** every one his brother their trespasses.*

19. I Vow to be Perfect before the Lord

Matthew 5:48 (KJV)

48 Be ye therefore perfect, even as your Father which is in heaven is perfect.

Ephesians 4:13 (KJV)

*13 Till we all come in the unity of the faith, and of the knowledge of the Son of God, **unto a perfect man**, unto the measure of the stature of the fulness of Christ:*

20. I Vow to Always Strive to Do the Perfect Will of God

Romans 12:1-2 (KJV)

1 I beseech you therefore, brethren, by the mercies of God, that ye present your bodies a living sacrifice, holy, acceptable unto God, which is your reasonable service. *2 And be not conformed to this world: but be ye transformed by the renewing of your mind, that ye may prove what is that good, and acceptable, and* **perfect, will of God.**

21. I VOW TO LIVE BY FAITH

Habakkuk 2:4 (KJV)
4 Behold, his soul which is lifted up is not upright in him: but **the just shall live by his faith.**

Hebrews 10:38 (KJV)
38 Now the just shall live by faith: but if any man draw back, my soul shall have no pleasure in him.

22. I VOW TO FIGHT THE GOOD FIGHT OF FAITH

1 Timothy 6:12 (KJV)
12 **Fight the good fight of faith,** *lay hold on eternal life, whereunto thou art also called, and hast professed a good profession before many witnesses.*

23. I VOW TO BE STRONG IN FAITH

Romans 4:20 (KJV)
20 He staggered not at the promise of God through unbelief; but **was strong in faith, giving glory to God;**

24. I VOW TO FEAR THE LORD

Proverbs 3:7 (KJV)
7 Be not wise in thine own eyes: **fear the Lord, and depart from evil.**

Proverbs 8:13 (KJV)

13 The fear of the Lord is to hate evil: pride, and arrogancy, and the evil way, and the froward mouth, do I hate.

25. I VOW TO DO THAT WHICH IS RIGHT IN THE SIGHT OF THE LORD

Exodus 15:26 (KJV)

*26 And said, If thou wilt diligently hearken to the voice of the Lord thy God, **and wilt do that which is right in his sight**, and wilt give ear to his commandments, and keep all his statutes, I will put none of these diseases upon thee, which I have brought upon the Egyptians: for I am the Lord that healeth thee.*

26. I VOW TO SERVE THE LORD WITH A PERFECT HEART

Psalm 101:2 (KJV)

*2 **I will behave myself wisely in a perfect way.** O when wilt thou come unto me? **I will walk within my house with a perfect heart.***

27. I VOW TO HELP THE ORPHANS AND WIDOWS

James 1:27 (KJV)

27 Pure religion and undefiled before God and the Father is this, To visit the fatherless and widows in their affliction, and to keep himself unspotted from the world.

28. I VOW TO HELP OTHERS WHEN THEY ARE IN NEED

1 John 3:17 (KJV)

17 But whoso hath this world's good, and seeth his brother have need, and shutteth up his bowels of compassion from him, how dwelleth the love of God in him?

29. I Vow to Walk Humbly Before God

Micah 6:8 (KJV)

*8 He hath shewed thee, O man, what is good; and what doth the Lord require of thee, but to do justly, and to love mercy, **and to walk humbly with thy God?***

1 Peter 5:6 (KJV)

6 Humble yourselves therefore under the mighty hand of God, that he may exalt you in due time:

30. I Vow to be Merciful

Matthew 5:7 (KJV)

7 Blessed are the merciful: for they shall obtain mercy.

31. I Vow to be a Peacemaker

Matthew 5:9 (KJV)

9 Blessed are the peacemakers: for they shall be called the children of God.

32. I Vow to give God Thanks in All Things

Ephesians 5:20 (KJV)

20 Giving thanks always for all things unto God and the Father in the name of our Lord Jesus Christ;

1 Thessalonians 5:18 (KJV)

18 In every thing give thanks: for this is the will of God in Christ Jesus concerning you.

33. I Vow to Preach the Gospel

Mark 16:15 (KJV)
15 And he said unto them, Go ye into all the world, and preach the gospel to every creature.

34. I Vow to Be Faithful to My Spouse

Exodus 20:14 (KJV)
14 Thou shalt not commit adultery.

35. I Vow to Not Lie

Ephesians 4:25 (KJV)
25 Wherefore putting away lying, speak every man truth with his neighbour: for we are members one of another.

Colossians 3:9 (KJV)
9 Lie not one to another, seeing that ye have put off the old man with his deeds;

36. I Vow to Not Steal

Ephesians 4:28 (KJV)
28 Let him that stole steal no more: but rather let him labour, working with his hands the thing which is good, that he may have to give to him that needeth.

37. I Vow to Honor the Lord with My Giving

Proverbs 3:9-10 (KJV)
9 Honour the Lord with thy substance, and with the firstfruits of all thine increase: 10 So shall thy barns be filled with plenty, and thy presses shall burst out with new wine.

38. I Vow to Protect My Heart

Proverbs 4:23 (KJV)

23 Keep thy heart with all diligence; for out of it are the issues of life.

39. I Vow to Keep Myself from Idols

1 John 5:21 (KJV)

21 Little children, keep yourselves from idols. Amen.

40. I Vow to Repent of Any Sin of Not Keeping these Vows

1 John 1:9 (KJV)

9 If we confess our sins, he is faithful and just to forgive us our sins, and to cleanse us from all unrighteousness.

Christians who are serious about their walk with the Lord and dwelling in the *Secret Place* will be passionately committed to keeping their vows. These vows are Commands from the Word of God. Many people don't dwell in the *Secret Place* because they are not willing to make any vows of commitment to God. The vows we proclaim and live by are essential in our New Covenant walk with the Lord.

In this chapter, I have revealed the power and purpose of vows. There are vows we can make as a sacrifice to God, and there are also New Covenant Marriage vows we can make to the Lord. Throughout history, every powerful man and woman of God lived by the Word of God and made personal vows to God. If you desire to dwell in the *Secret Place* and draw close to the Lord, make sure you are prepared to make and keep your vows to Him. Jesus is returning for a Bride who faithfully keeps their *Marriage Vows* to Him.

THE ENTRANCE OF THY WORDS GIVETH LIGHT;
IT GIVETH UNDERSTANDING UNTO THE SIMPLE.

PSALM 119:130

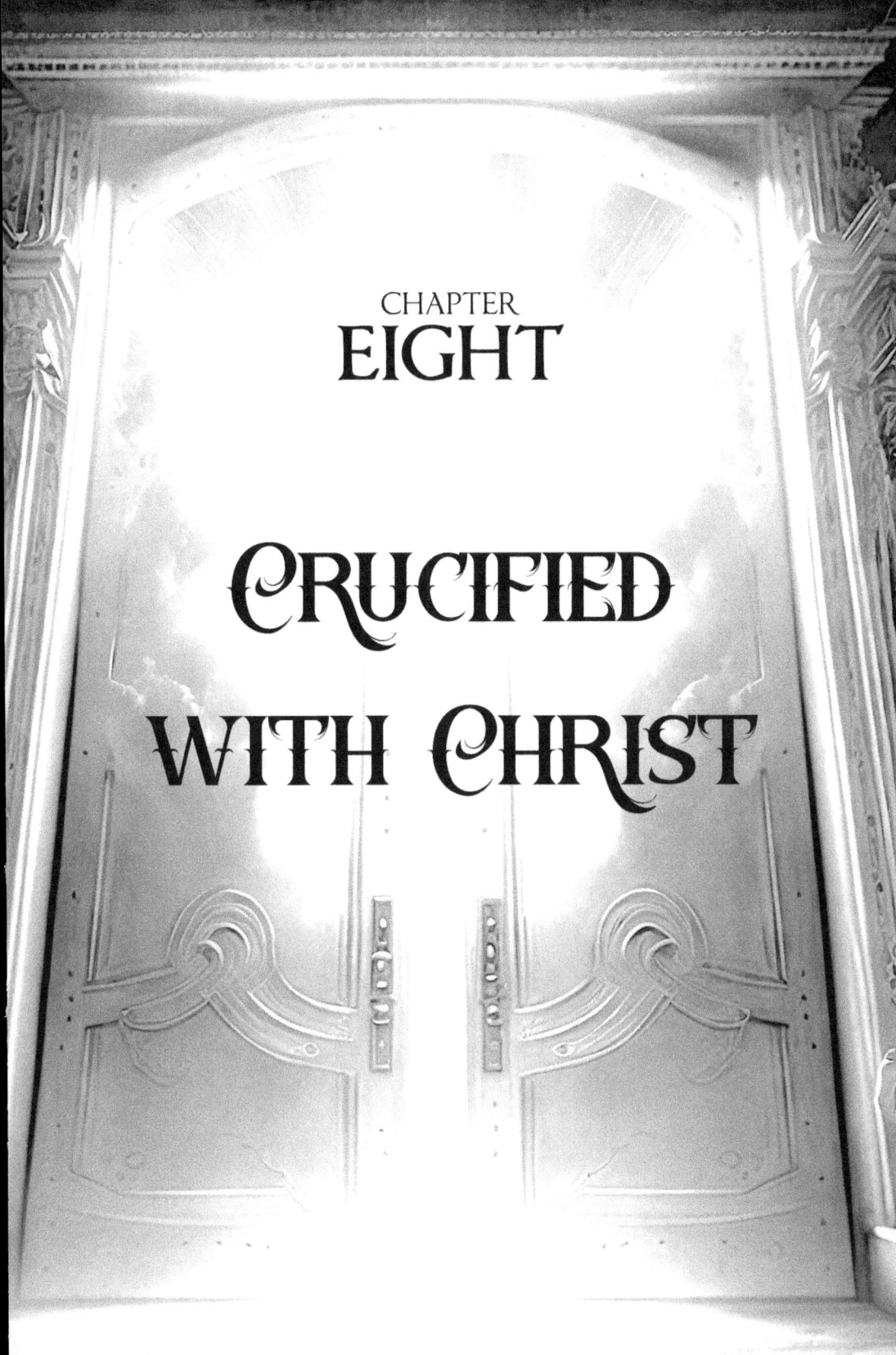

CHAPTER
EIGHT

CRUCIFIED
WITH CHRIST

The crucifixion, burial, and resurrection of Jesus are the most significant events in world history. These three events have impacted and influenced humankind and affected the entire world as we know it in more ways than one. Jesus is the most influential man to walk this Earth. His death, burial, and resurrection changed the course of humanity. In this chapter, we will explore the facts of the death of Jesus, His burial and resurrection, and what we must do in response to these life-changing events. I will also reveal the mysterious power of the Cross and how it applies to the *Secret Place*.

The only reason Jesus was sent to the Earth to die was because humankind had sinned and fallen away from God. The original sin was with Adam and Eve in the Garden of Eden when they ate of the Tree of the Knowledge of Good and Evil that God commanded them not to eat of. After the fall of Adam and Eve, the entire world was plunged into darkness and separated from the God who had created them. Worse of all, when anyone died, they were sent directly to hell, leaving them eternally separated from God.

The devil was given dominion over the Earth and the keys to death and hell after the fall of Adam. The devil is an evil, fallen angelic being who sinned against God before the world was created. Biblical history also records other angelic beings called "sons of God" who sinned against God, slept with the daughters of men, and produced giants on Earth that were very wicked. These giants were half man and half angelic. The sins of these fallen angels and evil giants caused God to flood the entire world and wipe everyone out except Noah and his family. Although God used Noah to repopulate the Earth, humanity was still fallen and prone to sin.

God, who is nothing but Holy and Good, was separated from His creation. The situation was dire, and God knew there needed to be a Divine answer. So, God the Father, The Son, and The Holy Spirit devised a secret plan to send Jesus (His

Only Begotten Son) on a mission to be born as a man and die as a man for all the sins of humanity. God's wrath and justice would be satisfied in the death of His own Son. Once Jesus rose from the dead, God allowed anyone who believed in Christ to be made righteous and could now go to Heaven. One of the first things they would have to do is believe in their heart that God raised Jesus from the dead and confess Jesus as their Lord, and they would be saved.

> *Romans 10:6-10 (KJV)*
>
> *6 But the righteousness which is of faith speaketh on this wise, Say not in thine heart, Who shall ascend into heaven? (that is, to bring Christ down from above:) 7 Or, Who shall descend into the deep? (that is, to bring up Christ again from the dead.) 8 But what saith it? The word is nigh thee, even in thy mouth, and in thy heart: that is, the word of faith, which we preach; 9 **That if thou shalt confess with thy mouth the Lord Jesus, and shalt believe in thine heart that God hath raised him from the dead, thou shalt be saved.** 10 For with the heart man believeth unto righteousness; and with the mouth confession is made unto salvation.*

Father Abraham played a key role in God sending Christ to the Earth. Abraham was a Hebrew in the Old Testament that God chose to make a Covenant with. This Covenant is called the Abrahamic Covenant. God promised to bless the entire world through his *SEED* in this Covenant. We know this *SEED* would be Christ, coming down from Abraham's family lineage.

> *Galatians 3:16 (KJV)*
>
> *16 Now to Abraham and his seed were the promises made. He saith not, And to seeds, as of many; but as of one, And to thy seed, which is Christ.*

We know through the Scriptures that the Blessing of Abraham was the preaching of the Gospel. The Gospel started with the *Good News* of the Kingdom of God, which came with miracles, signs, and wonders through Jesus' teaching and preaching.

Galatians 3:8 (KJV)
*8 And the scripture, foreseeing that God would justify the heathen through faith, **preached before the gospel unto Abraham, saying, In thee shall all nations be blessed.***

Matthew 4:23 (KJV)
*23 **And Jesus went about all Galilee, teaching in their synagogues, and preaching the gospel of the kingdom, and healing all manner of sickness and all manner of disease among the people.***

Today, the Gospel has everything to do with the blessings of God coming to those who not only believe Jesus is the Christ but believe what He did for them on the Cross and His resurrection. People who were healed before Jesus died on the Cross were being healed under the Abrahamic Covenant and Mosaic Covenant. The New Covenant that Jesus died for, which now allowed the Gentiles to be saved, is still a part of the Abrahamic Covenant. Only the Mosaic Covenant was done away with when Christ died and rose again.

1 Corinthians 15:1-4 (KJV)
*1 Moreover, brethren, **I declare unto you the gospel which I preached unto you**, which also ye have received, and wherein ye stand; 2 By which also ye are saved, if ye keep in memory what I preached unto you, unless ye have believed in vain. 3 For I delivered unto you first of all that which I also received, **how that***

Christ died for our sins according to the scriptures; 4 And that he was buried, and that he rose again the third day according to the scriptures:

In the Covenant that God made with Abraham, he was given a leadership role in the afterlife. God gave Abraham authority over a place called Abraham's Bosom. Abraham's Bosom was located in the center of the Earth next to tormenting hell. Abraham's Bosom was also called *Paradise* which was located in the middle of the Earth and was created as a holding place for any Old Testament believer who believed God for salvation after they died. No one could go to Heaven after the fall of Adam and Eve until Jesus paid the price. There is an insightful parable that Jesus spoke that describes Abraham's Bosom. This is the only parable that gives Divine revelation into what happened to Old Testament saints after they died.

Luke 16:19-31 (KJV)

*19 There was a certain rich man, which was clothed in purple and fine linen, and fared sumptuously every day: 20 And there was a certain beggar named Lazarus, which was laid at his gate, full of sores, 21 And desiring to be fed with the crumbs which fell from the rich man's table: moreover the dogs came and licked his sores. 22 And it came to pass, that the beggar died, and was carried by the angels into **Abraham's bosom**: the rich man also died, and was buried; 23 And in hell he lift up his eyes, being in torments, and seeth Abraham afar off, and Lazarus in his bosom. 24 And he cried and said, Father Abraham, have mercy on me, and send Lazarus, that he may dip the tip of his finger in water, and cool my tongue; for I am tormented in this flame. 25 But Abraham said, Son, remember that thou in thy lifetime receivedst thy good things, and* *likewise Lazarus evil things: but now he is comforted, and thou art tormented. 26 And beside all this, between us and you there is a great gulf fixed: so that they which would pass from hence to you cannot; neither can they pass to us, that would come from thence. 27 Then he said, I pray thee therefore, father, that thou wouldest send him to my father's house: 28 For I have five brethren; that he may testify unto them, lest they also come into this place of torment. 29 Abraham saith unto him, They have Moses and the prophets; let them hear them. 30 And he said, Nay, father Abraham: but if one went unto them from the dead, they will repent. 31 And he said unto him, If they hear not Moses and the prophets, neither will they be persuaded, though one rose from the dead.*

Abraham's Bosom was considered a part of hell because it was in the middle of the Earth next to tormenting hell, which was under the domain of the devil. The devil gained control of death and hell when Adam and Eve sinned against God. Everyone who died after the fall of Adam and Eve had to go either to Abraham's Bosom or tormenting hell. God saw the hopelessness of humanity and knew Jesus would have to die, be buried, and rise again to save humankind from the devil, death, and eternal damnation in hell.

The *Passion of Christ* refers to the suffering of our Lord that He endured for our redemption. I will walk through the events of the *Passion of Christ* to reveal all that transpired when Jesus died, was buried, and rose again. *Passion* means to suffer, endure, be tormented, be oppressed, be vexed, be subjected to evil, and be inflicted with harm. As New Testament believers, it is vital to know all of the details that Jesus went through during *His Passion*. The New Covenant was made between God and man when Jesus suffered, died, and rose again. Understanding all that Jesus went through in *His Passion* will give you a deeper insight into the New Covenant and how to dwell in the *Secret Place*.

> *Acts 1:1-3 (KJV)*
> *1 The former treatise have I made, O Theophilus, of all that Jesus began both to do and teach, 2 Until the day in which he was taken up, after that he through the Holy Ghost had given commandments unto the apostles whom he had chosen: 3 To whom also he shewed himself alive after **his passion** by many infallible proofs, being seen of them forty days, and speaking of the things pertaining to the kingdom of God:*

THE PASSION OF CHRIST

We know that Jesus had to die on a Wednesday to fulfill the prophesies that He would be three days and three nights in the middle of the Earth. Some Biblical scholars teach that Jesus died on a Friday and rose again on a Sunday, but the math of three days and three nights doesn't add up. You have to go back and study when the **Feast of Passover** landed during the last days of Christ leading up to His death. The closest **Feast of Passover** near *The Passion of Christ* landed on Wednesday, April 25th – 0031 A.D. (14th Month of Abib according to the Jewish Calendar).

> *Matthew 12:40 (KJV)*
> *40 For as Jonas was three days and three nights in the whale's belly; so shall the Son of man be three days and three nights in the heart of the Earth.*

The *Feast of Passover* celebrates God's protection from the death Angel by placing the blood of a lamb on the doorposts. God commanded the Israelites to sacrifice a lamb and put its blood on their doorposts. That night, a death Angel flew over the land of Egypt and slew all of the firstborn sons of the families that didn't have the blood of a lamb on their doorposts. The firstborn son of the Pharoah and all of the Egyptian families suffered the loss of their firstborn during this time because they didn't have the blood of a lamb on their doorposts. The judgment was so severe that Pharoah let the people of God go, who were under the slavery of Egypt at that time.

The sacrificed lamb's blood was symbolic of the Blood of Jesus that was going to be shed during *His Passion*. Pharoah symbolized the devil holding people under the slavery of sin. Anyone who believes in God raising Jesus from the dead and confessing Him as their Lord can now be released from the demonic bondage of satan and from the slavery to sin. The blood of Jesus ratified the New Covenant.

> *Hebrews 13:20-21 (KJV)*
> *20 Now the God of peace, that brought again from the dead our Lord Jesus, that great shepherd of the sheep, through the blood of the everlasting covenant, 21 Make you perfect in every good work to do his will, working in you that which is wellpleasing in his sight, through Jesus Christ; to whom be glory for ever and ever. Amen.*

Now, let's walk through the events and timeline of *The Passion of Christ*.

WEDNESDAY – THE FEAST OF PASSOVER
THE DAY OUR LORD WAS CRUCIFIED
14TH DAY OF THE MONTH OF ABIB

- Jesus Celebrates Passover with His Disciples (Luke 22:7-15)

- Communion is Instituted (Matthew 26:26-29)

- Jesus washes the feet of the Apostles (John 13:1-17)

- Jesus prays in the Garden of Gethsemane (Matthew 26:36-46)

- Jesus was strengthened by an angel (Luke 22:43)

- Judas Iscariot betrays Jesus with a kiss (Matthew 26:47-50)

- Peter cuts off the High Priest's servant's ear (John 18:10)

- Jesus heals the High Priest's servant's ear (Luke 22:51)

- 1st Trial of Jesus by Annas - Father-in-Law to the High Priest (John 18:12-13)

- 2nd Trial of Jesus by the High Priest Caiaphas (Matthew 26:57-68)

- First Time Jesus is injured by a strike of the High Priest officer (John 18:22)

- Jesus declares Himself to be the Son of God (Matthew 26:63-65)

- They spit in the face of Jesus, mock Him, and strike Him (Matthew 26:67-68)

- 3rd Trial of Jesus before the Elders of Israel, Chief Priests, and Scribes (Luke 22:66-71)

- Jesus declares Himself to be the Son of God again (Luke 22:66-71)

- 4th Trial of Jesus before Pontius Pilate – He finds Him not guilty (Luke 23:1-4)

- 5th Trial of Jesus before Herod (Luke 23:6-12)

- 6th Trial of Jesus before Pontius Pilate again (Matthew 27:11-14)

- 7th Trial of Jesus before the crowd (Matthew 27:15-26)

- The crowd chooses Barabbas over Jesus (Mark 15:6-14)

- Jesus was scourged with a whip by the Roman soldiers (Matthew 27:26)

- Jesus is stripped, and a scarlet robe is placed on Him (Matthew 27:28)

- A Crown of Thorns is placed on the head of Jesus (Matthew 27:29)

- The Roman soldiers place a reed in the right hand of Jesus (Matthew 27:29)

- The Roman soldiers bow their knees and mock Jesus, saying, Hail, King of the Jews! (Matthew 27:29)

- Roman soldiers Coronate Jesus as the King of the Jews (Matthew 27:27-29)

- Jesus was led away to Calvary to be crucified (Matthew 27:31)

- Jesus refuses to drink wine mingled with myrrh (Mark 15:23)

- Jesus was crucified (Matthew 27:35)

- This is Jesus the King of the Jews accusation placed on the Cross (Matthew 27:37)

- Jesus asks the Father to forgive them for they know not what they do (Luke 23:34)

- The Roman soldiers cast lots for Jesus' garments (John 19:23-24)

- Jesus tells a thief on a cross next to Him that he will be with Him in Paradise Today! (Luke 23:39-43)

- Jesus tells John to take care of His mother, Mary (John 19:25-27)

- Darkness covers the land (Matthew 27:45)

- Jesus cries out, "My God, My God, why have You forsaken Me" (Matthew 27:46-47)

- Jesus drinks vinegar from a sponge (Matthew 27:48)

- Jesus cries out, **"IT IS FINISHED"** (John 19:30)

- Jesus gives up His Spirit and dies (Matthew 27:50)

- The Old Covenant is Fulfilled (John 19:28)

- An Earthquake occurs (Matthew 27:51)

- The VEIL in the Temple is torn in two (Matthew 27:51)

- A centurion declares that Jesus was the Son of God (Mark 15:39)

- Roman soldiers pierced the side of Jesus to confirm He is dead (John 19:32-37)

- Joseph of Arimathea and Nicodemus request the body of Jesus from Pontius Pilot (Matthew 27:57-58)

- Jesus' body is wrapped in myrrh, aloes and spices (John 19:38-40)

- Jesus was placed in a rich man's tomb (Joseph of Arimathaea) (Matthew 27:60)

- Great stone was rolled over the door of Jesus' tomb and sealed (Matthew 27:60-66)

THURSDAY – HIGH SABBATH
FIRST FEAST DAY OF UNLEAVENED BREAD
15TH DAY OF THE MONTH OF ABIB

- High Holy Sabbath Day that follows Passover (Luke 23:54; Leviticus 23:5-7)

- No work to be done (John 19:31)

- Jesus is in Abraham's Bosom (Paradise) (Luke 23:43; Luke 16:19-31)

- Jesus preached the Gospel to the saints in Abraham's Bosom (1 Peter 4:6)

- Jesus preached to the disobedient spirits from the time of Noah (1 Peter 3:19-20)

FRIDAY
SECOND FEAST DAY OF UNLEAVENED BREAD
16TH DAY OF THE MONTH OF ABIB

- Mary Magdalene and Mary purchased spices and ointments for the body of Jesus (Mark 16:1)

- The women prepared the spices and the ointments (Luke 23:55-56)

SATURDAY – WEEKLY SABBATH
THIRD FEAST DAY OF UNLEAVENED BREAD
17TH DAY OF THE MONTH OF ABIB

- Day of rest, no work to be done (Luke 23:56)

- Jesus was promised that God would not leave His soul in hell (Psalm 16:10)

- Jesus was promised that His body would not decay (Acts 2:27)

SUNDAY – THE RESURRECTION
FOURTH FEAST DAY OF UNLEAVENED BREAD
18TH DAY OF THE MONTH OF ABIB

- Jesus was raised from the dead (Mark 16:9)

- Great Earthquake (Matthew 28:2)

- The stone rolled away (Matthew 28:2)

- Jesus took back the keys of death and hell from satan (Revelation 1:18)

- Jesus destroyed the devil (Hebrews 2:14)

- Jesus destroyed the works of the devil (1 John 3:8)

- Old Testament saints were resurrected from Abraham's Bosom (Matthew 27:52-53)

- Jesus triumphed over principalities and powers (Colossians 2:15)

- Jesus appeared to Mary Magdalene (John 20:11-18)

- Jesus ascended to our Heavenly Father (John 20:17)

- Jesus placed His Blood on the Mercy Seat in Heaven (Hebrews 9:7-12)

- Jesus was given a Name above every other name (Philippians 2:5-11)

- Jesus descended back to Earth and appeared to His Disciples (John 20:19-23)

- Jesus places His blood on the conscience of His Disciples (Hebrews 10:21-22)

- Disciples became Temples of the Holy Spirit when Jesus breathes on them (John 20:22)

After Jesus rose from the dead, He took His own blood into *The Throne Room of God* and placed His blood on the Mercy Seat of the Ark of the Covenant located in Heaven. Once He did this, the wrath and justice of God were satisfied, and believers in Christ were forgiven and allowed entrance into Heaven after they died. The Old Testament saints being held in Abraham's Bosom were resurrected and granted access to Heaven where they now dwell with God forever in new bodies.

When you fully comprehend why Jesus had to die, and the price He paid for your eternal salvation, your love and appreciation for Him will take on a whole new meaning. Jesus paid the ultimate price of death and went to hell so anyone could be saved and go to Heaven. Anyone who believes in Jesus does not go to Abraham's Bosom when they die any more; they go straight to Heaven. *Thank God for His unspeakable gift!*

Hebrews 9:11-12 (KJV)
*11 But Christ being come an high priest of good things to come, by a greater and more perfect tabernacle, not made with hands, that is to say, not of this building; 12 Neither by the blood of goats and calves, **but by his own blood he entered in once into the holy place, having obtained eternal redemption for us.***

Hebrews 9:24-26 (KJV)
24 For Christ is not entered into the holy places made with hands, which are the figures of the true; but into heaven itself, now to appear in the presence of God for us: 25 Nor yet that he should offer himself often, as the high priest entereth into the holy place

every year with blood of others; 26 For then must he often have suffered since the foundation of the world: but now once in the end of the world hath he appeared to put away sin by the sacrifice of himself.

Once Jesus offered His blood in Heaven, there was no need for a Temple on Earth, and the Old Testament (Law of Moses) was fulfilled and no longer needed. Jesus established a New Covenant where the Laws of God would be written on the hearts and minds of His believers. The blood of Jesus cleanses the conscience, which helps believers to know and do what is right before the Lord, according to the Laws of God written on their hearts and minds. New Testament believers now become the Temples of God. Jesus enters the believer's body and sprinkles His blood on their evil conscience, washes their body with pure water, and the Holy Spirit fills the Temple of their body with His glory.

Hebrews 10:15-22 (KJV)

15 Whereof the Holy Ghost also is a witness to us: for after that he had said before, 16 This is the covenant that I will make with them after those days, saith the Lord, I will put my laws into their hearts, and in their minds will I write them; 17 And their sins and iniquities will I remember no more. 18 Now where remission of these is, there is no more offering for sin. 19 Having therefore, brethren, boldness to enter into the holiest by the blood of Jesus, 20 By a new and living way, which he hath consecrated for us, through the veil, that is to say, his flesh; 21 And having an high priest over the house of God; 22 Let us draw near with a true heart in full assurance of faith, having our hearts sprinkled from an evil conscience, and our bodies washed with pure water.

The Holy of Holies is in the Temple of a believer's body and becomes the *Secret Place of the Most High* when Jesus applies His blood on the evil conscience. Jesus died, was buried, and rose again from the dead so the *Secret Place* could be found in the believer's body. This is the hidden mystery of the Cross and the *Secret Place*. Jesus died not only for you to go to Heaven but so that you could access the God of Heaven now within the *Secret Place* of your own Temple, which is your body.

Now, I will reveal why I titled this chapter **Crucified with Christ** and how it applies to the *Secret Place*. When Jesus was on the Earth before He died, He referred to Christians taking up their Cross, denying themselves, and following Him. He boldly proclaimed that anyone who didn't take up their Cross was not worthy of Him and couldn't be His disciple.

> *Matthew 10:38 (KJV)*
> *38 And he that taketh not his cross, and followeth after me, is not worthy of me.*

> *Matthew 16:24-26 (KJV)*
> *24 Then said Jesus unto his disciples, If any man will come after me, let him deny himself, and take up his cross, and follow me. 25 For whosoever will save his life shall lose it: and whosoever will lose his life for my sake shall find it. 26 For what is a man profited, if he shall gain the whole world, and lose his own soul? or what shall a man give in exchange for his soul?*

> *Luke 14:27 (KJV)*
> *27 And whosoever doth not bear his cross, and come after me, cannot be my disciple.*

When Jesus used the metaphor of taking up your Cross and following Him, He was speaking about people dying to sin. Another way to say this is He was saying they must put to death the works of the flesh. A big part of confessing Jesus as your Lord is making a covenant to die to your flesh daily and walk in the newness of life.

> *Romans 6:1-4 (KJV)*
>
> *1 What shall we say then? Shall we continue in sin, that grace may abound? 2 God forbid. How shall we, that are dead to sin, live any longer therein? 3 **Know ye not, that so many of us as were baptized into Jesus Christ were baptized into his death? 4 Therefore we are buried with him by baptism into death: that like as Christ was raised up from the dead by the glory of the Father, even so we also should walk in newness of life.***

After we experience salvation through confessing Christ as our Lord, we are commanded by God to get baptized in water. When the new believer in Christ is immersed in water, it symbolizes them dying to their flesh and old lifestyle. The old sinful nature is to stay dead and not come up out of the water. After they emerge from the water, it symbolizes them walking in the newness of life. From this point forward, they are committed to staying faithful to the Lord as a New Covenant believer, and their bodies become the Holy Temple of God.

The Bible is clear when it talks about what we are to die to. One of the main verses that list what we are to die to can be found in the Book of Colossians:

> *Colossians 3:5-10 (KJV)*
>
> *5 **Mortify** therefore your members which are upon the Earth; **fornication, uncleanness, inordinate affection, evil concupiscence,***

*and covetousness, which is idolatry: 6 For which things' sake the wrath of God cometh on the children of disobedience: 7 In the which ye also walked some time, when ye lived in them. 8 **But now ye also put off all these; anger, wrath, malice, blasphemy, filthy communication out of your mouth.** 9 Lie not one to another, seeing that ye have put off the old man with his deeds; 10 And have put on the new man, which is renewed in knowledge after the image of him that created him:*

Anyone not willing to crucify and put to death the works of the flesh is not worthy of being a disciple of Christ. This is what Jesus meant when He talked about people taking up their Cross, denying themselves, and following Him. The Book of Galatians also lists what we are to put to death.

Galatians 5:19-24 (KJV)
*19 Now the works of the flesh are manifest, which are these; Adultery, fornication, uncleanness, lasciviousness, 20 Idolatry, witchcraft, hatred, variance, emulations, wrath, strife, seditions, heresies, 21 Envyings, murders, drunkenness, revellings, and such like: of the which I tell you before, as I have also told you in time past, that they which do such things shall not inherit the kingdom of God. 22 But the fruit of the Spirit is love, joy, peace, longsuffering, gentleness, goodness, faith, 23 Meekness, temperance: against such there is no law. 24 **And they that are Christ's have crucified the flesh with the affections and lusts.***

The secret to entering the *Secret Place* is putting all the works of the flesh to death. Christ died on the Cross and offered His blood so you could access the *Secret Place.* All the works of the flesh must be put to death for you to enter and dwell in the *Secret Place of the Most High.* **THIS IS THE MYSTERIOUS POWER OF THE CROSS!**

The Apostle Paul said that he was crucified with Christ, and that Christ now lived in him.

> *Galatians 2:20 (KJV)*
> *20 I am crucified with Christ: nevertheless I live; yet not I, but Christ liveth in me: and the life which I now live in the flesh I live by the faith of the Son of God, who loved me, and gave himself for me.*

The Apostle Paul also said that the world was crucified unto him and he to the world.

> *Galatians 6:14 (KJV)*
> *14 But God forbid that I should glory, save in the cross of our Lord Jesus Christ, **by whom the world is crucified unto me, and I unto the world.***

Once you crucify and put to death the works of the flesh, you will start to walk in the newness of life.

> *Romans 6:4 (KJV)*
> *4 Therefore we are buried with him by baptism into death: **that like as Christ was raised up from the dead by the glory of the Father, even so we also should walk in newness of life.***

Anyone who walks in the Spirit will not fulfill the desires and lust of the flesh. You can spot someone dwelling in the *Secret Place* based on how they live. You will see a dramatic change in how they act, think, and speak. Anyone dwelling in the *Secret Place* will act, think, and talk like God. Another way to say this is that they will imitate God.

Galatians 5:16-18 (KJV)

16 This I say then, Walk in the Spirit, and ye shall not fulfil the lust of the flesh. 17 For the flesh lusteth against the Spirit, and the Spirit against the flesh: and these are contrary the one to the other: so that ye cannot do the things that ye would. 18 But if ye be led of the Spirit, ye are not under the law.

When you put the works of the flesh to death, you can live risen with Christ. You cannot walk in the newness of a risen life until you crucify your flesh. Crucifying and dying to yourself is not an option in Christianity. A genuine believer in Christ willfully dies to their flesh and sets their affections on things above where Christ sits on the right hand of the Father. The *Secret Place* is Heaven itself and the Throne Room of God. You can access the Throne Room of God in the *Secret Place* of your own body when you crucify your flesh. When you dwell in the *Secret Place* you are sitting in *Heavenly Places* in Christ Jesus.

Ephesians 2:4-6 (KJV)

4 But God, who is rich in mercy, for his great love wherewith he loved us, 5 Even when we were dead in sins, hath quickened us together with Christ, (by grace ye are saved;) 6 And hath raised us up together, and made us sit together in heavenly places in Christ Jesus:

Christ paid the ultimate price so you could go to Heaven and access the *Secret Place* in the Temple of your own body. Any believer who understands this truth would never willfully sin against God. Willful sin will kick you out of the *Secret Place* immediately. God is Holy and will not tolerate sin in His Presence. Numerous false teachers have taught that Christians can live in sin and still go to Heaven, or they teach hyper-grace. Avoid these false teachers if you want to dwell in the *Secret Place of the Most High* and go to Heaven. God will judge any believer who willfully sins and turns their back on Jesus and the Blood of the New Covenant.

> *Hebrews 10:26-31 (KJV)*
> *26 For if we sin wilfully after that we have received the knowledge of the truth, there remaineth no more sacrifice for sins, 27 But a certain fearful looking for of judgment and fiery indignation, which shall devour the adversaries. 28 He that despised Moses' law died without mercy under two or three witnesses: 29 Of how much sorer punishment, suppose ye, shall he be thought worthy, who hath trodden under foot the Son of God, and hath counted the blood of the covenant, wherewith he was sanctified, an unholy thing, and hath done despite unto the Spirit of grace? 30 For we know him that hath said, Vengeance belongeth unto me, I will recompense, saith the Lord. And again, The Lord shall judge his people. 31 It is a fearful thing to fall into the hands of the living God.*

The Bible teaches that those who fall away from God crucify to themselves the Son of God afresh.

> *Hebrews 6:4-8 (KJV)*
> *4 For it is impossible for those who were once enlightened, and have tasted of the heavenly gift, and were made partakers of the Holy Ghost, 5 And have tasted the good word of God, and the*

powers of the world to come, 6 If they shall fall away, to renew them again unto repentance; seeing they crucify to themselves the Son of God afresh, and put him to an open shame. 7 For the Earth which drinketh in the rain that cometh oft upon it, and bringeth forth herbs meet for them by whom it is dressed, receiveth blessing from God: 8 But that which beareth thorns and briers is rejected, and is nigh unto cursing; whose end is to be burned.

One of the greatest revelations of the *Mysterious Power of the Cross* is when we crucify our flesh; we are granted access to dwell in the *Secret Place*. The Cross of Christ was a prophetic event that symbolized our destiny. When Jesus died on the Cross and rose again, He went into Heaven and placed His blood on the Mercy Seat that sat on the Ark of the Covenant. When we take up our Cross, die to ourselves, and walk in the newness of life, we gain access to dwell in the Holy of Holies where the Ark of the Covenant is located, which is a representation of the Holy Spirit. The *Passion of Christ* is a prophetic portrait of the whole life of a New Testament believer.

We take up our Cross daily as He took up His Cross. Our old man stays dead, symbolized by Christ going to the middle of the Earth after He died. We walk in the newness of life as one risen from the dead from our old sinful lifestyle as Christ rose from the dead. We access Heaven as a born-again son of God, as Jesus now sits at the Father's right hand. We dwell in the *Secret Place* with Christ, our Saviour, the Father, and the Temple of our bodies is filled with the glorious Holy Spirit.

Colossians 3:1-4 (KJV)
1 If ye then be risen with Christ, seek those things which are above, where Christ sitteth on the right hand of God. 2 Set your affection

on things above, not on things on the Earth. 3 For ye are dead, and your life is hid with Christ in God. 4 When Christ, who is our life, shall appear, then shall ye also appear with him in glory.

In conclusion, believers who are seriously committed to their walk with God, dwelling in the *Secret Place,* and going to Heaven will crucify the works of the flesh. God calls His people to Himself and desires them to dwell in the *Secret Place*, but they must first take up their Cross daily, deny themselves, and follow Christ. Christ set the example and did everything in His power so you could dwell in the *Secret Place* and go to Heaven. It's a Divine privilege to accept God's *High Calling*, take up our Cross daily, deny yourself, and live for Him in the newness of life.

CHAPTER
NINE

BETTER
PROMISES

The *Passion of Christ* resulted in an abundance of blessings for believers. These abundant blessings are called the *Better Promises* of the New Covenant. Understanding all that was achieved for us in the *Passion of Christ* will change your life. If Jesus had not come and died for us, we would have no spiritual blessings and be destined to go to hell. As you study the Scriptures, you will discover numerous blessings given to us on Calvary. In this chapter, I will reveal by the Spirit of God all that was accomplished for us in the *Passion of Christ* and how anyone walking in the *Secret Place* can apply the New Covenant blessings of the *Better Promises* to their life.

The deep things of God are called mysteries in the Bible and can only be revealed to you by the Spirit of God. As you spend time in the *Secret Place*, God will reveal more of His secrets and hidden mysteries. This is one of the remarkable benefits of dwelling in the *Secret Place of the Most High*. As I spent time in the *Secret Place*, I sought the Lord for all that was accomplished and attained for us when Jesus died on the Cross. I knew there had to be more to what Jesus did, but I needed the Lord to reveal to me all He did for us during *His Passion*. God answered my prayer, and the Holy Spirit began to show me in the Scriptures the vast achievements Jesus accomplished for us when He died and rose again.

Gospel means *Good News*; when referring to Jesus, the *Good News* has to do with everything He did for us. The achievements and accomplishments of the *Passion of Christ* are the *Good News* of the Gospel. However, as remarkable as it is, many Christians don't know all that Jesus did for them, and many go without when they don't need to go without. What good is it to have something you don't know you have or understand how to access what you have?

The solution for God to help His people receive all He did on Calvary is by sending anointed preachers and teachers. God calls these preachers and teachers to help the people of God understand and receive what the Lord has done for them. God has sent me to help believers receive all He has done for them. Before receiving what the Lord has done for you, you must know all that was paid for at the Cross of Christ. The Bible says that God's people are destroyed for lack of knowledge.

Hosea 4:6a (KJV)
6 My people are destroyed for lack of knowledge: because thou hast rejected knowledge, I will also reject thee,...

When God finds someone hungry, available, and ready, He will send anointed preachers and teachers to them. The fact that you are reading this book reveals you are hungry for more of God. God can also teach you directly from the Word of God as you study the Scriptures by His Spirit. Our spiritual eyes and ears must be opened to comprehend all God has done for us. When your spiritual eyes and ears are opened, you will begin to see all the things freely given to you by God.

1 Corinthians 2:9-14 (KJV)
*9 But as it is written, Eye hath not seen, nor ear heard, neither have entered into the heart of man, the things which God hath prepared for them that love him. 10 But God hath revealed them unto us by his Spirit: for the Spirit searcheth all things, yea, the deep things of God. 11 For what man knoweth the things of a man, save the spirit of man which is in him? even so the things of God knoweth no man, but the Spirit of God. 12 **Now we have received, not the spirit of the world, but the spirit which is of God; that we might know the things that are freely given to us of God.** 13 Which things also we speak, not in the words which man's wisdom teacheth, but*

which the Holy Ghost teacheth; comparing spiritual things with spiritual. 14 But the natural man receiveth not the things of the Spirit of God: for they are foolishness unto him: neither can he know them, because they are spiritually discerned.

When Jesus died on the Cross, He established the New Covenant with His own Blood. A covenant is an agreement between two parties to agree to specific terms. If both parties meet the terms, both parties can partake in the promised blessings of the covenant they made with each other. Covenant promises between two parties are the benefits of adherence to the covenant. The Old Covenant was established on terms and, if kept, had promises to be enjoyed and curses if not obeyed.

We know from history that the Jews broke the Old Covenant and brought down many curses on themselves. These curses can be found in Deuteronomy 28 and Leviticus 26. God, however, never has and never will break a Covenant. *Psalm 89:34 (KJV) My covenant will I not break, nor alter the thing that is gone out of my lips.* Because the Jews broke the Old Covenant, God sent Jesus to establish the New Covenant. The New Covenant was established upon *Better Promises* than the Old Covenant.

Hebrews 8:6 (KJV)

*6 But now hath he obtained a more excellent ministry, by how much also he is the mediator of a **better covenant**, which was established upon **better promises**.*

In this New Covenant, we have commands to be obeyed and blessings to be enjoyed. The *Secret Place* has everything to do with the New Covenant of God, which is why God placed the Ark of the Covenant in the Holy of Holies. Previously, I have been teaching the terms and conditions of the New

Covenant. Now, by the Holy Spirit, I will teach you the things God has freely given us. The blessings freely given to us by God are the *Better Promises* that Jesus died for us to have. These *Better Promises* are the *Good News* of the Gospel. Anyone dwelling in the *Secret Place of the Most High* has access to the *Better Promises* of the New Covenant. When your spirit is enlightened to the *Better Promises* of God, you can claim all of them by faith and patience.

> *Hebrews 6:12 (KJV)*
> *12 That ye be not slothful, but followers of them who through faith and patience inherit the promises.*

Let's explore the depths of the Word of God and discover all that was accomplished for us by our Lord and Saviour, Jesus Christ. I pray God opens your spiritual eyes and ears to see and hear all that God has freely given you. I also pray you learn to claim by faith what you discover in the Word of God. The devil hates it when the children of God discover what they have been freely given and then learn how to claim all the *Precious Promises* of God by faith as they dwell in the *Secret Place*.

BETTER PROMISES
NEW COVENANT ACCOMPLISHMENTS

1. NEW COVENANT MADE BY BLOOD

When Jesus died and shed His Blood on the Cross, He did away with the Old Covenant and brought in a New Covenant. In the New Covenant, the Laws of God are written on our hearts and minds, God becomes our God, our sins are forgiven, and we can know God for ourselves.

Jeremiah 31:31-34 (KJV)

31 Behold, the days come, saith the Lord, that I will make a **new covenant** with the house of Israel, and with the house of Judah: 32 Not according to the covenant that I made with their fathers in the day that I took them by the hand to bring them out of the land of Egypt; which my covenant they brake, although I was an husband unto them, saith the Lord: 33 But this shall be the **covenant** that I will make with the house of Israel; After those days, saith the Lord, I will put my law in their inward parts, and write it in their hearts; and will be their God, and they shall be my people. 34 And they shall teach no more every man his neighbour, and every man his brother, saying, Know the Lord: for they shall all know me, from the least of them unto the greatest of them, saith the Lord: for I will forgive their iniquity, and I will remember their sin no more.

Matthew 26:26-28 (KJV)

26 And as they were eating, Jesus took bread, and blessed it, and brake it, and gave it to the disciples, and said, Take, eat; this is my body. 27 And he took the cup, and gave thanks, and gave it to them, saying, Drink ye all of it; 28 **For this is my blood of the new testament**, which is shed for many for the remission of sins.

2. RANSOMED US

THE PRICE WAS PAID

Adam sold humanity to the devil when he sinned in disobedience to God in the Garden of Eden. Because of the sin of Adam and Eve, all of their offspring were sold to the devil. To be freed from the devil as our master, a price had to be paid.

When Jesus died on the Cross, He paid that price with His blood to ransom us back to God.

Matthew 20:28 (KJV)

*28 Even as the Son of man came not to be ministered unto, but to minister, and to give his life a **ransom for many.***

Isaiah 35:10 (KJV)

*10 And **the ransomed of the Lord** shall return, and come to Zion with songs and everlasting joy upon their heads: they shall obtain joy and gladness, and sorrow and sighing shall flee away.*

3. REDEEMED US FROM THE CURSE OF THE LAW

When Adam and Eve sinned, it brought a curse on the Earth and all of humanity. God established a covenant with Abraham where he and his descendants could be blessed. This is known as the Abrahamic Covenant. Later, when God established the Law through Moses, He listed out what those curses would be if they broke the Law. When Jesus died on the Cross, He became a curse for us, and all those who believe in Him can be freed from the curse of the Law and receive the blessings of God through the Gospel. Redeemed means Jesus paid the price for the curse not to be in your life anymore.

Galatians 3:13-14 (KJV)

*13 **Christ hath redeemed us from the curse of the law, being made a curse for us:** for it is written, Cursed is every one that hangeth on a tree: 14 That the blessing of Abraham might come on the Gentiles through Jesus Christ; that we might receive the promise of the Spirit through faith.*

4. RECONCILED US TO GOD

THE JUSTICE OF GOD WAS SATISFIED

When Jesus died on the Cross, He became sin for us and substituted Himself in our place to satisfy the Justice of God. God's Justice had to be satisfied because He is a Holy God. The wrath of God abides on anyone who does not accept the atoning blood of Jesus. Through the death, burial, and resurrection of Jesus, we are reconciled to back to God and Christ becomes our righteousness.

2 Corinthians 5:19-21 (KJV)

*19 To wit, that God was in Christ, **reconciling the world unto himself, not imputing their trespasses unto them**; and hath committed unto us the word of **reconciliation**. 20 Now then we are ambassadors for Christ, as though God did beseech you by us: we pray you in Christ's stead, **be ye reconciled to God**. 21 For he hath made him to be sin for us, who knew no sin; that we might be made the righteousness of God in him.*

5. FREED US FROM THE SLAVERY OF SIN

WE ARE NOW SERVANTS TO RIGHTEOUSNESS

When someone sins, they become a slave to sin. This means they no longer have the power or ability to stop sinning. When Jesus died on the Cross and forgave people their sins, they were born again as new creatures and were given the power to stop sinning if they repented. When you have been set free from sin by the Son of God, you have become a servant of righteousness.

John 8:34-36 (KJV)

*34 Jesus answered them, Verily, verily, I say unto you, **Whosoever committeth sin is the servant of sin**. 35 And the servant abideth not in the house for ever: but the Son abideth ever. 36 **If the Son therefore shall make you free, ye shall be free indeed.***

Romans 6:17-20 (KJV)

*17 But God be thanked, that ye were the **servants of sin**, but ye have obeyed from the heart that form of doctrine which was delivered you. 18 Being then made free from sin, ye became the **servants of righteousness**. 19 I speak after the manner of men because of the infirmity of your flesh: for as ye have yielded your members **servants to uncleanness and to iniquity unto iniquity; even so now yield your members servants to righteousness unto holiness.** 20 For when ye were the servants of sin, ye were free from righteousness.*

6. DESTROYED THE WORKS OF THE DEVIL

When Adam and Eve sinned, all of humanity was brought under the rulership of the devil. The devil was an oppressive ruler who ruled through fear, terror, injustice, sickness, disease, poverty, and death. When Jesus entered the world and died on the Cross, He took on the devil in a cosmic war. Jesus had to fight the devil to free people from the devil's evil oppression. Jesus destroyed the works of the devil at every turn through the anointing during His Earthly ministry. The works of the devil are curses, disease, sickness, poverty, oppression, depression, possession, death, hell, and more. Jesus then defeated all the works of the devil by dying on the Cross, being buried, and then resurrecting from the dead.

Acts 10:38 (KJV)

*38 How God anointed Jesus of Nazareth with the Holy Ghost and with power: **who went about doing good, and healing all that were oppressed of the devil;** for God was with him.*

1 John 3:8 (KJV)

8 He that committeth sin is of the devil; for the devil sinneth from the beginning. For this purpose the Son of God was manifested, that he might destroy the works of the devil.

7. ADOPTED US AS SONS OF GOD

When Adam and Eve sinned, everyone born after them was born into sin and were no longer the children of God but became sons of disobedience. The devil became the father of all those who disobeyed God. All of humankind lost their sonship with God. When Jesus died on the Cross, sinners could now be adopted back into the family of God and become sons of God once they received and believed on His Name.

John 1:12 (KJV)

12 But as many as received him, to them gave he power to become the sons of God, even to them that believe on his name:

Galatians 4:6-7 (KJV)

6 And because ye are sons, God hath sent forth the Spirit of his Son into your hearts, crying, Abba, Father. 7 Wherefore thou art no more a servant, but a son; and if a son, then an heir of God through Christ.

8. ESTABLISHED THE KINGDOM OF GOD ON THE EARTH

When Jesus was on the Earth, He preached that the Kingdom of God was at hand. Jesus was coronated as King by the Roman soldiers right before He was crucified. When Jesus rose from the dead and was seated at the right hand of God the Father, He was given all authority in Heaven and on Earth. Jesus sits on the throne of King David as the rightful heir to his throne, and the Kingdom of God is now established on the Earth. When Jesus returns, He will enforce His authority and Kingdom on the kingdom of darkness with all that was paid for on the Cross.

Revelation 12:10-11 (KJV)

*10 And I heard a loud voice saying in heaven, **Now is come salvation, and strength, and the kingdom of our God, and the power of his Christ**: for the accuser of our brethren is cast down, which accused them before our God day and night. 11 And they overcame him by the blood of the Lamb, and by the word of their testimony; and they loved not their lives unto the death.*

9. GIVEN US ETERNAL LIFE

The Children of God can now live forever because of the death and the resurrection of Jesus. When we go to Heaven, we will be granted free access to partake of the Tree of Life and the Water of Life, which enables us to live Eternally with God.

John 3:16 (KJV)

*16 **For God so loved the world, that he gave his only begotten Son, that whosoever believeth in him should not perish, but have everlasting life.***

Revelation 2:7 (KJV)

*7 He that hath an ear, let him hear what the Spirit saith unto the churches; **To him that overcometh will I give to eat of the tree of life, which is in the midst of the paradise of God.***

Revelation 22:17 (KJV)

*17 And the Spirit and the bride say, Come. And let him that heareth say, Come. And let him that is athirst come. **And whosoever will, let him take the water of life freely.***

10. GRANTED US ACCESS TO GOD

THE VEIL WAS TORN IN TWO

When Jesus died, the Veil of the Temple was torn in two, representing that believers in Christ now have access to God once again. We can access God by prayer while we live on this Earth, and we have access to God when we go to Heaven. The Veil being torn also represented our ability to access the *Secret Place* within the Temple of our bodies.

Luke 23:44-46 (KJV)

*44 And it was about the sixth hour, and there was a darkness over all the earth until the ninth hour. 45 And the sun was darkened, **and the veil of the temple was rent in the midst.** 46 And when Jesus had cried with a loud voice, he said, Father, into thy hands I commend my spirit: and having said thus, he gave up the ghost.*

Hebrews 10:19-20 (KJV)

*19 **Having therefore, brethren, boldness to enter into the holiest by the blood of Jesus, 20 By a new and living way, which he hath consecrated for us, through the veil, that is to say, his flesh;** with pure water.*

11. SEATED US IN HEAVENLY PLACES IN CHRIST JESUS

Believers who take up their Cross and die to themselves daily can sit in *Heavenly Places* in Christ Jesus. This means we now have access and authority to operate on this Earth as a son of God. We don't have to wait to go to Heaven to sit in *Heavenly Places.*

Ephesians 2:4-7 (KJV)

*4 But God, who is rich in mercy, for his great love wherewith he loved us, 5 Even when we were dead in sins, hath quickened us together with Christ, (by grace ye are saved;) 6 And hath raised us up together, **and made us sit together in heavenly places in Christ Jesus:** 7 That in the ages to come he might shew the exceeding riches of his grace in his kindness toward us through Christ Jesus.*

Colossians 3:1 (KJV)

1 If ye then be risen with Christ, seek those things which are above, where Christ sitteth on the right hand of God.

12. CREATED US AS NEW CREATIONS

We were not just restored to the original state of Adam and Eve when we were saved! We are created as *New Creatures* in the very image of Christ Himself. When we see Him, we will be made like unto the very image of the Resurrected Lord Jesus Christ.

2 Corinthians 5:17 (KJV)

17 Therefore if any man be in Christ, he is a new creature: old things are passed away; behold, all things are become new

1 John 3:1-2 (KJV)

*1 Behold, what manner of love the Father hath bestowed upon us, that we should be called the sons of God: therefore the world knoweth us not, because it knew him not. 2 **Beloved, now are we the sons of God, and it doth not yet appear what we shall be: but*** *we know that, when he shall appear, we shall be like him; for we shall see him as he is.*

13. BELIEVERS BECAME THE TEMPLE OF GOD

God destroyed the Temple located in Jerusalem and made New Testament Christian's bodies His new Temple. The Body of Christ, which is the Church, is also collectively the Temple of God.

1 Corinthians 3:16-17 (KJV)
*16 **Know ye not that ye are the temple of God, and that the Spirit of God dwelleth in you?** 17 If any man defile the temple of God, him shall God destroy; for the temple of God is holy, **which temple ye are.***

Ephesians 2:22 (KJV)
*22 **In whom ye also are builded together for an habitation of God through the Spirit.***

14. HOLY SPIRIT GIVEN TO BELIEVERS

When Jesus rose from the dead, the Holy Spirit was restored to all the believers in Christ. The Holy Spirit is now our Comforter, Teacher, Covenant Enabler, Covenant Enforcer, and the One who Anoints us with power.

John 14:15-17 (KJV)
*15 If ye love me, keep my commandments. 16 **And I will pray the Father, and he shall give you another Comforter, that he may abide with you for ever;** 17 Even the Spirit of truth; whom the world cannot receive, because it seeth him not, neither knoweth him: but ye know him; for he dwelleth with you, and shall be in you.*

15. The Power of the Spirit Given to the Church

The Holy Spirit empowers believers to work miracles by the power of God in the New Testament. The power of God works through the nine gifts of the Holy Spirit.

> *Acts 1:8 (KJV)*
>
> *8 But ye shall receive power, after that the Holy Ghost is come upon you: and ye shall be witnesses unto me both in Jerusalem, and in all Judaea, and in Samaria, and unto the uttermost part of the earth.*

> *1 Corinthians 12:7-11 (KJV)*
>
> *7 But the manifestation of the Spirit is given to every man to profit withal. 8 For to one is given by the Spirit the word of wisdom; to another the word of knowledge by the same Spirit; 9 To another faith by the same Spirit; to another the gifts of healing by the same Spirit; 10 To another the working of miracles; to another prophecy; to another discerning of spirits; to another divers kinds of tongues; to another the interpretation of tongues: 11 But all these worketh that one and the selfsame Spirit, dividing to every man severally as he will.*

16. Ability to Know the Truth

The Holy Spirit leads us into all *Truth*. We are given the *Truth* of God and no longer have to tolerate being lied to by the devil and his demons.

> *John 16:12-13 (KJV)*
>
> *12 I have yet many things to say unto you, but ye cannot bear them now. 13 Howbeit when he, the Spirit of truth, is come, he will guide you into all truth: for he shall not speak of himself; but*

whatsoever he shall hear, that shall he speak: and he will shew you things to come.

17. DIVINE HEALING

When Jesus took stripes upon His back, He paid the price for everyone to be healed of anything and everything.

> *1 Peter 2:24 (KJV)*
> *24 Who his own self bare our sins in his own body on the tree, that we, being dead to sins, should live unto righteousness: **by whose stripes ye were healed.***

18. SUPERNATURAL PROVISION

DIVINE PROSPERITY

It is the will of God that we prosper financially and be in health. God has promised to supply all our needs according to His riches in glory by Christ Jesus.

> *3 John 1:2 (KJV)*
> *2 Beloved, I wish above all things that thou mayest prosper and be in health, even as thy soul prospereth.*

> *Philippians 4:19 (KJV)*
> *19 But my God shall supply all your need according to his riches in glory by Christ Jesus.*

19. GIVEN THE GLORY OF GOD

The Glory of God is the splendor of the unchanging Pure Essence of Who He is. The Glory of God goes beyond His honor and gets into how He shines from the Holiness and Grandeur of His Being. When we receive the Glory of God, we become one with God. The night before Jesus was crucified, He said He gave the Church God's Glory so they may be one with God.

John 17:20-23 (KJV)

*20 Neither pray I for these alone, but for them also which shall believe on me through their word; 21 That they all may be one; as thou, Father, art in me, and I in thee, that they also may be one in us: that the world may believe that thou hast sent me. 22 **And the glory which thou gavest me I have given them; that they may be one, even as we are one:** 23 I in them, and thou in me, that they may be made perfect in one; and that the world may know that thou hast sent me, and hast loved them, as thou hast loved me.*

20. GIVEN A NEW HEART & NEW SPIRIT

When we make Jesus our Lord, He gives us a *new heart* and *new spirit*. When He does this, He takes away our stoney hearts, enabling us to walk in the Laws of God.

Ezekiel 36:25-27 (KJV)

*25 Then will I sprinkle clean water upon you, and ye shall be clean: from all your filthiness, and from all your idols, will I cleanse you. 26 **A new heart also will I give you, and a new spirit will I put within you: and I will take away the stony heart out of your flesh, and I will give you an heart of flesh. 27 And I will put my spirit within you, and cause you to walk in my statutes, and ye shall keep my judgments, and do them.***

21. MADE KINGS & PRIESTS UNTO GOD

As new believers in Christ, we are made kings and priests unto God. We will be granted the right to rule and reign with Christ as kings over the nations. We are also given access to God to minister to Him as priests.

Revelation 1:5-6 (KJV)

5 And from Jesus Christ, who is the faithful witness, and the first begotten of the dead, and the prince of the kings of the earth. Unto him that loved us, and washed us from our sins in his own blood,

*6 **And hath made us kings and priests unto God and his Father**; to him be glory and dominion for ever and ever. Amen.*

22. GRANTED HEAVENLY CITIZENSHIP

As New Testament believers, we have been given citizenship with the saints of Heaven.

Ephesians 2:19 (KJV)

*19 Now therefore ye are no more strangers and foreigners, **but fellowcitizens with the saints**, and of the household of God;*

23. GIVEN THE BLESSINGS OF ABRAHAM

As children of God, we have been given access to the blessings of Abraham through faith in Christ.

Galatians 3:6-9 (KJV)

*6 Even as Abraham believed God, and it was accounted to him for righteousness. 7 **Know ye therefore that they which are of faith, the same are the children of Abraham.** 8 And the scripture, foreseeing that God would justify the heathen through faith, preached before the gospel unto Abraham, saying, In thee shall all nations be blessed. 9 **So then they which be of faith are blessed with faithful Abraham.***

24. GENTILES CAN NOW BE SAVED WITH THE JEWS

When Jesus died on the Cross and rose again from the dead, He made a way for the Gentiles to be saved with the Jews.

> *Ephesians 2:11-14 (KJV)*
>
> *11 Wherefore remember, that ye being in time past Gentiles in the flesh, who are called Uncircumcision by that which is called the Circumcision in the flesh made by hands; 12 That at that time ye were without Christ, being aliens from the commonwealth of Israel, and strangers from the covenants of promise, having no hope, and without God in the world: 13 **But now in Christ Jesus ye who sometimes were far off are made nigh by the blood of Christ. 14 For he is our peace, who hath made both one, and hath broken down the middle wall of partition between us;***

25. ABILITY TO ENTER GOD'S REST

There is a *Rest* for the people of God. This *Rest* is for us to enter into now as we inherit the promises of God, and there is also an *Eternal Rest* with God throughout Eternity.

> *Hebrews 4:1-3 (KJV)*
>
> *1 **Let us therefore fear, lest, a promise being left us of entering into his rest, any of you should seem to come short of it.** 2 For unto us was the gospel preached, as well as unto them: but the word preached did not profit them, not being mixed with faith in them that heard it. 3 **For we which have believed do enter into rest,** as he said, As I have sworn in my wrath, if they shall enter into my **rest:** although the works were finished from the foundation of the world.*

26. FIVE-FOLD MINISTRIES GIVEN AS A GIFT

Jesus established the Five-Fold ministry as a gift to the body of Christ for the perfecting of the saints, for the work of the ministry, and for the edifying of the Body of Christ.

Ephesians 4:7-12 (KJV)

*7 But unto every one of us is given grace according to the measure of the gift of Christ. 8 Wherefore he saith, When he ascended up on high, he led captivity captive, **and gave gifts unto men**. 9 (Now that he ascended, what is it but that he also descended first into the lower parts of the earth? 10 He that descended is the same also that ascended up far above all heavens, that he might fill all things.)11 **And he gave some, apostles; and some, prophets; and some, evangelists; and some, pastors and teachers;** 12 For the perfecting of the saints, for the work of the ministry, for the edifying of the body of Christ:*

27. CHURCH ESTABLISHED AS THE BRIDE OF CHRIST

The New Testament Church was saved and destined to be the *Eternal Bride of Christ.*

Ephesians 5:31-32 (KJV)

*31 For this cause shall a man leave his father and mother, and shall be joined unto his wife, and they two shall be one flesh. 32 **This is a great mystery: but I speak concerning Christ and the church.***

Revelation 21:9 (KJV)

*9 And there came unto me one of the seven angels which had the seven vials full of the seven last plagues, and talked with me, saying, **Come hither, I will shew thee the bride, the Lamb's wife.***

28. Allowed Entrance into the Heavenly Jerusalem

Anyone whose name is written in the Lamb's Book of Life will be allowed entrance into the New Jerusalem.

Revelation 21:23-27 (KJV)

*23 And the city had no need of the sun, neither of the moon, to shine in it: for the glory of God did lighten it, and the Lamb is the light thereof. 24 And the nations of them which are saved shall walk in the light of it: and the kings of the earth do bring their glory and honour into it. 25 And the gates of it shall not be shut at all by day: for there shall be no night there. 26 And they shall bring the glory and honour of the nations into it. 27 **And there shall in no wise enter into it any thing that defileth, neither whatsoever worketh abomination, or maketh a lie: but they which are written in the Lamb's book of life.***

29. Ability to See God's Face and Live

When Adam and Eve sinned, humankind was no longer able to look into the Holy *Face* of God and live. As born-again believers we will be able to look in the *Face* of God and live.

Exodus 33:20 (KJV)

20 And he said, Thou canst not see my face: for there shall no man see me, and live.

Revelation 22:3-4 (KJV)

*3 And there shall be no more curse: but the throne of God and of the Lamb shall be in it; and his servants shall serve him: 4 **And they shall see his face;** and his name shall be in their foreheads.*

30. GIVEN GOD'S ARMOUR & SWORD

We no longer have to face the devil in our own strength. God has not only given us His Holy Spirit, but He has also given us His *Heavenly Armour* to fight the devil, fallen angels, and the evil hosts of demons.

Ephesians 6:13-17 (KJV)
13 Wherefore take unto you the whole armour of God, that ye may be able to withstand in the evil day, and having done all, to stand. 14 Stand therefore, having your loins girt about with truth, and having on the breastplate of righteousness; 15 And your feet shod with the preparation of the gospel of peace; 16 Above all, taking the shield of faith, wherewith ye shall be able to quench all the fiery darts of the wicked. 17 And take the helmet of salvation, and the sword of the Spirit, which is the word of God:

31. DIVINE ANGELIC PROTECTION

The angel of the Lord encamps around us and delivers us. When you dwell in the *Secret Place* God will protect you with His angels.

Psalm 34:7 (KJV)
7 The angel of the Lord encampeth round about them that fear him, and delivereth them.

Psalm 91:11-12 (KJV)
11 For he shall give his angels charge over thee, to keep thee in all thy ways. 12 They shall bear thee up in their hands, lest thou dash thy foot against a stone.

32. GIVEN THE KINGDOM OF GOD

When we first seek the Kingdom of God, He will provide for all our needs. The Eternal Kingdom of God is the answer to all of our needs. The Kingdom of God is also within us, and we can access it now through the power of the Holy Spirit.

> *Luke 12:31-32 (KJV)*
>
> *31 But rather seek ye the kingdom of God; and all these things shall be added unto you. 32 Fear not, little flock;* **for it is your Father's good pleasure to give you the kingdom.**

33. INHERIT ALL THINGS

When we become overcoming born-again sons of God, we will inherit all things. Those who choose God above His creation will inherit all of creation.

> *Revelation 21:7 (KJV)*
>
> *7 He that overcometh shall inherit all things; and I will be his God, and he shall be my son.*

34. ANSWERS TO OUR PRAYERS

The night before Jesus died on the Cross, He told His disciples that if they abided in His Words, they could ask what they wanted, and it would be done for them.

> *John 15:7 (KJV)*
>
> *7 If ye abide in me, and my words abide in you, ye shall ask what ye will, and it shall be done unto you.*

35. GAVE US ALL PROMISES FOUND IN THE WORD OF GOD

All of the Promises of God are yea and amen in Christ Jesus. If you can find a promise in God's Word, you can believe to receive it. The one dwelling in the *Secret Place* can claim any promise in God's Word. Jesus died, was buried, and rose again so we could claim all of the Promises of God in the Old and New Testaments. God is glorified when we inherit His promises.

> *2 Corinthians 1:20 (KJV)*
> *20 For all the promises of God in him are yea, and in him Amen, unto the glory of God by us.*

Jesus paid a very heavy price so we could have all these blessings. I am amazed at all the wonderful things Jesus accomplished for us because of *His Passion*. Your life will never be the same once you get a revelation of all that Jesus has done for you.

THE POWER OF GOD

The Bible says that the preaching of the Cross IS the *Power of God* (Romans 1:16). It doesn't say the preaching of the Cross talks about the *Power of God;* it says the preaching of the Cross IS the *Power of God*. Why is the preaching of the Cross the *Power of God?* To answer this question, we must ask, What is the *Power* of God? The *Power of God* is the anointing of the Holy Spirit to work Miracles. Jesus was working miracles through the Power of the Holy Spirit, also called the anointing.

> *Acts 10:38 (KJV)*
> *38 How God anointed Jesus of Nazareth with the Holy Ghost and with power: who went about doing good, and healing all that were oppressed of the devil; for God was with him.*

The preaching of the Cross IS the *Power* because when people believe what is preached about what Jesus did on the Cross and the *Better Promises* freely given to them, they can receive by the *Power* of the Anointing through the

Holy Spirit the Blessings of the Gospel. The preaching of the Cross has the same powerful impact as the events of the Cross. God has ordained that through the foolishness of preaching the Cross, the anointing of the Holy Spirit will be imparted. The *Power of the Holy Spirit* imparts the *Better Promises* of the *New Covenant* through the foolishness of preaching the Gospel.

> *1 Corinthians 1:18 (KJV)*
> *18 For the preaching of the cross is to them that perish foolishness; but unto us which are saved it is the power of God.*

The Good News of the Gospel is the *Power* of God unto salvation to all who believe. When people hear the preaching of the Gospel, they can receive the *Better Promises* of the New Covenant once they believe.

> *Romans 1:16 (KJV)*
> *16 For I am not ashamed of the gospel of Christ: for it is the power of God unto salvation to every one that believeth; to the Jew first, and also to the Greek.*

The Gospel is the Good News of what Jesus paid for in His death, burial, and resurrection so we could inherit the blessings of the *New Covenant*. Jesus anointed His disciples with the *Power of the Holy Spirit* so they could preach and be a witness to all that He paid for in His *Passion*. The Holy Spirit, by His *Anointed Power* freely gives us the blessings of the *Better Promises* whenever the Gospel is preached.

> *Acts 1:8 (KJV)*
> *8 But ye shall receive power, after that the Holy Ghost is come upon you: and ye shall be witnesses unto me both in Jerusalem, and*

in all Judaea, and in Samaria, and unto the uttermost part of the earth.

The *Better Promises* of the Gospel are the miracles we receive from the New Covenant. A miracle is when God intervenes with His **Anointed Divine Power** in the affairs of believers with impossible answers to prayers of faith that defy logic, scientific reasoning, doctor reports, negative bank accounts, physical laws of nature, demonic oppression, human ability, and the natural course of life experience. Another definition of a miracle is the release of God's *Supernatural Power* to deliver the *Better Promises* of the New Covenant by the *Power* of the Holy Spirit to someone in need.

It is amazing beyond all comprehension what Jesus has done for us. Jesus paid the ultimate price of death on a Cross so we could receive the *Better Promises* of the New Covenant. The Bible says the angels desire to look into what is given to us through the preaching of the Gospel by the Holy Spirit that was sent down to us from Heaven.

> *1 Peter 1:12 (KJV)*
> *12 Unto whom it was revealed, that not unto themselves, but unto us they did minister the things, **which are now reported unto you by them that have preached the gospel unto you with the Holy Ghost sent down from heaven; which things the angels desire to look into.***

In conclusion, ending a chapter like this isn't easy because of the impact of these wondrous revelations. When the eyes of your understanding are opened to the reality of all that Jesus has done for us and what is freely given to us by God, you are never the same. The Gospel is a dream come true for a lost and dying world. All we must do to inherit the *Better Promises* is walk in the New Covenant, dwell in the *Secret Place,* and believe God to perform all He accomplished for us in the *Passion of Christ.* We cannot thank Jesus Christ enough for what He was willing to suffer for us to be *eternally blessed* by God. Thank you, God, for all you have done for us so we can inherit the Abrahamic Blessings of the *Better Promises* of the New Covenant.

AND JESUS ANSWERED HIM, SAYING, IT IS WRITTEN,
THAT MAN SHALL NOT LIVE BY BREAD ALONE,
BUT BY EVERY WORD OF GOD.

LUKE 4:4

CHAPTER
TEN

ASKING
GOD

What the Bible teaches about asking God for *Anything* in prayer is astounding! There are amazing promises found in the Word of God regarding prayer that stagger the natural mind. God loves to answer the prayers of His obedient children with miracles. However, as much as God loves to answer our prayers, He has a set of necessary requirements before He hears and answers our petitions. In this chapter, I will teach God's profound promises for asking *Anything* from Him when we pray, the parameters He requires when we ask, and how this applies to the *Secret Place*.

The Word of God has established *Prayer Parameters* that must be adhered to before God will answer our prayers. *Prayer Parameters* are God's rules, laws, and guidelines that govern our asking. When God's Biblical *Prayer Parameters* are satisfied, He is ready and willing to answer any prayer. It is imperative that we learn His rules, laws, and guidelines when asking if we want our prayers answered by God.

The night before Jesus died on the Cross, He taught His disciples that if they *Abided* in Him and His Words *Abided* in them, they could ask *Whatever* they wanted, and it would be done for them.

> *John 15:7 (KJV)*
> *7 If ye abide in me, and my words abide in you, ye shall ask what ye will, and it shall be done unto you.*

One parameter to reflect on is what it means to *Abide* in Christ. We know that when Jesus taught about *"Abiding in Him,"* He was referring to the *Secret Place*. The *Secret Place* and the *Abiding* are the same place. Psalms 91:1 (KJV) says: *"He that dwelleth in the **secret place** of the most High shall **abide** under the shadow of the Almighty."* When you dwell in the *Secret Place*, you *Abide* under the Shadow of the Almighty. Jesus taught that to dwell in the *Secret Place* of *Abiding* in Him; His Words must be *Abiding* in you.

Dwelling in the *Secret Place* means you are dying to your flesh daily and are obeying everything Jesus Commanded us to live by. An essential parameter to your prayers being answered is you must be obeying all the Words of Christ. Once you are *Abiding* in the Words of Christ, you can inherit the precious promise of having your prayers answered. Obeying all the Words of Christ is vital to dwelling in the *Secret Place*. You cannot believe God to answer your prayers if you are disobeying His Word. The Bible teaches that the Lord will not hear us if we regard iniquity in our heart.

> *Psalm 66:18 (KJV)*
> *18 If I regard iniquity in my heart, the Lord will not hear me:*

The Bible also says that God will hide His Face and not hear because of iniquity and sin. You cannot expect God to listen to you and answer your prayers if you don't listen to Him regarding iniquity and sin. Iniquity is disobedience to His Commands by doing evil in His sight. Sin is an immoral act against God's Divine Laws found in His Word.

> *Isaiah 59:1-2 (KJV)*
> *1 Behold, the Lord's hand is not shortened, that it cannot save; neither his ear heavy, that it cannot hear: 2 But your iniquities have separated between you and your God, and your sins have hid his face from you, that he will not hear.*

The *Secret Place* is the Holy of Holies, and just like in the Old Testament, the Altar of Incense was placed before the Ark of the Covenant in the Tabernacle and Temple. As I revealed in a previous chapter, the smoke of the incense burning on the Altar of Incense represents the prayers of the saints ascending up before God.

Revelation 8:3-4 (KJV)

*3 And another angel came and stood at the altar, having a golden censer; and there was given unto him much incense, **that he should offer it with the prayers of all saints upon the golden altar which was before the throne. 4 And the smoke of the incense, which came with the prayers of the saints, ascended up before God out of the angel's hand.***

The mystery of the Altar of Incense is the prayers that God hears, and answers must be prayed in the Holy Place *(Secret Place)*. However, you cannot enter the Holy Place unless your sins are dealt with in the Outer Court, where the Bronze Altar and Bronze Laver is located. The Bronze Altar is where sin is dealt with by the sacrifice of Christ when He died on the Cross. You must also be cleaned from the water in the Bronze Laver, which is the washing of the water of the Word before entering the Holy Place. We must be forgiven of our sins and cleansed by the Word of God before entering the *Secret Place.*

It is vital to understand that when Jesus died on the Cross, the Veil in the Temple was torn in two, making the Inner Court and Holy of Holies one place. The *Secret Place* is now the Holy Place (Inner Court) and Holy of Holies within the Temple of your body. There is no more Veil separating these two holy locations. Jesus made them one place after His death, giving anyone dwelling in the *Secret Place* access to God, who hovers over the Mercy Seat that sits on top of the Ark of the Covenant. God revealed in the pattern of the Temple in a New Testament believer that for their prayers to be answered, they must be dwelling in the *Secret Place.*

A Christian living in sin by not *Abiding* in the Words of Christ cannot expect God to hear and answer their prayers because they are not dwelling in the *Secret Place.* A Christian living in sin is still in the Outer Court and must deal with their sins before they can enter the *Secret Place* (Holy Place & Holy of Holies). Once sin is dealt with at the Bronze Altar, a Christian who is *Abiding* in all the Words of Christ (washed at the Bronze Laver) can dwell in the *Secret Place* and pray petitions from the Altar of Incense before the Ark of the Covenant that God will hear. The pattern of the Tabernacle of Moses and the Temple that King Solomon built served to establish the *Prayer Parameters* of dwelling in the *Secret Place* for prayers to be heard and answered by God.

> ### Psalm 141:1-2 (KJV)
> *1 Lord, I cry unto thee: make haste unto me; give ear unto my voice, when I cry unto thee. 2* **Let my prayer be set forth before thee as incense;** *and the lifting up of my hands as the evening sacrifice.*

There are more *Prayer Parameters* that must be met once dwelling in the *Secret Place,* which I will teach in this chapter. Before I reveal **ALL** the conditions that must be met when we pray, we need to know **WHAT** we can ask God for when we come before His Presence in the *Secret Place.* What do we have a right to ask God for when dwelling in *the Secret Place of the Most High?* The Scriptures reveal that God not only has *Prayer Parameters* but also set a boundary on **WHAT** we can ask Him for.

You will be astonished and amazed when you discover the set boundary of **WHAT** we can ask God for in prayer. Jesus taught that we could ask God for

ANYTHING. Wait a minute, did Jesus say *ANYTHING?* Yes, *ANYTHING!* Another way to say *ANYTHING* is *WHATSOEVER!* What does *WHATSOEVER* mean? *WHATSOEVER* means *WHATSOEVER!* What does *ANYTHING* mean? *ANYTHING* means *ANYTHING!* This sounds like a blank check, and that is precisely what it is. Rather than God mapping out item by item what you could ask Him for in prayer, He made it open-ended. If you can dream it up, you can ask Him for it.

Here are some Scriptures that Jesus spoke that reveal and confirm this amazing truth:

John 14:14 (KJV)
*14 If ye shall ask **any thing** in my name, I will do it.*

John 16:23-24 (KJV)
*23 And in that day ye shall ask me nothing. Verily, verily, I say unto you, **Whatsoever** ye shall ask the Father in my name, he will give it you. 24 Hitherto have ye asked nothing in my name: ask, and ye shall receive, that your joy may be full.*

These two Scriptures reveal another parameter to our prayers being answered when asking God for *Anything*; you also have to ask in His Name. Asking in His Name has to do with the Name Jesus was going to receive after He arose from the dead. When Jesus rose from the dead, He was given a Name above every other name. The Name Jesus received after He arose from the dead was the **Lord Jesus Christ**. Jesus had to fulfill all of the Old Testament prophesies about the Messiah including the ones concerning His death, burial, and resurrection, before He could officially take on the Name Christ. Once He completed His Passion, He was officially Named by the Father, the **Lord Jesus Christ**.

Acts 2:36 (KJV)

*36 Therefore let all the house of Israel know assuredly, that **God** **hath** **made** **the** **same** **Jesus,** **whom** **ye** **have** **crucified,** **both Lord and Christ.***

When you ask in the Name of the **Lord Jesus Christ**, you are requesting by the right of everything He paid for in *His Passion*. Jesus died, was buried, and rose again so that you could have the right and privilege to ask God for *Anything*. His new Name represents everything He paid for when He died for us on the Cross. Asking in the Name of the **Lord Jesus Christ** means calling upon the New Covenant and what was paid for through *His Passion*. God exalted Jesus with a Name above every name when He rose Him from the dead, and every knee should bow to Him of things in Heaven, in Earth, and under the Earth.

Philippians 2:8-11 (KJV)

*8 And being found in fashion as a man, he humbled himself, and became obedient unto death, even the death of the cross. 9 **Wherefore God also hath highly exalted him, and given him a name which is above every name:** 10 That at **the name of Jesus every knee should bow, of things in heaven, and things in earth, and things under the earth; 11 And that every tongue should confess that Jesus Christ is Lord,** to the glory of God the Father.*

Jesus kept the revelation of His new Name He would be given after *His Passion* a secret during His ministry. It wasn't until the night before Jesus went to the Cross that He revealed to His disciples His new Name. While revealing His new Name to His disciples, Jesus revealed they could ask for *Anything* in His new Name. His new Name permitted them to ask God for

Anything if they were dwelling in the *Secret Place (Abiding in Him)* because of what He was about to do in *His Passion*.

John 14:12-14 (KJV)

*12 Verily, verily, I say unto you, He that believeth on me, the works that I do shall he do also; and greater works than these shall he do; because I go unto my Father. 13 **And whatsoever ye shall ask in my name, that will I do**, that the Father may be glorified in the Son. 14 **If ye shall ask any thing in my name, I will do it.***

John 15:16 (KJV)

*16 Ye have not chosen me, but I have chosen you, and ordained you, that ye should go and bring forth fruit, and that your fruit should remain: **that whatsoever ye shall ask of the Father in my name, he may give it you.***

Jesus also taught His disciples that their joy would be full when they asked for *"Whatsoever"* in His new Name. There is no greater joy than to ask God for something in the Name of the **Lord Jesus Christ** and receive an answer. It is unspeakable joy when God answers your prayers as you *Abide* in Christ in the *Secret Place*, especially when you need a miracle. When God answers prayers with miracles, it fills the believer *Abiding* in the *Secret Place* with abundant joy.

John 16:23-24 (KJV)

*23 And in that day ye shall ask me nothing. Verily, verily, I say unto you, **Whatsoever ye shall ask the Father in my name, he will give it you.** 24 **Hitherto have ye asked nothing in my name: ask, and ye shall receive, that your joy may be full.***

During His ministry, Jesus taught His disciples that they could speak to a Mountain, and it would move if they had faith and didn't doubt. When you dwell in the *Secret Place,* you have a Divine right to speak to Mountains, but we must speak to them to be removed and cast into the sea. Jesus used a Mountain as something symbolically insurmountable standing in our way. Speaking to the Mountain is a metaphor, meaning we must speak to impossible situations for them to move. However, the Mountain will only move if you are dwelling in the *Secret Place of the Most High.*

> *Matthew 21:21-22 (KJV)*
> *21 Jesus answered and said unto them, Verily I say unto you, If ye have faith, and doubt not, ye shall not only do this which is done to the fig tree,* **but also if ye shall say unto this mountain, Be thou removed, and be thou cast into the sea; it shall be done. 22 And all things, whatsoever ye shall ask in prayer, believing, ye shall receive.**

One of the best places to understand the truth of prayer and speaking to a Mountain is found in the story of when Jesus raised Lazarus from the dead. When Jesus stood before the tomb of Lazarus, Martha said to Jesus that *Whatever* He asked God for, God would give it to Him. This statement provides great insight into the ministry of Jesus and how He was working miracles. Jesus was performing miracles by asking God for them and speaking to Mountains. He was dwelling in the *Secret Place,* and God was answering His prayers of faith that were offered up on the Altar of Incense.

> *John 11:21-22 (KJV)*
> *21 Then said Martha unto Jesus, Lord, if thou hadst been here, my brother had not died. 22* **But I know, that even now, whatsoever thou wilt ask of God, God will give it thee.**

Jesus told Martha that if she believed, she would see the glory of God. Then, in front of the tomb of Lazarus, Jesus made a bold statement. He declared that the Father always hears Him. Jesus was living in the *Secret Place*, obeying His Father's Commands, and meeting all of the *Prayer Parameters* for His prayers to be answered.

> ### *John 11:41-42 (KJV)*
> *41 Then they took away the stone from the place where the dead was laid. **And Jesus lifted up his eyes, and said, Father, I thank thee that thou hast heard me. 42 And I knew that thou hearest me always:** but because of the people which stand by I said it, that they may believe that thou hast sent me.*

Interestingly, this passage reveals that the Father had already heard Jesus concerning Lazarus being raised from the dead. Jesus prayed to God, and God heard Him, but Lazarus was still dead because Jesus needed to speak to the Mountain for Lazarus to be raised from the dead. This reveals that when we ask God for *"Whatsoever"* in prayer, for us to receive it, we must also speak to the impossible situation (Mountain) standing in our way. Jesus had to call Lazarus forth for His prayer to come to pass. It's not enough to just ask God in prayer for something; we must speak to the Mountain after we know God heard our prayer in the *Secret Place*.

> ### *John 11:43 (KJV)*
> *43 And when he thus had spoken, he cried with a loud voice, Lazarus, come forth.*

Jesus was very bold and audacious in His asking the Father for miracles. Jesus asked the Father for not only dead people to be raised from the dead but for blind eyes to see. Jesus asked the Father for demons to come out of people, for missing limbs to be restored, and for storms to be calmed. Jesus even went as far as to ask the Father to allow Him to open the eyes of someone born blind. The Father heard and answered all of Jesus' bold *Secret Place* prayers.

The Father also asked Jesus to ask Him to give Him the heathen for His inheritance and the uttermost parts of the Earth for His possession.

> *Psalm 2:7-9 (KJV)*
> *7 I will declare the decree: the Lord hath said unto me,* **Thou art my Son; this day have I begotten thee. 8 Ask of me, and I shall give thee the heathen for thine inheritance, and the uttermost parts of the earth for thy possession.** *9 Thou shalt break them with a rod of iron; thou shalt dash them in pieces like a potter's vessel.*

We know this verse was fulfilled after the resurrection of Jesus because it is quoted in the Book of Acts by the Apostle Paul after the *Passion of Christ.*

> *Acts 13:30-33 (KJV)*
> *30* **But God raised him from the dead:** *31 And he was seen many days of them which came up with him from Galilee to Jerusalem, who are his witnesses unto the people. 32 And we declare unto you glad tidings, how that the promise which was made unto the fathers, 33* **God hath fulfilled the same unto us their children, in that he hath raised up Jesus again; as it is also written in the second psalm, Thou art my Son, this day have I begotten thee.**

The Gentiles came into the inheritance of salvation by faith because of the **Lord Jesus Christ's** *Passion.*

Matthew 28:18-20 (KJV)

*18 And Jesus came and spake unto them, saying, **All power is given unto me in heaven and in earth**. 19 **Go ye therefore, and teach all nations**, baptizing them in the name of the Father, and of the Son, and of the Holy Ghost: 20 Teaching them to observe all things whatsoever I have commanded you: and, lo, I am with you always, even unto the end of the world. Amen.*

In the Book of Acts, the Apostles prayed and asked God to do miracles in the new Name of His Holy Son Jesus. The Apostles were under constant attack from the Jewish religious leaders at that time, who were trying to stop them from speaking or teaching in the Name of the **Lord Jesus Christ**. God granted the Apostles their request, and extraordinary miracles were performed by the hands of the Apostles, and they continued to speak the Word of God boldly.

Acts 4:29-33 (KJV)

*29 And now, Lord, behold their threatenings: **and grant unto thy servants, that with all boldness they may speak thy word, 30 By stretching forth thine hand to heal; and that signs and wonders may be done by the name of thy holy child Jesus.** 31 And when they had prayed, the place was shaken where they were assembled together; **and they were all filled with the Holy Ghost, and they spake the word of God with boldness.** 32 And the multitude of them that believed were of one heart and of one soul: neither said any of them that ought of the things which he possessed was his own; but they had all things common. 33 **And with great power gave the apostles witness of the resurrection of the Lord Jesus: and great grace was upon them all.***

In the Book of James, the Bible reveals more important parameters when asking God for *Anything* in prayer. Some people don't have because they don't ask. Don't expect God to answer your prayer if He doesn't know what you are asking Him for. You must be specific when making requests to God. You have to let God know exactly what you are asking for. Another parameter is you also can't ask to consume it upon your lust; this is called asking amiss. Lust means evil desires that don't align with Christ's Words. Whatever you ask must align with Christ's Commands, Words, holiness, purity, and selflessness.

James 4:1-3 (KJV)

*1 From whence come wars and fightings among you? come they not hence, even of your lusts that war in your members? 2 Ye lust, and have not: ye kill, and desire to have, and cannot obtain: ye fight and war, **yet ye have not, because ye ask not. 3 Ye ask, and receive not, because ye ask amiss, that ye may consume it upon your lusts.***

There is a powerful story in the Old Testament where God allowed a king to ask for whatever he wanted. God gave this king a blank check to ask for *ANYTHING*. You can gain great insight into what to ask God for by studying how this king responded to God. This king was King Solomon, one of Israel's most influential and powerful kings. Let's observe how King Solomon answered God when He permitted him to ask for *ANYTHING*.

1 Kings 3:5-14 (KJV)

*5 In Gibeon the Lord appeared to Solomon in a dream by night: **and God said, Ask what I shall give thee.** 6 And Solomon said, Thou hast shewed unto thy servant David my father great mercy, according as he walked before thee in truth, and in righteousness,* *and in uprightness of heart with thee; and thou hast kept for him this great kindness, that thou hast given him a son to sit on his throne, as it is this day. 7 And now, O Lord my God, thou hast made thy servant king instead of David my father: and I am but a little child: I know not how to go out or come in. 8 And thy servant is in the midst of thy people which thou hast chosen, a great people, that cannot be numbered nor counted for multitude. 9 Give therefore thy servant an understanding heart to judge thy people, that I may discern between good and bad: for who is able to judge this thy so great a people? 10 And the speech pleased the Lord, that Solomon had asked this thing. 11 And God said unto him, Because thou hast asked this thing, and hast not asked for thyself long life; neither hast asked riches for thyself, nor hast asked the life of thine enemies; but hast asked for thyself understanding to discern judgment; 12 Behold, I have done according to thy words: lo, I have given thee a wise and an understanding heart; so that there was none like thee before thee, neither after thee shall any arise like unto thee. 13 And I have also given thee that which thou hast not asked, both riches, and honour: so that there shall not be any among the kings like unto thee all thy days. 14 And if thou wilt walk in my ways, to keep my statutes and my commandments, as thy father David did walk, then I will lengthen thy days.*

King Solomon responded to God by asking for something selfless. King Solomon didn't ask anything for himself; he asked God for an understanding heart to judge God's people. King Solomon's response caused God to go beyond what he asked for and blessed him beyond measure. King Solomon's selflessness in what he asked God for caused the Lord to make him one of the wisest and wealthiest kings ever to live and gave him great honor, so there was no other king like him.

Believers become more selfless when they get close to God in the *Secret Place* because God is selfless. When you look at the life of Jesus, most of His asking God for petitions was for other people's needs. Even when Jesus was getting ready to die on the Cross, He prayed if there was any other way this cup of suffering could pass from Him. But Jesus knew there was no other way, and He selflessly submitted to the will of God to die for us by going to the Cross. Jesus was very selfless in all that He did and asked God for. This is why God gave Him a Name above every other name!

When you become selfless and pray for the needs of others, God will look after you, just like He looked after King Solomon and gave him beyond what he asked for. God can do exceedingly abundantly above all that we ask or think according to the power that works in us.

Ephesians 3:20 (KJV)
20 Now unto him that is able to do exceeding abundantly above all that we ask or think, according to the power that worketh in us,

When Elisha asked Elijah for a *double portion* of his spirit, this had to do with helping others. Elisha knew the *double portion* would be for him to be used by God as a prophet to help others. Elisha was selfless in his request. After Elisha received the *double portion* of Elijah's mantle, he went on to help many people by the power of God.

2 Kings 2:9-15 (KJV)
*9 And it came to pass, when they were gone over, that Elijah said unto Elisha, **Ask what I shall do for thee**, before I be taken away*

*from thee. **And Elisha said, I pray thee, let a double portion of thy spirit be upon me.** 10 And he said, Thou hast asked a hard thing: nevertheless, if thou see me when I am taken from thee, it shall be so unto thee; but if not, it shall not be so. 11 And it came to pass, as they still went on, and talked, that, behold, there appeared a chariot of fire, and horses of fire, and parted them both asunder; and Elijah went up by a whirlwind into heaven. 12 And Elisha saw it, and he cried, My father, my father, the chariot of Israel, and the horsemen thereof. And he saw him no more: and he took hold of his own clothes, and rent them in two pieces. 13 He took up also the mantle of Elijah that fell from him, and went back, and stood by the bank of Jordan; 14 And he took the mantle of Elijah that fell from him, and smote the waters, and said, Where is the Lord God of Elijah? and when he also had smitten the waters, they parted hither and thither: and Elisha went over. 15 And when the sons of the prophets which were to view at Jericho saw him, they said, **The spirit of Elijah doth rest on Elisha.** And they came to meet him, and bowed themselves to the ground before him.*

One of the greatest prayers you can pray is to ask God for wisdom and understanding like King Solomon asked for. The wisdom of God will help you in everything you do in this life, and prepare you for Judgment Day and the afterlife. When you become wise and selfless, God can use you in a mighty way, like He used the mighty men and women of the Bible. Just make sure when you ask God for wisdom, you ask in faith, nothing wavering.

James 1:5-8 (KJV)
5 If any of you lack wisdom, let him ask of God, that giveth to all men liberally, and upbraideth not; and it shall be given him. 6 But

let him ask in faith, nothing wavering. For he that wavereth is like a wave of the sea driven with the wind and tossed. 7 For let not that man think that he shall receive any thing of the Lord. 8 A double minded man is unstable in all his ways.

God also loves persistence when asking Him for *Anything*. Jesus taught people to persist and keep asking until they received an answer to their prayer. He even went as far as to say we must bug God and be importunate in our asking. Importunity means to be insistent, troublesome, frequent, forceful, and persistent to the point of annoyance in asking God for an answer to a prayer.

Luke 11:5-13 (KJV)

5 And he said unto them, Which of you shall have a friend, and shall go unto him at midnight, and say unto him, Friend, lend me three loaves; 6 For a friend of mine in his journey is come to me, and I have nothing to set before him? 7 And he from within shall answer and say, Trouble me not: the door is now shut, and my children are with me in bed; I cannot rise and give thee. 8 I say unto you, Though he will not rise and give him, because he is his friend, yet because of his importunity he will rise and give him as many as he needeth. 9 And I say unto you, Ask, and it shall be given you; seek, and ye shall find; knock, and it shall be opened unto you. 10 For every one that asketh receiveth; and he that seeketh findeth; and to him that knocketh it shall be opened. 11 If a son shall ask bread of any of you that is a father, will he give him a stone? or if he ask a fish, will he for a fish give him a serpent? 12 Or if he shall ask an egg, will he offer him a scorpion? 13 If ye then, being evil, know how to give good gifts unto your children: how much more shall your heavenly Father give the Holy Spirit to them that ask him?

If we want God to hear us and answer our prayers, we must also ask according to His will. Asking according to the will of God is a vital *Prayer Parameter*. You can never go wrong if you ask according to God's revealed will in His Word.

1 John 5:14-15 (KJV)

*14 And this is the confidence that we have in him, that, **if we ask any thing according to his will, he heareth us: 15 And if we know that he hear us, whatsoever we ask, we know that we have the petitions that we desired of him.***

When we come before God asking for *Anything* in prayer, it must also be with the confidence of a clean conscience. When our conscience is clean, we have the confidence to ask God for *Anything*. When we keep the Commands of God, do things that are pleasing in His sight, and have a clean conscience, we will receive *Whatever* we ask of Him.

1 John 3:19-22 (KJV)

*19 And hereby we know that we are of the truth, and shall assure our hearts before him. 20 For if our heart condemn us, God is greater than our heart, and knoweth all things. 21 **Beloved, if our heart condemn us not, then have we confidence toward God. 22 And whatsoever we ask, we receive of him, because we keep his commandments, and do those things that are pleasing in his sight.***

Another important factor when praying to God is that we must forgive anyone we have ought against. Forgiving people who have sinned against you is vital because God will not forgive you if you don't forgive others. God will forgive you in the same way you forgive others. Dwelling in the *Secret Place* means you are forgiven and have forgiven others. If you are not forgiven of your sins, you cannot come before the Presence of God in the *Secret Place* and offer up prayers on the Altar of Incense because God doesn't hear sinners. *John 9:31 (KJV) Now we know that God heareth not sinners: but if any man be a worshipper of God, and doeth his will, him he heareth.*

> *Mark 11:25-26 (KJV)*
> *25 And when ye stand praying, forgive, if ye have ought against any: that your Father also which is in heaven may forgive you your trespasses. 26 But if ye do not forgive, neither will your Father which is in heaven forgive your trespasses.*

God promises He will answer **ANYTHING** we ask for in prayer when we keep all of His *Prayer Parameters*. God is looking for selfless believers who will ask Him for **ANYTHING**, and they will start to see miracles beyond all comprehension. Below is a list of all of the *Prayer Parameters* I mentioned in this chapter:

PRAYER PARAMETERS

1. Must be Abiding in Christ

2. Must be Dwelling in the *Secret Place*

3. The Words of Christ Must be Abiding in you

4. You cannot be in disobedience to ANY of the Words of Christ

5. Can't regard iniquity in your heart

6. Can't be living in sin or iniquity when asking

7. Must ask in the Name of the Lord Jesus Christ

8. Must believe when we ask

9. Must not waiver in our faith when we ask

10. Must speak to the Mountain after we ask

11. Can't have any doubt in our hearts when speaking to the Mountain

12. We must believe whatever we say shall come to pass

13. We must believe we have received whatever we are asking for

14. You must be forgiven of your sin before you ask

15. You must be washed with the water of the Word

16. When you are praying, you must forgive anyone you have ought against

17. Must ask and not assume God knows what you want

18. Must be specific when you ask

19. Must not ask to consume it upon your lusts (evil desire)

20. Must ask in faith

21. We must keep asking and be persistent until we receive

22. We must bug God and be importunate when asking

23. We must ask according to the will of God

24. We must have a clean conscience when we ask

25. Must be keeping the Commands of God

26. Must be doing that which is pleasing in His sight when asking

An important question is, if I ask God for *Anything*, does He have the power to do *Anything*? This is a fundamental question to ask when it comes to asking God for *Anything*. Why would we ask God for *Anything* if He didn't have the power to do *Anything*? The Bible says that nothing is too hard for the Lord.

> *Genesis 18:14a (KJV)*
> *14 Is any thing too hard for the Lord?...*

> *Jeremiah 32:27 (KJV)*
> *27 Behold, I am the Lord, the God of all flesh: **is there any thing too hard for me?***

Let me explain why nothing is too hard for the Lord and how He can do *Anything* we ask Him to do in prayer. God can create or turn anything into another thing with His spoken Words. God can turn rocks into bread with His spoken Word. Even the devil knew Jesus had control over physical matter with His Words when he tempted Him in the wilderness to turn a stone into bread.

> *Luke 4:2-4 (KJV)*
> *2 Being forty days tempted of the devil. And in those days he did eat nothing: and when they were ended, he afterward hungered. 3 And the devil said unto him, **If thou be the Son of God, command this stone that it be made bread.** 4 And Jesus answered him, saying, It is written, That man shall not live by bread alone, but by every word of God.*

When God called Moses to lead the children of Israel out of Egypt, He first revealed to Moses that He had miraculous power and control over all matter.

God revealed this by first commanding Moses to cast his staff to the ground; when Moses did this, his staff became a serpent. Then God told him to pick the serpent up, and it became a rod again in his hand.

Exodus 4:2-4 (KJV)

2 And the Lord said unto him, What is that in thine hand? And he said, A rod. 3 And he said, Cast it on the ground. And he cast it on the ground, and it became a serpent; and Moses fled from before it. 4 And the Lord said unto Moses, Put forth thine hand, and take it by the tail. And he put forth his hand, and caught it, and it became a rod in his hand:

Next, God told Moses to put his hand in his bosom and take it out. When he took it out, his hand was leprous. Then God told him to put his hand back in his bosom and take it out again, and when he did this it was normal.

Exodus 4:6-7 (KJV)

6 And the Lord said furthermore unto him, Put now thine hand into thy bosom. And he put his hand into his bosom: and when he took it out, behold, his hand was leprous as snow. 7 And he said, Put thine hand into thy bosom again. And he put his hand into his bosom again; and plucked it out of his bosom, and, behold, it was turned again as his other flesh.

The final sign that God used to show Moses He had complete power and control over all matter was to have him take water from the river on the dry ground, and He would turn it into blood before the children of Israel.

Exodus 4:8-9 (KJV)

*8 And it shall come to pass, if they will not believe thee, neither hearken to the voice of the first sign, that they will believe the voice of the latter sign. 9 And it shall come to pass, if they will not believe also these two signs, neither hearken unto thy voice, **that thou shalt take of the water of the river, and pour it upon the dry land: and the water which thou takest out of the river shall become blood upon the dry land.***

All creation is virtual to God and can be manipulated entirely at the Command of His voice. What I mean by virtual is all of God's creation is not solid as we see and know it to be. God's faith created all matter, and He controls all of His creation at a spiritual level with His Words. Nothing is too hard for the Lord because He has complete control over **EVERYTHING**, even deeper than at a molecular level. Miracles are as easy for God to perform because all He has to do is speak a Word to make them happen. God can make anything appear, disappear, or be transformed at His Word. The Word of His power upholds all things. God has complete control over everything created in His universe.

Hebrews 1:3 (KJV)

*3 Who being the brightness of his glory, and the express image of his person, **and upholding all things by the word of his power,** when he had by himself purged our sins, sat down on the right hand of the Majesty on high:*

Nothing is too hard for the Lord because He has the power to do *ANYTHING* He wants by creatively speaking to it. God creates and controls all of His creation with the power of His Words. Once you fully understand

God's power and ability with His Words, your faith will increase in asking God for *Anything*! God has the power to do *Anything* He wants to do and is willing and ready to answer your impossible prayers. All you have to do is meet the *Prayer Parameters* and ask Him to do it. Anyone living in the *Secret Place* knows that God loves to answer prayers and perform miracles for those who love Him.

> *Luke 1:37 (KJV)*
> *37 For with God nothing shall be impossible.*

We serve and worship a *Mighty* God who wants to answer our prayers in a *BIG* way! It is amazing what God will do in response to our prayers as we dwell in the *Secret Place of the Most High*. God seeks selfless believers who will go beyond the status quo and ask Him for the miraculous. There is nothing God won't do for His children who come to Him in faith. God is a God of miracles, and it is high time we call upon Him to do great and mighty things.

> *Jeremiah 33:3 (KJV)*
> *3 Call unto me, and I will answer thee, and show thee great and mighty things, which thou knowest not.*

Once you realize God is ready and waiting on His Throne for His children to come and ask Him for **ANYTHING**, your faith will be increased as you reach for the stars in your asking. It's God's job to deliver Divine answers to anyone who meets His requirements for asking in prayer while dwelling in the *Secret Place*. Only God can answer prayers and do miracles that confound all who see and experience them.

Anyone filled with the Holy Spirit will be extraordinary and not be afraid to come boldly before the **Throne of Grace** and ask God for *ANYTHING.* Believers dwelling in the *Secret Place* are filled with a faith that hopes against hope. They are like Father Abraham, who believed God he would be a father of a multitude when he didn't have a rightful heir and was past the age of having children along with his wife, Sarah. The Bible abounds with stories of people of faith who asked God for miracles beyond their natural capabilities and received answers to their prayers.

Don't be shy about asking God for *Anything* in your prayers. You are called to soar like an eagle in your prayers with God in the *Secret Place*. God wants you to dream big when coming to Him. Yes, we can't be selfish in our asking, but this doesn't mean we can't be bold and daring when coming to the **Throne of Grace** in our time of need. There is profound boldness only found in the *Secret Place* to believe you have received *WHATSOEVER* you ask in the Name of the **Lord Jesus Christ**. This boldness comes from knowing you have a New Covenantal right to ask for *ANYTHING* and speak to it, and it will obey you because of what Jesus paid for on the Cross.

> *Hebrews 4:16 (KJV)*
> *16 Let us therefore come boldly unto the throne of grace, that we may obtain mercy, and find grace to help in time of need.*

In conclusion, the Bible clearly states that we can ask God for *ANYTHING* if we meet His *Prayer Parameters*. God's promise to answer our impossible prayers is breathtaking to the natural man. Only God can make a miracle come out of nowhere and save the day in answer to our prayers. The God of the universe has made a New Covenant Promise to answer any prayer for the believer dwelling in the *Secret Place*. As you spend time in the *Secret Place*, you will discover a generous God who loves to answer prayers. God delights in answering impossible prayers of the one dwelling in the *Secret Place of the Most High.* Let your prayers ascend before God as a sweet-smelling aroma off of the Altar of Incense before the Ark of the Covenant in the Holy of Holies. Now is the time to dream *BIG* and not be afraid to ask God for *ANYTHING!*

Exodus 34:10 (KJV)

10 And he said, Behold, I make a covenant: before all thy people I will do marvels, such as have not been done in all the earth, nor in any nation: and all the people among which thou art shall see the work of the Lord: for it is a terrible thing that I will do with thee.

LET
MY
PRAYER
BE
SET
FORTH
BEFORE
THEE
AS
INCENSE...
PSALM 141:2A

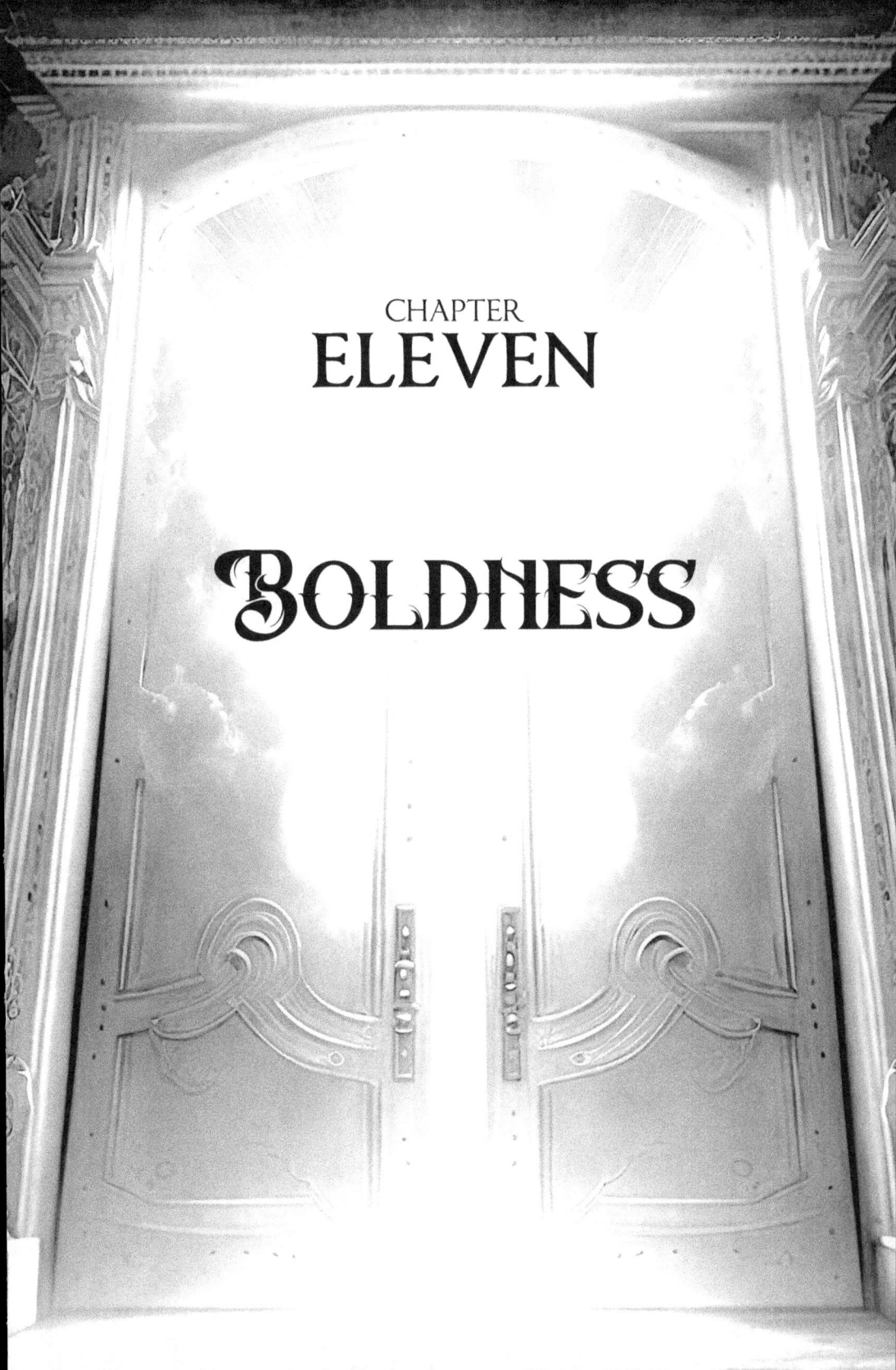

CHAPTER
ELEVEN

BOLDNESS

S piritual *boldness* comes from being filled with the Holy Spirit in the *Secret Place.* As you study the Scriptures daily, pray without ceasing, and commune with God in the *Secret Place,* the Holy Spirit fills the Temple of your body with His glorious strength. You are strengthened with the knowledge that God is with you and is pleased with you because you are in His perfect will. There is an unmistakable difference with someone filled with the Holy Spirit who knows God and is walking in *Secret Place Boldness.* When you dwell in the *Secret Place* with the Ark of the Covenant (the Holy Spirit) in the Temple of your body, you are filled with courage, strength, confidence, and power. In this chapter, I will teach you the *supernatural boldness* that only comes by being filled with the Holy Spirit in the *Secret Place.*

The night before Jesus went to the Cross, He said He would send us a Comforter from the Father. The Holy Spirit is the Comforter that was given to the Church after Jesus rose from the dead. Jesus was leaving the Earth, but the Comforter (Holy Spirit) would be sent to abide with us forever, teach us all things, and bring to our remembrance what Jesus taught. The word for Comforter in the Greek language is *Paraklētos,* which means Advocate. Advocate means one who defends and pleads for the cause of another and offers aid of any kind.

> *John 16:7 (KJV)*
> *7 Nevertheless I tell you the truth; It is expedient for you that I go away: for if I go not away, the Comforter will not come unto you; but if I depart, I will send him unto you.*

Jesus also said on that eventful night before He went to the Cross that the Holy Spirit would reprove the world of sin, righteousness, and judgment.

John 16:8-11 (KJV)

8 And when he is come, he will reprove the world of sin, and of righteousness, and of judgment: 9 Of sin, because they believe not on me; 10 Of righteousness, because I go to my Father, and ye see me no more; 11 Of judgment, because the prince of this world is judged.

The Holy Spirit can only fill you with *boldness* when you walk in the holiness and righteousness of God. God is *Bold* because He is perfect in all of His ways. When we imitate God, we become *Bold* like He is. You cannot walk in authentic spiritual *boldness* if anything in you condemns yourself in your actions. A spiritually *bold* person knows that all their actions are established on obeying all of the Commands of Christ. If you want to be filled with the Holy Spirit and walk in **Secret Place Boldness**, you must always do what is right in the sight of the Lord. This is why the Bible says that the **Righteous** are as *Bold* as a lion.

Proverbs 28:1 (KJV)

1 The wicked flee when no man pursueth: **but the righteous are bold as a lion.**

When the Jewish religious leaders attacked the Apostles after Jesus ascended to Heaven, they realized there was something different about them. They recognized they were not weak men who could be pushed around but had the same *boldness* they saw in Jesus. Jesus was *Bold* because He was filled with the Holy Spirit. Jesus taught the Apostles how to walk in the Spirit and be *bold* like He was. After the Holy Spirit filled the Apostles on the Day of Pentecost, they were empowered with supernatural *boldness.* People will recognize a *boldness* in you as you are filled with God's glorious Holy Spirit from dwelling in the *Secret Place of the Most High.*

> *Acts 4:13 (KJV)*
> *13 Now when they saw the boldness of Peter and John, and perceived that they were unlearned and ignorant men, they marvelled; and they took knowledge of them, that they had been with Jesus.*

Real *boldness* is not the conquering of fear but rather the absence of fear. Genuine *boldness* in Christ is not defeating fear but the non-existence of fear. You will have no fear when you walk in God's perfect love. The Holy Spirit is fearless, and as you are filled with the Holy Spirit, you become fearless.

> *1 John 4:18 (KJV)*
> *18 There is no fear in love; but perfect love casteth out fear: because fear hath torment. He that feareth is not made perfect in love.*

You can become so confident in your relationship with God that you no longer fear anything. You no longer fear anything because you know the Holy Spirit is with you. The Holy Spirit is with you because you walk in His righteousness by faith, and God always backs what is right. If anything, or anyone comes against you as you dwell in the *Secret Place of the Most High*, your heart overflows with *boldness* knowing the Holy Spirit is with you to deliver you because you have set your love upon God. God becomes the strength of your heart.

> *Psalm 91:14-16 (KJV)*
> *14 Because he hath set his love upon me, therefore will I deliver him: I will set him on high, because he hath known my name. 15 He*

shall call upon me, and I will answer him: I will be with him in
trouble; I will deliver him, and honour him. 16 With long life will
I satisfy him, and shew him my salvation.

Even if an army comes against you, you are not afraid. You are confident because you are filled with the Holy Spirit and dwelling in the *Secret Place*. The *Secret Place* is a place of *boldness*, confidence, and protection in your intimate relationship with the Lord. No enemy can penetrate and overcome you if you dwell in the *Secret Place*. Your relationship with God and the Holy Spirit is your *Hiding Place* when war or trouble arises against you.

Psalm 27:3-6 (KJV)
3 Though an host should encamp against me, my heart shall not
fear: though war should rise against me, in this will I be confident.
4 One thing have I desired of the Lord, that will I seek after; that I
may dwell in the house of the Lord all the days of my life, to behold
the beauty of the Lord, and to enquire in his temple. 5 For in the
time of trouble he shall hide me in his pavilion: in the secret of his
tabernacle shall he hide me; he shall set me up upon a rock. 6 And
now shall mine head be lifted up above mine enemies round about
me: therefore will I offer in his tabernacle sacrifices of joy; I will
sing, yea, I will sing praises unto the Lord.

When I first became a believer, I was not *bold*. I was timid, feared most things in this life, lacked confidence, and didn't know who I was. I was desperately in need of spiritual Fathering. I can honestly say that God has Fathered me and brought me into a place of *boldness* throughout the years. The *boldness* I now walk in resulted from being filled with the Holy Spirit as He built up my confidence in knowing Him. I was filled with *boldness* as the Holy Spirit taught me secrets from the Word of God. The Holy Spirit also taught me how to pray. As I prayed, the Holy Spirit filled the Temple of my body with His glory. I will teach you what I learned about **Secret Place Boldness** from years of spending alone time with the Lord.

Whenever I found myself in a challenging situation, God repeatedly came through for me. I know the power, confidence, courage, strength, and *boldness* I now walk in comes entirely from the Holy Spirit dwelling inside of me. God changed me as I spent years studying His Word and praying in the *Secret Place of the Most High*. I am no longer that weak and beggarly young kid I used to be. I give God all the glory because I know I am not a self-made man but a God-made man. If God can make me supernaturally *bold*, I know He can make anyone *bold*. A big part of my supernatural *boldness* was established by knowing God through His Word, which was given to us by the Holy Spirit. You can't push someone around who is filled with the Holy Spirit and equipped with the knowledge of God's Word.

> *Ephesians 4:13-15 (KJV)*
>
> *13 Till we all come in the unity of the faith, and of the knowledge of the Son of God, unto a perfect man, unto the measure of the stature of the fulness of Christ: 14 **That we henceforth be no more children, tossed to and fro, and carried about with every wind of doctrine, by the sleight of men, and cunning craftiness, whereby they lie in wait to deceive;** 15 But speaking the truth in love, may grow up into him in all things, which is the head, even Christ:*

SECRET PLACE BOLDNESS

I will reveal all the ways and areas in which God will make you supernaturally *bold* as you spend time being transformed by Him in the *Secret Place*. You cannot get close to the Lord in the *Secret Place* and not be changed from glory to glory and from faith to faith as you behold His glory. The Holy Spirit is the one who sets you free and fills you with supernatural courage.

> *2 Corinthians 3:17-18 (KJV)*
>
> *17 Now the Lord is that Spirit: and where the Spirit of the Lord is, there is liberty. 18 But we all, with open face beholding as in a glass the glory of the Lord, are changed into the same image from glory to glory, even as by the Spirit of the Lord.*

> *Romans 1:16-17 (KJV)*
>
> *16 For I am not ashamed of the gospel of Christ: for it is the power of God unto salvation to every one that believeth; to the Jew first, and also to the Greek. 17 **For therein is the righteousness of God revealed from faith to faith: as it is written, The just shall live by faith.***

1. BOLDNESS IN PRAYER

The Holy Spirit was given to us to help us pray. We don't always know what we should pray, but the Holy Spirit helps our infirmities and makes intercession for us with groanings that cannot be uttered. The Holy Spirit makes intercession for us according to the will of God.

> *Romans 8:26-27 (KJV)*
>
> *26 Likewise the Spirit also helpeth our infirmities: for we know not what we should pray for as we ought: but the Spirit itself maketh intercession for us with groanings which cannot be uttered. 27 And he that searcheth the hearts knoweth what is the mind of the Spirit, because he maketh intercession for the saints according to the will of God.*

God wants us to come *boldly* before His Throne of Grace to help us in our time of need. The Holy Spirit, who is our Advocate, is the one who stands with us before God and helps us plead our cause.

Hebrews 4:16 (KJV)
16 Let us therefore come boldly unto the throne of grace, that we may obtain mercy, and find grace to help in time of need.

God has given access to Himself in the *Secret Place* of the Temple of our bodies. God wants you to confidently come before Him in prayer, believing and knowing He will hear and answer your prayers.

Ephesians 3:12 (KJV)
12 In whom we have boldness and access with confidence by the faith of him.

A person walking in Holy Spirit *Boldness* will be filled with faith in knowing how to ask God for a promise and then speak to the mountain by faith. You can only get to this kind of mountain-moving faith by spending time with God in the *Secret Place*. Spending time in the *Secret Place* with God's Word teaches you not to doubt. All doubt is eradicated when you know God through His Word and learn to communicate with Him by faith in the Spirit.

Mark 11:22-24 (KJV)
*22 And Jesus answering saith unto them, **Have faith in God**. 23 For verily I say unto you, **That whosoever shall say unto this mountain, Be thou removed, and be thou cast into the sea; and shall not doubt in his heart, but shall believe that those things which he saith shall come to pass; he shall have whatsoever he saith**. 24 Therefore I say*

unto you, What things soever ye desire, when ye pray, believe that ye receive them, and ye shall have them.

The *Secret Place* is a place where God puts His supernatural strength into you. As you wait upon the Lord in prayer, you renew your strength by His Spirit. The beauty of God is He never gets weary or faints. There is no one as strong as God. Those who come to know God become strong like He is as He imparts His strength to them. The strength that God gives you while you wait on Him in the *Secret Place* is supernatural and can't be imitated.

> *Isaiah 40:28-31 (KJV)*
>
> *28 Hast thou not known? hast thou not heard, **that the everlasting God, the Lord, the Creator of the ends of the earth, fainteth not, neither is weary?** there is no searching of his understanding. 29 **He giveth power to the faint; and to them that have no might he increaseth strength.** 30 Even the youths shall faint and be weary, and the young men shall utterly fall: 31 **But they that wait upon the Lord shall renew their strength; they shall mount up with wings as eagles; they shall run, and not be weary; and they shall walk, and not faint.***

2. BOLDNESS IN SPEECH

A sign that someone is spending time in the *Secret Place* and filled with God's Holy Spirit is they will speak *boldly.* The devil and religious leaders love to shut the mouths of God's saints. However, when someone knows God, they will not be afraid to speak the TRUTH. A Holy Spirit *Boldness* comes upon anyone who spends time in the *Secret Place*, and they *boldly* proclaim the Word of God.

Ephesians 6:19-20 (KJV)

19 And for me, that utterance may be given unto me, that I may open my mouth boldly, to make known the mystery of the gospel, 20 For which I am an ambassador in bonds: that therein I may speak boldly, as I ought to speak.

In the Book of Acts, the Jewish religious leaders who killed Jesus tried to stop the mouths of His disciples. These religious leaders did not want to hear the truth that they had their Messiah killed. They did everything they could to stop the Apostles from *boldly* proclaiming the Word of God. The Apostles, however, prayed to God for *boldness*. God answered their prayer by filling them with a *boldness* from the Holy Spirit. From that point on, they went out and *boldly* preached the Gospel with signs following. It takes *Boldness* from the Holy Spirit to stand up against religious leaders of your day and minister God's Word with authority and power to a lost generation.

Acts 4:23-31 (KJV)

23 And being let go, they went to their own company, and reported all that the chief priests and elders had said unto them. 24 And when they heard that, they lifted up their voice to God with one accord, and said, Lord, thou art God, which hast made heaven, and earth, and the sea, and all that in them is: 25 Who by the mouth of thy servant David hast said, Why did the heathen rage, and the people imagine vain things? 26 The kings of the earth stood up, and the rulers were gathered together against the Lord, and against his Christ. 27 For of a truth against thy holy child Jesus, whom thou hast anointed, both Herod, and Pontius Pilate, with the Gentiles, and the people of Israel, were gathered together, 28 For to do whatsoever thy hand and thy counsel determined before to be done. *29 And now, Lord, behold their threatenings: and grant unto thy servants, that with all boldness they may speak thy word, 30 By stretching forth thine hand to heal; and that signs and wonders may be done by the name of thy holy child Jesus. 31 And when they had prayed, the place was shaken where they were assembled together; and they were all filled with the Holy Ghost, and they spake the word of God with boldness.*

3. CLEAN CONSCIENCE BOLDNESS

You will enjoy powerful confidence and *boldness* as you protect and keep your conscience clean. Jesus came to set you free from the dominion of sin. When someone sins, they are a slave to sin. The taskmaster of sin, which is the devil, beats people up for their sins. People bound by sin are tortured by their conscience, which is why they lack *boldness* and confidence. When Jesus sets you free, and you begin to walk in the newness of life by obeying His Commands, you become *boldly* confident. You become confident because your heart no longer condemns you but empowers you because you are doing what is right in the sight of the Lord.

> *1 John 3:19-21 (KJV)*
> *19 And hereby we know that we are of the truth, and shall assure our hearts before him. 20 For if our heart condemn us, God is greater than our heart, and knoweth all things. 21 Beloved, if our heart condemn us not, then have we confidence toward God.*

There is no condemnation to them which are in Christ Jesus, who walk not after the flesh but after the Spirit.

Romans 8:1-2 (KJV)

1 There is therefore now no condemnation to them which are in Christ Jesus, who walk not after the flesh, but after the Spirit. 2 For the law of the Spirit of life in Christ Jesus hath made me free from the law of sin and death.

4. BOLDNESS IN DOING THE WILL OF GOD

Anyone dwelling in the *Secret Place* will be doing the perfect will of God for their life. *Boldness* comes to those who know they are in and doing the perfect will of God. God has a perfect will for your life; when you discover and enter the perfect will of God, you will have a great *boldness* in who you are and what you are doing.

Romans 12:1-2 (KJV)

*1 I beseech you therefore, brethren, by the mercies of God, that ye present your bodies a living sacrifice, holy, acceptable unto God, which is your reasonable service. 2 And be not conformed to this world: but be ye transformed by the renewing of your mind, **that ye may prove what is that good, and acceptable, and perfect, will of God.***

You must understand that doing the will of God is not just about your calling but living according to the Commands of God and doing what is right before the Lord. Someone could be doing what God has called them to do but not be in the perfect will of God by living in sin. A big part of doing the will of God is how you treat God and others. When you do the will of God by treating others right while doing what God has called you to do, you will have great *boldness*.

1 Thessalonians 4:3-7 (KJV)

3 For this is the will of God, even your sanctification, that ye should abstain from fornication: 4 That every one of you should know how to possess his vessel in sanctification and honour; 5 Not in the lust of concupiscence, even as the Gentiles which know not God: 6 That no man go beyond and defraud his brother in any matter: because that the Lord is the avenger of all such, as we also have forewarned you and testified. 7 For God hath not called us unto uncleanness, but unto holiness.

The Holy Spirit was given to us to help us and makes intercession for the saints according to the will of God.

Romans 8:27 (KJV)

27 And he that searcheth the hearts knoweth what is the mind of the Spirit, because he maketh intercession for the saints according to the will of God.

5. BOLDNESS BY BEING LED BY THE HOLY SPIRIT

The Word of God teaches that those who the Spirit of God leads are the sons of God. You will have great *boldness* in all that you do when you know the Holy Spirit is leading you. Being led by the Holy Spirit is also how we stay in the perfect will of God. As you dwell in the *Secret Place*, God will lead you by His Spirit in how to live, speak, and act. He will also lead you to what He has called you to do.

Romans 8:14 (KJV)

14 For as many as are led by the Spirit of God, they are the sons of God.

Sometimes, the Holy Spirit may lead you in a direction you don't understand. It may not make sense to the natural mind where He is leading you to go, but obeying what He tells you to do or where He tells you to go is imperative.

> *Proverbs 3:5-7 (KJV)*
> *5 Trust in the Lord with all thine heart; and lean not unto thine own understanding. 6 In all thy ways acknowledge him, and he shall direct thy paths. 7 Be not wise in thine own eyes: fear the Lord, and depart from evil.*

If the Holy Spirit continually leads you, you will always be in the right place at the right time. Ultimately, you will always see the wisdom of God as to why He led you the way He did. There is great *boldness* in knowing the Holy Spirit is leading you in everything you do. God delights in those who are led by His Spirit.

> *Psalm 37:23 (KJV)*
> *23 The steps of a good man are ordered by the Lord: and he delighteth in his way.*

6. BOLDNESS IN THE FEAR OF THE LORD

The only fear found in the *Secret Place* is the *Fear of the Lord*. When you *Fear* God, you will be *bold* and not fear anyone or anything. In the *Fear of the Lord*, you understand that God will not fail you, which causes you to walk in supernatural *boldness*. God reveals His secrets and Covenant to you in the Holy of Holies *(Secret Place),* where the Ark of the Covenant rests when you *Fear the Lord*. You know that God made a Covenant with you and will never break His Word or Covenant, which fills your heart with *boldness*.

Psalm 25:14 (KJV)
14 The secret of the Lord is with them that fear him; and he will shew them his covenant.

We *Fear the Lord* by obeying all of the Words of Christ, taking up our Cross daily by dying to our flesh, being led by the Holy Spirit, and keeping our conscience clean. When you *Fear the Lord*, you will hate and depart from evil. You know the judgment and power of God that He executes against evildoers. Jesus taught His disciples to *Fear* the one who, after He kills the body, has the power to cast someone into hell.

Luke 12:4-5 (KJV)
4 And I say unto you my friends, Be not afraid of them that kill the body, and after that have no more that they can do. 5 But I will forewarn you whom ye shall fear: **Fear him, which after he hath killed hath power to cast into hell; yea, I say unto you, Fear him.**

Moses told the children of Israel not to fear, for God had come to prove them, and that His *Fear* may be before their faces so that they wouldn't sin. Natural fear is unlike the *Fear of the Lord* in that the *Fear of the Lord* causes you not to sin.

Exodus 20:20 (KJV)
20 And Moses said unto the people, Fear not: for God is come to prove you, and that his fear may be before your faces, that ye sin not.

This is what the Book of Proverbs has to say about the *Fear of the Lord*:

- The *Fear of the Lord* is the beginning of knowledge (Proverbs 1:7)

- The *Fear of the Lord* is to hate evil – pride, arrogancy, the evil way, and a froward mouth (Proverbs 8:13)

- The *Fear of the Lord* is the beginning of wisdom (Proverbs 9:10)

- The *Fear of the Lord* prolongeth days (Proverbs 10:27)

- In the *Fear of the Lord* is strong confidence (Proverbs 14:26)

- The *Fear of the Lord* is a fountain of life (Proverbs 14:27)

- Better is a little with the *Fear of the Lord* than great treasures and trouble therewith (Proverbs 15:16)

- The *Fear of the Lord* is the instruction of wisdom (Proverbs 15:33)

- By the *Fear of the Lord*, men depart from evil (Proverbs 16:6)

- The *Fear of the Lord* tendeth to life (Proverbs 19:23)

- Whoever has the *Fear of the Lord* will be satisfied (Proverbs 19:23)

- Whoever has the *Fear of the Lord* will not be visited with evil (Proverbs 19:23)

- By humility and the *Fear of the Lord* are riches, honour, and life (Proverbs 22:4)

- We are to be in the *Fear of the Lord* all day long (Proverbs 23:17)

The *Fear of the Lord* is His treasure because without the *Fear of the Lord*, people would not know how to dwell with God in the *Secret Place* and do those things that are pleasing in His sight.

Isaiah 33:6 (KJV)
6 And wisdom and knowledge shall be the stability of thy times, and strength of salvation: **the fear of the Lord is His treasure.**

When you walk in the *Fear of the Lord* in the *Secret Place*, you will have strong confidence. The *Fear of the Lord* gives you strong *boldness* as you *Fearfully* walk humbly in the wisdom of God. God is a place of refuge *(Secret Place)* for all those who *Fear* Him, and He gives them *boldness*, wisdom, and confidence. When you *Fear the Lord* in the *Secret Place,* you will no longer *Fear* anything or anyone because God is your confidence and has become your place of refuge.

> *Proverbs 14:26 (KJV)*
> *26 In the fear of the Lord is strong confidence: and his children shall have a place of refuge.*

7. BOLDNESS ON JUDGMENT DAY

The beauty of dwelling in the *Secret Place* all the days of your life is your reward on Judgement Day. When you dwell in the *Secret Place of the Most High*, you don't have to fear Judgment Day. God wants to prepare you by His Spirit for that Great Day. Everyone will die someday and have to give an account of their life on Judgment Day. Don't you want to prepare yourself now? When you dwell in the *Secret Place*, you will have a *boldness* and not be ashamed on Judgment Day.

> *1 John 4:16-18 (KJV)*
> *16 And we have known and believed the love that God hath to us. God is love; and he that dwelleth in love dwelleth in God, and God in him. 17 **Herein is our love made perfect, that we may have boldness in the day of judgment:** because as he is, so are we in this world. 18 There is no fear in love; but perfect love casteth out fear: because fear hath torment. He that feareth is not made perfect in love.*

Those who dwell with God in the *Secret Place* are being prepared for the afterlife. Before you can enter the next life, you have to stand before God and give an account of what you did during this life. God is writing down everything you say and do in books. On Judgment Day, those books will be opened, and you will be rewarded if you lived in the *Secret Place*. The number one Book you want to be found in is the Book of Life. The Book of Life is the book that has the names of everyone who accepted Jesus as their Lord.

> *Revelation 20:12 (KJV)*
> *12 And I saw the dead, small and great, stand before God; **and the books were opened: and another book was opcncd, which is the book of life: and the dead were judged out of those things which were written in the books, according to their works.***

> *Daniel 7:10 (KJV)*
> *10 A fiery stream issued and came forth from before him: thousand thousands ministered unto him, and ten thousand times ten thousand stood before him: **the judgment was set, and the books were opened.***

The Apostle Peter wrote in His first epistle what we were to add to our faith. In his letter, he said people were blind and could not see afar off if they didn't do the things he listed. Being able to see afar off is about Judgement Day and the afterlife. Those who listened to what he wrote down would be prepared for the everlasting Kingdom of our Lord and Saviour Jesus Christ. He promised that those who did the things he listed would have an abundant entrance ministered to them into the Kingdom of God.

2 Peter 1:5-12 (KJV)

5 And beside this, giving all diligence, add to your faith virtue; and to virtue knowledge; 6 And to knowledge temperance; and to temperance patience; and to patience godliness; 7 And to godliness brotherly kindness; and to brotherly kindness charity. 8 For if these things be in you, and abound, they make you that ye shall neither be barren nor unfruitful in the knowledge of our Lord Jesus Christ. 9 But he that lacketh these things is blind, and cannot see afar off, and hath forgotten that he was purged from his old sins. 10 Wherefore the rather, brethren, give diligence to make your calling and election sure: for if ye do these things, ye shall never fall: 11 For so an entrance shall be ministered unto you abundantly into the everlasting kingdom of our Lord and Saviour Jesus Christ. 12 Wherefore I will not be negligent to put you always in remembrance of these things, though ye know them, and be established in the present truth.

GOD IS WITH YOU

Before Joshua entered the Promised Land, God commanded him to be strong and courageous in observing the Law of Moses. God told him that the Book of the Law was not to depart from his mouth, but he was to meditate on it day and night to observe all that was written in it. Then God commanded Joshua again to be strong and of good courage and not to be afraid or dismayed. Joshua was strong and courageous because God said He would be with Him wherever he went.

Joshua 1:6-9 (KJV)

6 Be strong and of a good courage: for unto this people shalt thou divide for an inheritance the land, which I sware unto their fathers *to give them. 7 **Only be thou strong and very courageous, that thou mayest observe to do according to all the law, which Moses my servant commanded thee: turn not from it to the right hand or to the left, that thou mayest prosper withersoever thou goest.** 8 This book of the law shall not depart out of thy mouth; but thou shalt meditate therein day and night, that thou mayest observe to do according to all that is written therein: for then thou shalt make thy way prosperous, and then thou shalt have good success. 9 **Have not I commanded thee? Be strong and of a good courage; be not afraid, neither be thou dismayed: for the Lord thy God is with thee whithersoever thou goest.***

Throughout the Bible, whenever God sent someone on a mission or raised them up as a leader, He told them He would be with them. The statement **The Lord Is With You** is extremely meaningful and powerful. When God said He was with someone, it meant He would be with them in trouble, deliver them, be with them in battle, and cause them to be successful. But, for the Lord to be with them, they had to be with the Lord. They had to be with the Lord by obeying His Commands. A prophet prophesied to one of the kings of Israel named Asa that the Lord was with him while he was with the Lord.

2 Chronicles 15:1-2 (KJV)
*1 And the Spirit of God came upon Azariah the son of Oded: 2 And he went out to meet Asa, and said unto him, Hear ye me, Asa, and all Judah and Benjamin; **The Lord is with you, while ye be with him; and if ye seek him, he will be found of you; but if ye forsake him, he will forsake you.***

For the Lord to be with you, you have to be with the Lord. In the New Testament, for the Lord to be with you, you must obey all of the Words of Christ with a pure conscience. When you obey the Lord, He promises to be with you. This promise of being with you imparts great *boldness* because you know who can be against you if God is for you.

> *Romans 8:31 (KJV)*
> *31 What shall we then say to these things? **If God be for us, who can be against us?***

One of the Names given to Jesus at His birth is Emmanuel, which means *GOD WITH US.*

> *Matthew 1:22-23 (KJV)*
> *22 Now all this was done, that it might be fulfilled which was spoken of the Lord by the prophet, saying, 23 Behold, a virgin shall be with child, and shall bring forth a son, **and they shall call his name Emmanuel, which being interpreted is, God with us.***

The Apostle Peter preached that God was with Jesus by Anointing Him with the Holy Spirit and power. God shows you He is with you by Anointing you with His Holy Spirit and power.

> *Acts 10:38 (KJV)*
> *38 How God anointed Jesus of Nazareth with the Holy Ghost and with power: who went about doing good, and healing all that were oppressed of the devil; for God was with him.*

There is great *boldness* in the Anointing of the Holy Spirit. The Anointing is when the Spirit of the Lord comes upon a man or woman of God with the power to work miracles. The word for *Power* in Greek is *Dúnamis,* which means might, strength, violence, mighty work, spiritual gifts, and specifically miraculous power. The Anointed man or woman of God is filled with *boldness*, knowing they have power through the Holy Spirit to defeat the works of the devil and his demons.

> *Luke 24:49 (KJV)*
> *49 And, behold, I send the promise of my Father upon you: but tarry ye in the city of Jerusalem, until ye be endued with power from on high.*

> *Acts 1:8 (KJV)*
> *8 But ye shall receive power, after that the Holy Ghost is come upon you: and ye shall be witnesses unto me both in Jerusalem, and in all Judaea, and in Samaria, and unto the uttermost part of the earth.*

Knowing and having God be with you and for you creates supernatural *boldness* within you. No matter what you face, God promises to be there for you as you are with Him. When you face a trial, attack, tribulation, sickness, debt, or an enemy, God shows up and delivers you by His Spirit in your time of need. The Lord promises to be with you as you dwell in the *Secret Place* and set your love upon Him. God being with you causes you to have a supernatural *boldness.*

> *Psalm 91:14-16 (KJV)*
> *14 Because he hath set his love upon me, therefore will I deliver him: I will set him on high, because he hath known my name. 15 He shall call upon me, and I will answer him: I will be with him in*

trouble; I will deliver him, and honour him. 16 With long life will I satisfy him, and shew him my salvation.

Displaying **Secret Place Boldness** in your time of need can only come by knowing God and being filled with His Spirit. God is *Bold* and imparts His strength and courage in you when you face an enemy. This is how King David ran at the giant Goliath and defeated him. King David knew God was with him. King David went on to win many battles for the children of Israel because he set his love upon the Lord, and God always delivered him.

1 Samuel 17:45-50 (KJV)

*45 Then said David to the Philistine, Thou comest to me with a sword, and with a spear, and with a shield: **but I come to thee in the name of the Lord of hosts, the God of the armies of Israel, whom thou hast defied.** 46 This day will the Lord deliver thee into mine hand; and I will smite thee, and take thine head from thee; and I will give the carcases of the host of the Philistines this day unto the fowls of the air, and to the wild beasts of the earth; that all the earth may know that there is a God in Israel. 47 And all this assembly shall know that the Lord saveth not with sword and spear: **for the battle is the Lord's,** and he will give you into our hands. 48 And it came to pass, when the Philistine arose, and came, and drew nigh to meet David, that David hastened, and ran toward the army to meet the Philistine. 49 And David put his hand in his bag, and took thence a stone, and slang it, and smote the Philistine in his forehead, that the stone sunk into his forehead; and he fell upon his face to the earth. 50 **So David prevailed over the Philistine with a sling and with a stone, and smote the Philistine,** and slew him; but there was no sword in the hand of David.*

Prior to David facing the giant Goliath, he was Anointed by Samuel to be the king of Israel. King David was not alone but faced Goliath with the Anointing of the Holy Spirit. The Holy Spirit imparted *boldness* to King David to where he had no fear when facing this giant. The Holy Spirit gave King David the victory.

> *1 Samuel 16:13 (KJV)*
> *13 **Then Samuel took the horn of oil, and anointed him in the midst of his brethren: and the Spirit of the Lord came upon David from that day forward.** So Samuel rose up, and went to Ramah.*

The benefit of dwelling in the *Secret Place* is to have God be with you. If God is with you, you have nothing to fear. God told the children of Israel in the Old Testament that He would send an Angel before them to keep them in the way. They were warned to obey this Angel's voice and not provoke Him by transgression. If they obeyed this Angel's voice, God said He would be an enemy to their enemies and an adversary to their adversaries.

> *Exodus 23:20-22 (KJV)*
> *20 **Behold, I send an Angel before thee**, to keep thee in the way, and to bring thee into the place which I have prepared. 21 **Beware of him, and obey his voice, provoke him not; for he will not pardon your transgressions:** for my name is in him. 22 But if thou shalt indeed obey his voice, and do all that I speak; **then I will be an enemy unto thine enemies, and an adversary unto thine adversaries.***

There is Divine Angelic protection for anyone dwelling in the *Secret Place*. God promises in Psalm 91 to give His angels charge over you to keep you in all your ways. They will bear you up in their hands lest you dash your foot against a stone.

Psalm 91:11-12 (KJV)
11 For he shall give his angels charge over thee, to keep thee in all thy ways. 12 They shall bear thee up in their hands, lest thou dash thy foot against a stone.

There is no safer place to be than in the *Secret Place*. When you know God is with you and His Angels are given charge over you, you will have great supernatural *boldness*. God wants His children to be *bold* like lions, but this *boldness* will only come if you dwell in the *Secret Place of the Most High*. As you obey God and show you are with Him as much as He is with you, the Holy Spirit will fill you with a supernatural *boldness* that is not of this Earth.

You have angelic protection in the *Secret Place*, and God strengthens your heart through His Spirit. God strengthens the believer's heart and removes all fear as He assures them that He is with them to deliver them. One can face many dangers in this lifetime, but God strengthens the one dwelling in the *Secret Place* with a *boldness* that will run the devil off. The courage God gives the one dwelling in the *Secret Place* is a weapon in and of itself. Only God can fill someone with courage and strength when battling an enemy or facing impossible odds.

Psalm 27:14 (KJV)
14 Wait on the Lord: be of good courage, and he shall strengthen thine heart: wait, I say, on the Lord.

Ephesians 3:16 (KJV)

16 That he would grant you, according to the riches of his glory, to be strengthened with might by his Spirit in the inner man;

In conclusion, *Secret Place Boldness* comes to those who are filled with God's Holy Spirit. God Himself becomes your *boldness* by His Holy Spirit as you dwell in the *Secret Place*. Without God, we would all be helpless and sitting ducks to the attacks of the enemy. But, with God, you become a giant slayer who is more than ready to go to battle with the devil and his legions. The Holy Spirit endues the believer with power and supernatural *boldness* that causes them to be feared, as the enemies of Israel feared the Ark of the Covenant in the Old Testament. The Ark of the Covenant symbolized the power of God's Holy Spirit being with His people as they kept His Covenant and dwelled in the *Secret Place of the Most High*. The Holy Spirit is the *ONE* who fights your battles, and this is why you are filled with supernatural *boldness*. Thank you, God, for giving us Your precious Holy Spirit.

THE WICKED FLEE
WHEN NO MAN PURSUETH:
BUT THE RIGHTEOUS
ARE BOLD AS A LION.
PROVERBS 28:1

CHAPTER
TWELVE

Final Secret Thoughts

Anyone who dwells in the *Secret Place* will experience a paradigm shift in how they think, speak, and act. As you dwell in the *Secret Place,* you will live differently than most people on the Earth. When you are in close contact with God, nothing about your life will be normal. Believers who dwell in the *Secret Place* will experience Heaven on Earth while the rest of the world misses out on the blessings of God. In this final chapter, I will reveal some final secret thoughts about dwelling in the *Secret Place* that will have a powerful impact on your life.

To dwell in the *Secret Place,* you must die to your old life as you have known it. God has rules and regulations that cannot be violated if someone wants to be near Him in the *Secret Place* and inherit the Kingdom of God. These rules and regulations are contrary to how most people live their lives on this Earth. God gave us the Bible to help teach us how to dwell in the *Secret Place* and ultimately live with Him in Heaven. God's thoughts are higher than our thoughts, and His ways are higher than our ways. You must think and act like God to dwell in the *Secret Place.*

> *Isaiah 55:8-9 (KJV)*
> *8 For my thoughts are not your thoughts, neither are your ways my ways, saith the Lord. 9 For as the heavens are higher than the earth, so are my ways higher than your ways, and my thoughts than your thoughts.*

We need the Holy Spirit to open our spiritual eyes to see the mysteries and hidden wonders in the Word of God about the *Secret Place.* God has to teach you all there is to know about the *Secret Place* so that you can successfully dwell there. Your life will be deeply enriched and blessed with the *Better Promises* of the New Covenant the more you learn about the *Secret Place.*

Below are additional *Secret Place Revelations* to help you with your walk with God.

SECRET PLACE REVELATIONS

1. FAMILY OF GOD

Jesus made it very clear that His true family was those who did the Will of God. One day, Jesus' earthly family came to Him as He was talking to His disciples. At that moment, Jesus declared, who is my mother or brethren? He then looked around and said that whoever did God's Will was His brother, sister, and mother. When you dwell in the *Secret Place*, your new family is anyone doing the Will of God.

> *Matthew 12:46-50 (KJV)*
> *46 While he yet talked to the people, behold, his mother and his brethren stood without, desiring to speak with him. 47 Then one said unto him, Behold, thy mother and thy brethren stand without, desiring to speak with thee. 48 But he answered and said unto him that told him, **Who is my mother? and who are my brethren?** 49 And he stretched forth his hand toward his disciples, and said, **Behold my mother and my brethren! 50 For whosoever shall do the will of my Father which is in heaven, the same is my brother, and sister, and mother.***

We are born again into the Kingdom of God once we accept Jesus Christ as our Lord. As much as we may love our earthly family if they don't accept Christ and do the Will of God, they will not go to Heaven and be a part of the family of God. Jesus taught that whoever left their family, lands, and lives for the Gospel would receive a hundredfold now in this time of houses, lands, and a new family.

Mark 10:29-30 (KJV)

*29 And Jesus answered and said, Verily I say unto you, **There is no man that hath left house, or brethren, or sisters, or father, or mother, or wife, or children, or lands, for my sake, and the gospel's, 30 But he shall receive an hundredfold now in this time, houses, and brethren, and sisters, and mothers, and children, and lands, with persecutions; and in the world to come eternal life.***

This may be a hard pill for some to swallow, but it is the Gospel truth. Jesus declared that He came to bring a sword and that family members would be divided because of Him. He also said that if anyone loved a family member more than Him, they were not worthy of Him. Loving God and sometimes leaving unbelieving family members is what you have to do for the Gospel and to dwell in the *Secret Place*. Dwelling in the *Secret Place* will cost you everything. Why would you want to fellowship with someone who says they are your family and hates your Messiah?

Matthew 10:34-38 (KJV)

*34 Think not that I am come to send peace on earth: I came not to send peace, but a sword. 35 **For I am come to set a man at variance against his father, and the daughter against her mother, and the daughter in law against her mother in law. 36 And a man's foes shall be they of his own household. 37 He that loveth father or mother more than me is not worthy of me: and he that loveth son or daughter more than me is not worthy of me.** 38 And he that taketh not his cross, and followeth after me, is not worthy of me.*

The *Secret Place* is very relationship-driven. In the *Secret Place,* we become a son to the Father, the Bride of Christ, and a friend of God. The Holy Spirit is our Comforter, and the Body of Christ becomes our family.

2. FRIEND OF GOD

One of the blessings of dwelling in the *Secret Place* is the privilege of being God's friend. The night before Jesus was crucified, He told His disciples that He no longer called them servants but friends. He said they would be His friends if they did whatsoever He commanded them to do. He also said that in this friendship, He would make known all things He heard from His Heavenly Father.

> *John 15:14-15 (KJV)*
>
> *14 Ye are my friends, if ye do whatsoever I command you.*
> *15 Henceforth I call you not servants; for the servant knoweth not what his lord doeth: **but I have called you friends; for all things that I have heard of my Father I have made known unto you.***

An important aspect of our friendship with God while dwelling in the *Secret Place* is our faith. Abraham was called the Friend of God when he believed God when He said his seed would be as many as the stars of Heaven. When God told Abraham this, he and his wife were well beyond the years of having children. Later, Abraham was tested to offer up his son Isaac, who was born to him through the promise of God, as a sacrifice. It was only a test, but Abraham was willing to obey God. Abraham's faith was perfected when he was willing to offer up his son as a sacrifice in obedience to God. In this story, we can see being a friend of God means you will believe what He says no matter how audacious it is, and you will obey God to do anything He asks of you.

> *James 2:22-23 (KJV)*
>
> *22 Seest thou how faith wrought with his works, and by works was faith made perfect? 23 And the scripture was fulfilled which saith,*

Abraham believed God, and it was imputed unto him for righteousness: and he was called the Friend of God.

God is looking for **FRIENDS** to dwell with Him in the *Secret Place*.

3. SERVANT'S HEART

Anyone who dwells in the *Secret Place* will have a servant's heart. Jesus taught His disciples that the greatest among them would be a minister. Minister means to serve. Jesus said He came not to be ministered unto but to serve. He also washed His disciples' feet the night before He went to the Cross. Anyone who wants to get close to God in the *Secret Place* will have a servant's heart. God is the greatest servant of all; when He answers prayers, that is Him serving humanity.

> *Matthew 20:25-28 (KJV)*
>
> *25 But Jesus called them unto him, and said, Ye know that the princes of the Gentiles exercise dominion over them, and they that are great exercise authority upon them. 26 But it shall not be so among you: but whosoever will be great among you, let him be your minister; 27 And whosoever will be chief among you, let him be your servant: 28 Even as the Son of man came not to be ministered unto, but to minister, and to give his life a ransom for many.*

4. FIRE OF GOD

The fire of God represents His glory and His *Jealousy*. God is a Holy God and is very *jealous* of His people. There is no betrayal in God, and He will not tolerate any betrayal in those close to Him. When you dwell in the *Secret Place*, God will be very *jealous* of you. God takes you being in Covenant with Him very seriously and expects you to do the same.

Deuteronomy 4:24 (KJV)

24 For the Lord thy God is a consuming fire, even a jealous God.

God's Jealousy is called a *Godly Jealousy.* The Apostle Paul said he was jealous of the Church with *Godly Jealousy* because the Church was to be espoused as a chaste virgin to Christ. Because we are the Bride of Christ, we cannot do anything that would make the Lord *jealous* of us. Faithfulness, trustworthiness, and loyalty are paramount to anyone dwelling in the *Secret Place.* In the Bible, James calls believer's adulterers and adulteresses for being friends with the world.

James 4:4-5 (KJV)

4 Ye adulterers and adulteresses, know ye not that the friendship of the world is enmity with God? whosoever therefore will be a friend of the world is the enemy of God. 5 Do ye think that the scripture saith in vain, The spirit that dwelleth in us lusteth to envy?

Jehoshaphat was a King of Judah who loved the Lord but was friends with Ahab, the King of Israel. Ahab hated the Lord and served other gods. A prophet came to Jehoshaphat and rebuked him, saying, "Shouldest thou help the ungodly and love them that hate the Lord?" The prophet announced that the wrath of God was on him for this because God is *jealous* of His people.

2 Chronicles 19:2-3 (KJV)

2 And Jehu the son of Hanani the seer went out to meet him, and said to king Jehoshaphat, Shouldest thou help the ungodly, and love them that hate the Lord? therefore is wrath upon thee from before the Lord. 3 Nevertheless there are good things found in thee, in that thou hast taken away the groves out of the land, and hast prepared thine heart to seek God.

5. FORGIVENESS

Anyone who dwells in the *Secret Place* is a very forgiving person. They are forgiving because they know the only way they made it into the *Secret Place* was by God forgiving them. Forgiveness came from Jesus dying on the Cross and accepting Him as your Lord. Jesus paid a heavy price with His blood so you could be forgiven and dwell in the *Secret Place*. Jesus taught that offenses would come, but we were to forgive anyone up to seventy times seven a day. Jesus forgave us of our sins, and we must forgive anyone who sins against us.

> *Matthew 18:21-22 (KJV)*
> *21 Then came Peter to him, and said, Lord, how oft shall my brother sin against me, and I forgive him? till seven times? 22 Jesus saith unto him, I say not unto thee, Until seven times: but, Until seventy times seven.*

When I was younger, I was a very hurt person with a broken heart. Whenever I felt someone did something wrong against me, it would take me months to forgive them, if I forgave them at all. When I became a Christian, God taught me more about His forgiveness. I knew God forgave me of my sins, but I was having a tough time in my forgiveness of others. God taught me to think of anything that could be done to me in advance. Then, He told me to forgive everyone in advance for anything anyone would do to me in the future. I did what the Lord Commanded me to do and was set free.

The concept of forgiving in advance was a shift in my thinking and acting. I no longer have to work to forgive people because now I am a forgiving person. I tell people now when they do something against me that I already forgave them over 30 years ago. It is empowering when you do this. I no longer have to work through forgiveness because I have already forgiven everyone in advance.

> *Ephesians 4:32 (KJV)*
>
> *32 And be ye kind one to another, tenderhearted, **forgiving one another, even as God for Christ's sake hath forgiven you.***

The Mercy Seat in the Holy of Holies that was placed on the Ark of the Covenant reveals that God is abundant in Mercy for those who dwell in the *Secret Place of the Most High*.

> *Exodus 26:34 (KJV)*
>
> *34 **And thou shalt put the mercy seat upon the ark of the testimony in the most holy place.***

6. REVELATION KNOWLEDGE

When you dwell in the *Secret Place of the Most High*, God will give you Revelation Knowledge in His Word. God will open your mind to Divine Revelations. Jesus opened up the understanding of His Apostles after He rose from the dead so they could understand the Scriptures.

> *Luke 24:44-45 (KJV)*
>
> *44 And he said unto them, These are the words which I spake unto you, while I was yet with you, that all things must be fulfilled, which were written in the law of Moses, and in the prophets, and in the psalms, concerning me. 45 **Then opened he their understanding, that they might understand the scriptures,***

When we receive profound revelations of God, we must ensure they align with *Sound Doctrine*. A *Sound Doctrine* is a Divine teaching from God's

Word that contains a truth that has been researched and confirmed by the Holy Spirit. *Sound Doctrines* include teachings that rightly divide the truth about God, Jesus Christ, the Holy Spirit, His Kingdom, His Character, and what He requires of humankind to be saved. All *Sound Doctrine* will bring you closer to God, cause you to love your neighbor, open your spiritual eyes, and make you holy like God is holy. The Apostle Paul taught in the Last Days that people will not endure *Sound Doctrine*. The preaching of the Word of God is given to us to help us fight false doctrines.

2 Timothy 4:1-3 (KJV)
*1 I charge thee therefore before God, and the Lord Jesus Christ, who shall judge the quick and the dead at his appearing and his kingdom; 2 **Preach the word**; be instant in season, out of season; reprove, rebuke, **exhort with all long suffering and doctrine**. 3 **For the time will come when they will not endure sound doctrine;** but after their own lusts shall they heap to themselves teachers, having itching ears;*

Titus 2:1 (KJV)
*1 **But speak thou the things which become sound doctrine:***

I have received many revelations from God while dwelling in the *Secret Place* and was a Valedictorian Bible College graduate. I have studied the Word of God for years, and some of the revelations in this book or any of my other books may challenge some people and their traditional and religious ways of thinking that don't align with the Word of God. When you go deeper with God, you will see things that many religious leaders of your day don't see. Even during the time of Jesus, the religious leaders challenged the doctrines of Christ. Jesus declared that His doctrines were not His but His who sent Him. He said you would know of the doctrine if it was of God or if He spoke of Himself. All sound doctrine glorifies God, is true, and has no unrighteousness in it.

> *John 7:16-18 (KJV)*
>
> *16 Jesus answered them, and said, **My doctrine is not mine, but his that sent me. 17 If any man will do his will, he shall know of the doctrine, whether it be of God, or whether I speak of myself. 18 He that speaketh of himself seeketh his own glory: but he that seeketh his glory that sent him, the same is true, and no unrighteousness is in him.***

Sound Doctrine is vital as you spend time in the *Secret Place* with God. God desires to reveal secrets to you in the *Secret Place* from His Word, but they must be proven to be from the Lord. I am adding a list of what I call the *Sound Doctrine Formula* to help people know they are adhering to *Sound Doctrine*. A *Sound Doctrine Formula* is a set of checks and balances to help guide you when studying God's Word and when He is giving you prophetic revelations from His Word. This *Formula* can be applied to any teaching, doctrine, or revelation you believe you are receiving from God. Following this *Formula* will help guide you to stay within the boundaries of *Sound Doctrine* as you study God's Holy Scriptures.

SOUND DOCTRINE FORMULA

- It must be formulated only by the established 66 books of the Bible. No other outside sources, books, or commentaries can be used to establish *Sound Doctrine*. All doctrines needed for humankind's salvation originate from God's mind and are recorded in the Word of God.

- Christ and His teachings must be interwoven within the doctrine. *Sound Doctrine* will not violate any of the teachings of Christ. All Scriptures and doctrines must testify of Jesus and what He taught.

- It will glorify God – The Father, Son, and Holy Spirit.

- Scripture must interpret Scripture and establish a doctrine. A *Sound Doctrine* must be built and founded on multiple Scriptures. You can't use an isolated Scripture to formulate a *Sound Doctrine*. A *Sound Doctrine* has been researched from Genesis to Revelation and studied wherever it can be located in the Bible. *Sound Doctrine* is consistent with the whole of the Scriptures.

- When studying words and definitions from the Word of God, you must return to the original Hebrew, Aramaic, and Greek definitions within the word study. The definition of a word must line up within the context of the Scripture in which it is found because there are multiple definitions for words.

- The *Sound Doctrines* of God must be understood based on the timing and dispensation in which it was written. God revealed more of who He is and the plan of salvation through time and through the revelation of His Covenants. New Testament believers are not living in the same revelations of God as the saints living in the Old Testament. God has progressively revealed His plan of salvation and doctrines through the dispensation of time.

- A *Sound Doctrine* must stay within the context of a passage of Scripture. You have to read what is before and after a passage of

Scripture to establish a doctrinal truth. You cannot take a verse out of context to establish a doctrinal truth.

- An interpretation of a *Sound Doctrine* from the Scriptures must be viewed in light of who it was written to and why it was written.

- A *Sound Doctrine* must align with God's revealed Character and Holy Nature.

- A mature group of 5-fold Christian leaders will confirm the validity of the doctrine being taught and that all of the above guidelines were followed to establish a *Sound Doctrine.*

- All *Sound Doctrine* will lead you to spiritual maturity and growth, deep faith in God, sanctification, a pure conscience, a sensitivity to the Voice of God, make you act and talk more like God, cause you to imitate Christ, keep all the Words of Christ, teach you how to be led by the Holy Spirit, be more dedicated to God, make you more selfless, teach you to die to your flesh, endue you with the wisdom of God, make you alive to good works, prepare you for Judgement Day, and bring you to a closer walk with God.

- The Holy Spirit confirms, and bears witness to whether the doctrine being taught and preached is true. All *Sound Doctrine* comes from and is confirmed by the Spirit of Truth. The Holy Spirit was sent to teach and lead us into all truth.

When you sit at the feet of Jesus in the *Secret Place,* He will reveal secrets that cannot be taken from you. The revelations that God gives you are what define and change your life. Whenever God gives a secret revelation from His Word while dwelling in the *Secret Place,* it will help you gain greater access to Himself and His *Precious Promises.* To grow in your walk with God and know Him more intimately, you need Him to reveal secret revelations to you from His Word. The profound revelations of God and His Covenants will only come to those dwelling in the *Secret Place.* Many people are distracted by the things of this life, as Martha was during the time of Christ, but Mary was wise in putting Christ and His Words first. Distractions of this life will rob you of receiving God's hidden mysteries in His Word.

Luke 10:38-42 (KJV)
*38 Now it came to pass, as they went, that he entered into a certain village: and a certain woman named Martha received him into her house. 39 **And she had a sister called Mary, which also sat at Jesus' feet, and heard his word.** 40 But Martha was cumbered about much serving, and came to him, and said, Lord, dost thou not care that my sister hath left me to serve alone? bid her therefore that she help me. 41 And Jesus answered and said unto her, Martha, Martha, thou art careful and troubled about many things: 42 **But one thing is needful: and Mary hath chosen that good part, which shall not be taken away from her.***

7. GIVING

Everyone dwelling in the *Secret Place* will be a giver. Giving is a main attribute of God's character. Giving is at the heart of God and the *Secret Place.* The more you become like God, the more of a giver you will become. God loves to give, and He loves a cheerful giver.

2 Corinthians 9:7 (KJV)

7 Every man according as he purposeth in his heart, so let him give; not grudgingly, or of necessity: for God loveth a cheerful giver.

There is more to giving than just money. A person dwelling in the *Secret Place* gives in all areas of their life, such as their time, resources, ministering in the Spirit to others, emotional support, acts of service, and more. Giving comes from who you are and your willingness to help others in whatever they need, as God has helped you.

The beauty of giving is God always gives back to the giver dwelling in the *Secret Place* with the same measure that they give.

Luke 6:38 (KJV)

38 Give, and it shall be given unto you; good measure, pressed down, and shaken together, and running over, shall men give into your bosom. For with the same measure that ye mete withal it shall be measured to you again.

8. THE JOY OF THE LORD

Anyone dwelling in the *Secret Place of the Most High* will be filled with the joy of the Lord. The joy of the Lord is not natural human joy. The joy of the Lord is supernatural. A believer who has the joy of the Lord will be filled with an unspeakable joy that only comes from knowing God. The joy of the Lord becomes your strength that frees you from fear, stress, anxiety, grief, and sorrow that weakens the soul. The supernatural joy of the Lord strengthens you because you know God is taking care of you. In the Presence of God is fullness of joy!

Psalm 16:11 (KJV)

11 Thou wilt shew me the path of life: **in thy presence is fulness of joy;** *at thy right hand there are pleasures for evermore.*

The night Jesus was betrayed, He taught His Disciples about the joy of the Lord. He told them they would *Abide* in His love if they kept His commandments. He went on to say the things He said to them would cause their joy to be full, and His joy would remain in them.

John 15:10-11 (KJV)

10 If ye keep my commandments, ye shall abide in my love; even as I have kept my Father's commandments, and abide in his love. 11 **These things have I spoken unto you, that my joy might remain in you, and that your joy might be full.**

We don't physically see God with our eyes now, but someday we will. Our faith in God fills us with joy unspeakable and causes us to be full of glory.

1 Peter 1:8 (KJV)

8 Whom having not seen, ye love; in whom, though now ye see him not, yet believing, **ye rejoice with joy unspeakable and full of glory:**

9. PEACE OF GOD

Another benefit of dwelling in the *Secret Place* is being filled with the peace of God. The peace of God transcends all human understanding. Someone dwelling in the *Secret Place* will be peaceful, even if they are going through hell on Earth. The peace of God fills your soul, knowing everything will be alright because God is with you.

The Book of Philippians says not to worry about anything and goes on to say in everything, by prayer and supplication with thanksgiving, we are to let our requests be made known to God. Those who do this will keep their hearts and minds by the peace of God that passes all understanding. You are not stressed in your trial because you know God has heard your prayer, giving you peace.

> *Philippians 4:6-7 (KJV)*
> *6 Be careful for nothing; but in every thing by prayer and supplication with thanksgiving let your requests be made known unto God. 7 And the peace of God, which passeth all understanding, shall keep your hearts and minds through Christ Jesus.*

The Bible also says that God will keep the mind who stayed on Him in perfect peace because they trust Him.

> *Isaiah 26:3 (KJV)*
> *3 Thou wilt keep him in perfect peace, whose mind is stayed on thee: because he trusteth in thee.*

The Hebrew Word for peace is *Shalom. Shalom* means happy, prosperous, uninjured, healthy, safe, blessed, whole, and sound.

10. STRONG IN THE LORD

Whoever dwells in the *Secret Place* will be strong in the Lord and the power of His might. Being strong in the Lord means you are filled with supernatural strength from the Holy Spirit that empowers you to overcome any trial or enemy. Someone strong in the Lord who dwells in the *Secret Place* will be mentally tough. A spiritually strong person is free from fear, overcomes opposition, and is unyielding when engaged in warfare. They are resolute in their determination to stand against the devil as they put on the whole armour of God. The *Secret Place* is not just a place of protection, but a place filled with the strength of God to battle and overcome any attack from the enemy.

> *Ephesians 6:10-11 (KJV)*
> *10 Finally, my brethren, be strong in the Lord, and in the power of his might. 11 Put on the whole armour of God, that ye may be able to stand against the wiles of the devil.*

11. POWER OF GOD

Anyone dwelling in the *Secret Place* will have the *Power* of God on their life. Jesus returned in the *Power* of the Holy Spirit when He came out of His testing by the devil in the wilderness (Luke 4:14). The Holy Spirit anointed Jesus with His *Power* to destroy the works of the devil. As you dwell in the *Secret Place*, God will anoint you with the same *Power* of the Holy Spirit that Jesus walked in to be a witness of His resurrection. The *Power* of the Holy Spirit gives you the ability to work miracles and defeat the devil.

> *Acts 1:8 (KJV)*
> *8 But ye shall receive power, after that the Holy Ghost is come upon you: and ye shall be witnesses unto me both in Jerusalem, and in all Judaea, and in Samaria, and unto the uttermost part of the earth.*

12. GIFTS OF THE SPIRIT

There are nine gifts of the Holy Spirit revealed in the Scriptures. The Holy Spirit manifests His Presence through these nine gifts. As we dwell in the *Secret Place,* the Holy Spirit can use you in one or more of these gifts. These nine gifts of the Holy Spirit fall into three categories: **1. Revelation Gifts**

(Word of Wisdom, Word of Knowledge, and Discerning of Spirits) **2. Inspiration Gifts** (Prophecy, Diverse Kinds of Tongues, and Interpretation of Tongues) **3. Power Gifts** (Gift of Faith, Gifts of Healing, and Working of Miracles).

> *1 Corinthians 12:7-11 (KJV)*
> *7 But the manifestation of the Spirit is given to every man to profit withal. 8 For to one is given by the Spirit the word of wisdom; to another the word of knowledge by the same Spirit; 9 To another faith by the same Spirit; to another the gifts of healing by the same Spirit; 10 To another the working of miracles; to another prophecy; to another discerning of spirits; to another divers kinds of tongues; to another the interpretation of tongues: 11 But all these worketh that one and the selfsame Spirit, dividing to every man severally as he will.*

13. VOICE OF GOD

A privilege of dwelling in the *Secret Place* is the ability to hear God's Voice. When you dwell in the *Secret Place,* you can hear God speak to you from above the Ark of the Covenant in the Holy of Holies of the Temple of your body. As believers, we can hear the still small voice of God daily as we dwell in the *Secret Place* like Moses heard God speak. God will speak to you from within the Holy of Holies in your body.

> *Numbers 7:89 (KJV)*
> *89 And when Moses was gone into the tabernacle of the congregation to speak with him, then he heard the voice of one speaking unto him from off the mercy seat that was upon the ark of testimony, from between the two cherubims: and he spake unto him.*

Jesus taught His disciples that they were like sheep who would hear His Voice and follow Him. Believers dwelling in the *Secret Place* hear the Voice of God and will not listen to the voice of strangers.

> *John 10:2-5 (KJV)*
> *2 But he that entereth in by the door is the shepherd of the sheep. 3 To him the porter openeth;* **and the sheep hear his voice:** *and he calleth his own sheep by name, and leadeth them out. 4 And when he putteth forth his own sheep, he goeth before them, and the sheep follow him:* **for they know his voice.** *5 And a stranger will they not follow, but will flee from him: for they know not the voice of strangers.*

When you dwell in the *Secret Place,* you will not only hear God speak to you, but God will also speak through you. When you walk in the Covenant of God and dwell in the *Secret Place*, God will put His Words in your mouth by the Spirit of the Lord.

> *Isaiah 59:21 (KJV)*
> *21* **As for me, this is my covenant with them, saith the Lord; My spirit that is upon thee, and my words which I have put in thy mouth, shall not depart out of thy mouth,** *nor out of the mouth of thy seed, nor out of the mouth of thy seed's seed, saith the Lord, from henceforth and for ever.*

14. FAITH IN GOD

Everything about God and the *Secret Place* is supernatural, so we must have faith to dwell with Him. Only by faith can we dwell in the *Secret Place* and inherit the *Precious Promises* of the New Covenant. The *Better Promises* of the New Covenant are so astounding they stagger the natural mind. To dwell with the Lord in the *Secret Place*, you must be prepared to believe God for the miraculous. You must also believe anything and everything the Lord speaks to you about in the *Secret Place* because when you get near God, He always has mind-boggling miracles that He wants to do, and we must believe Him for them to be performed. The *Secret Place* is filled with faith because God is a God of *Faith*, and it takes faith for miracles to manifest.

> *Hebrews 11:6 (KJV)*
> *6 But without faith it is impossible to please him: for he that cometh to God must believe that he is, and that he is a rewarder of them that diligently seek him.*

Men and women of God in the Bible believed God when He made astonishing promises to them. Abraham believed God to have a child with his barren wife in their old age. Moses believed God to deliver the children of Israel from Pharoah and his armies. Mary believed she would give birth to the Son of God without knowing a man. Elijah believed God to call down fire on his enemies, and Elisha believed God to raise the dead. All these people of faith dwelled in the *Secret Place of the Most High* and believed God for astonishing miracles.

God will make a legend out of anyone dwelling in the *Secret Place* as they use their faith to move mountains and work miracles. God is pleased when we believe Him to fulfill His New Covenant Promises. Jesus pleased the Father with His faith, and as you spend time with God in the *Secret Place*, you will begin to do the works that Jesus did. Jesus went to the Father so His followers could do even greater works than He did, but we must have faith for them to manifest.

John 14:12 (KJV)

12 Verily, verily, I say unto you, He that believeth on me, the works that I do shall he do also; and greater works than these shall he do; because I go unto my Father.

For a miracle from the New Covenant to manifest, you must believe you received it. Once you know by faith what you believe God for from His revealed New Covenant, you have a right to call it into existence. You also have a Divine right to speak to Mountains that stand in the way of the New Covenant and make them move.

Mark 11:22-24 (KJV)

*22 And Jesus answering saith unto them, **Have faith in God.** 23 For verily I say unto you, That whosoever shall say unto this mountain, Be thou removed, and be thou cast into the sea; and shall not doubt in his heart, but shall believe that those things which he saith shall come to pass; he shall have whatsoever he saith. 24 Therefore I say unto you, What things soever ye desire, when ye pray, believe that ye receive them, and ye shall have them.*

15. WISDOM OF GOD

The atmosphere in the *Secret Place* is saturated with God's eternal wisdom. God is wise beyond all comprehension and has infinite knowledge and understanding of what He created in the seen and unseen realm. God shares His Eternal wisdom with those who dwell in the *Secret Place*. God's wisdom allows you to see beyond the limitations of the material world and lets you see into the mind of God and His Everlasting Kingdom.

Proverbs 3:19 (KJV)
19 The Lord by wisdom hath founded the earth; by understanding hath he established the heavens.

Anyone dwelling in the *Secret Place* is given the wisdom of God to see beyond the fleeting pleasures of this world. A higher understanding of the ways of God transforms your heart and mind. The wisdom of God gives you insight in how to live in a way that pleases Him. You know the importance of saying no to all this world has to offer through the devil's deception. One of the greatest blessings of the *Secret Place* is to hear God teach you His wisdom, knowledge, and understanding.

Proverbs 2:6-11 (KJV)
6 For the Lord giveth wisdom: out of his mouth cometh knowledge and understanding. 7 He layeth up sound wisdom for the righteous: he is a buckler to them that walk uprightly. 8 He keepeth the paths of judgment, and preserveth the way of his saints. 9 Then shalt thou understand righteousness, and judgment, and equity; yea, every good path. 10 When wisdom entereth into thine heart, and knowledge is pleasant unto thy soul; 11 Discretion shall preserve thee, understanding shall keep thee:

The wisdom of God gives you the insight to know the outcome of your actions before you make a decision. God's wisdom gives you the knowledge and understanding to govern your affairs in a way that is pleasing to the Lord. Nothing on this Earth is more valuable than the wisdom of God found in the *Secret Place.*

Proverbs 8:11 (KJV)
11 For wisdom is better than rubies; and all the things that may be desired are not to be compared to it.

16. THANKFULNESS

Thankfulness is a fruit of dwelling in the *Secret Place*. When God blesses you for dwelling in the *Secret Place*, all you can do is be thankful. A thankful person is free from complaining. Complaining is what kept the children of Israel from inheriting the Promised Land. Anyone dwelling in the *Secret Place* will have a heart full of thanksgiving. No one wants to be around a complainer, not even God.

> *Colossians 3:15 (KJV)*
> *15 And let the peace of God rule in your hearts, to the which also ye are called in one body; and be ye thankful.*

The only way to approach God in the *Secret Place* is with thanksgiving and praise.

> *Psalm 100:4 (KJV)*
> *4 Enter into his gates with thanksgiving, and into his courts with praise: be thankful unto him, and bless his name.*

The Bible also teaches that we are to thank God for **EVERYTHING**. Yes, **EVERYTHING!** We thank God for **EVERYTHING** because we know all things work together for good to those who love God and are called according to His purpose (Romans 8:28). God does not allow complainers into the *Secret Place*. The *Secret Place* is a place of thanksgiving, and giving thanks in *all things* is the will of God.

> *Ephesians 5:20 (KJV)*
> *20 Giving thanks always for all things unto God and the Father in the name of our Lord Jesus Christ;*

1 Thessalonians 5:18 (KJV)

18 In every thing give thanks: for this is the will of God in Christ Jesus concerning you.

17. KINGDOM OF GOD

While Jesus ministered on the Earth, He had much to say about the Kingdom of God. Jesus taught that the Kingdom of God was at hand and that you must be born again to enter the Kingdom of God. Jesus spoke using parables, and most of these parables were used to help describe the Kingdom of God. He also taught us to seek God's Kingdom and His righteousness first.

Matthew 6:33 (KJV)

33 But seek ye first the kingdom of God, and his righteousness; and all these things shall be added unto you.

One day, Jesus revealed a mystery about the Kingdom of God. He told those listening that the Kingdom of God is within you. Jesus was using this analogy to talk about the *Secret Place*. The *Secret Place* is within you. The Kingdom of God can be defined as the rule and reign of God by His Spirit. Another way to describe the *Secret Place* is to say that God rules and reigns by His Spirit within the heart of the believer. This teaching aligns with the Ark of the Covenant, which symbolizes the Holy Spirit inside your Holy of Holies. The Kingdom of God is within any believer who obeys God's Commands. The believer is filled with God Himself, and their body is the Temple of the Holy Spirit.

Luke 17:20-21 (KJV)

20 And when he was demanded of the Pharisees, when the **kingdom of God** *should come, he answered them and said, The* **kingdom of God** *cometh not with observation: 21 Neither shall* they say, Lo here! or, lo there! for, behold, **the kingdom of God is within you.**

PRESENCE & GLORY OF GOD

What sets the *Secret Place* apart from any other place on the Earth is the privilege of dwelling in the manifested *Presence of God* and beholding the *Glory of God.* God is Omnipresent, which means He is everywhere at the same time. However, God can manifest His Omnipresent Being in the *Secret Place* where believers can experience *His Presence* personally and intimately. The *Secret Place* is where you behold the beauty of the Lord and see the *Glory* of Who He is.

> *Psalm 27:4 (KJV)*
> *4 One thing have I desired of the Lord, that will I seek after; that I may dwell in the house of the Lord all the days of my life, **to behold the beauty of the Lord**, and to enquire in his temple.*

While Moses was dwelling in *God's Presence* in the *Secret Place* on Mount Sinai (The Mountain of God), he asked to see God's *Glory.* Moses was dwelling in *God's Presence* and didn't want to go into the Promised Land without the *Presence of God.* God reassured Him that *His Presence* would go with him and the children of Israel. It was at this time Moses asked to see God's *Glory.*

> *Exodus 33:14-23 (KJV)*
> *14 And he said, **My presence shall go with thee, and I will give thee rest.** 15 And he said unto him, **If thy presence go not with me, carry us not up hence.** 16 For wherein shall it be known here that I and thy people have found grace in thy sight? is it not in that thou goest with us? so shall we be separated, I and thy people, from all the*

*people that are upon the face of the earth. 17 And the Lord said unto Moses, I will do this thing also that thou hast spoken: for thou hast found grace in my sight, and I know thee by name. 18 And he said, **I beseech thee, shew me thy glory.** 19 And he said, I will make all my goodness pass before thee, and I will proclaim the name of the Lord before thee; and will be gracious to whom I will be gracious, and will shew mercy on whom I will shew mercy. 20 And he said, Thou canst not see my face: for there shall no man see me, and live. 21 And the Lord said, Behold, there is a place by me, and thou shalt stand upon a rock: 22 And it shall come to pass, while my glory passeth by, that I will put thee in a clift of the rock, and will cover thee with my hand while I pass by: 23 And I will take away mine hand, and thou shalt see my back parts: but my face shall not be seen.*

God revealed His *Glory* to Moses, and as He did, He revealed who He was, giving us great insight into what the *Glory of God* is. The *Glory of God* is the *Essence* of His *Nature* and is at the core of His *Being*, which makes Him radiant with a *Supernatural Light* that we cannot look into while in an earthly body.

Exodus 34:5-7 (KJV)

5 And the Lord descended in the cloud, and stood with him there, and proclaimed the name of the Lord. 6 And the Lord passed by before him, and proclaimed, The Lord, The Lord God, merciful and gracious, longsuffering, and abundant in goodness and truth, 7 Keeping mercy for thousands, forgiving iniquity and transgression and sin, and that will by no means clear the guilty; visiting the iniquity of the fathers upon the children, and upon the children's children, unto the third and to the fourth generation.

Moses was dwelling in the *Secret Place* and was given the privilege of experiencing God's manifested *Presence* and His *Glory*. As we dwell in the *Secret Place*, we, too, can experience the *Presence of God* and His *Glory*. We are eternally changed when we are saturated in the *Presence of God* and *Glory of God* in the *Secret Place*. We can see the *Glory of God* in the *Face of Jesus Christ* as we dwell in the *Secret Place*. God shows you who He is in the *Secret Place*, which changes you. You are changed into the very image of the *Glory of God* you experience in the *Secret Place*.

> *2 Corinthians 4:6-7 (KJV)*
> *6 For God, who commanded the light to shine out of darkness, hath shined in our hearts, to give the light of the knowledge of the glory of God in the face of Jesus Christ. 7 But we have this treasure in earthen vessels, that the excellency of the power may be of God, and not of us.*

There are times while dwelling in the *Secret Place* that the *Presence of God* is so remarkable and wonderful you don't even want to talk or leave that moment. No earthly words can express what you are feeling and experiencing in the Holy of Holies. Sometimes, glorious tears will roll down your face as you behold the *Glory of God*. You bond with the Lord and become one with Him in these precious moments. Your heart will exalt God as you are being still and knowing He is God.

> *Psalm 46:10 (KJV)*
> *10 Be still, and know that I am God: I will be exalted among the heathen, I will be exalted in the earth.*

FINAL SECRET PLACE THOUGHTS

There is so much more to the *Secret Place* than what meets the eye. This book was written to help you understand the mysteries of the *Secret Place*. Once you learn the mysteries of the *Secret Place*, you can apply all these truths to help you dwell in this *Sacred Location* all the days of your life. You cannot live in something you know nothing about, but the more you understand something, the more you can live in it.

The *Secret Place* is revealed in the Scriptures as a hidden place where you can enjoy a *Private Covenant Relationship* with God. God had Moses construct a Tabernacle and had King Solomon build a Temple to reveal a hidden place where the Ark of the Covenant could rest. This resting place is called the Holy of Holies. The Ark of the Covenant represented the Holy Spirit. The hidden mystery behind the Tabernacle and the Temple is that they represented the New Testament believer's body where the Holy Spirit would dwell. To dwell in the Holy of Holies *(Secret Place)* in the Temple of your body, you must be in Covenant with God.

Every Covenant between two parties had Laws to be obeyed and promises to be enjoyed. Jesus died so a New Testament believer could enter a Holy Covenant with God. If this Covenant was kept, the New Testament believer could dwell in the *Secret Place* where the Holy Spirit resides and enjoy the Presence and protection of God, just like the Ark of the Covenant represented God's Presence and protection in the Old Covenant.

In the Old Covenant, the Ark of the Covenant was given to the children of Israel as a symbol of God Himself. The Ark of the Covenant was used in battle, guidance, and daily worship. Now, the Holy Spirit helps the New Covenant believer in battle, guidance, and daily worship. Jesus died so the

Holy Spirit could dwell in the hearts of His followers and be there for them in their time of need. The hidden mystery of the *Secret Place* is our ability to now enter a Holy Covenant with God where we can meet with Him daily in the Temple of our own body. As we keep the New Covenant with God in the *Secret Place*, we are given all of the blessings of having the Holy Spirit in our lives.

The Holy Spirit was given as a *Comforter, Protecter, Teacher, Guide*, and *Answer* to all our needs. The Holy Spirit was sent to always be there for any believer who was dwelling in the *Secret Place* by keeping the New Covenant. This is one of the greatest mysteries of the *Secret Place*. God is with you by His Spirit and will answer all of your prayers when you are in need if you keep His New Covenant.

When you dwell in the *Secret Place*, you choose God above *anyone* and *everything*. Your relationship with God means more to you than anything this world has to offer. The *Secret Place* is where God becomes your everything, and He is more valuable to you than life itself. Jesus said anyone who understood what He was offering would sell everything they had to be a part of His Kingdom.

> *Matthew 13:44 (KJV)*
> *44 Again, the kingdom of heaven is like unto treasure hid in a field; the which when a man hath found, he hideth, **and for joy thereof goeth and selleth all that he hath, and buyeth that field.***

Jesus came to this Earth as the ***Messenger of the Covenant*** to offer humanity the opportunity to accept His High Call and dwell in the *Secret Place*. Your most valuable possession is your Covenant with God.

Malachi 3:1 (KJV)

1 Behold, I will send my messenger, and he shall prepare the way before me: **and the Lord, whom ye seek, shall suddenly come to his temple, even the messenger of the covenant,** *whom ye delight in: behold, he shall come, saith the Lord of hosts.*

The *Secret Place* is a place of intimacy and commitment where you seek God with all your heart, find Christ within you, and make Him your Lord. You understand all that Jesus went through on the Cross of Calvary so you can be in a relationship with Him. In this relationship, you forsake all and put God first as you obey His Commandments. You are also given a wonderful new family who has chosen God and His Kingdom first and dwells in the *Secret Place.*

Your Covenant with God in the *Secret Place* will sometimes come under attack, but this is where God is your hiding place. As you trust God in the middle of a storm, God will reassure you that He is with you to deliver you. The *Secret Place* is the only place you can dwell in for spiritual protection and answers from God. As you keep Covenant with God, God will keep His Covenant with you.

In conclusion, guard the *Secret Place*, for all the hidden treasures of Heaven are found in your private Covenant relationship with God. As you dwell in the *Secret Place*, the Holy Spirit, as represented by the Ark of the Covenant, will comfort, and aid you in any trial you may face. God, Himself, is your *Hiding Place.* When you forsake everything and put God first, you will find Him when you seek Him with all of your heart. I pray God gives you the key of knowledge to open the door to the *Secret Place* within yourself so you may dwell there all the days of your life.

There is no place

like the

Secret Place

ABOUT THE AUTHOR

Vince Baker was born in Southern California and later lived on 17 acres just north of Sacramento. As a child, Vince was raised as a Southern Baptist. Vince was always drawn to the Lord and even said he wanted to be a preacher at an early age.

Vince's life was uneventful until, one day, he encountered God while driving in his car at the age of 17. God manifested Himself to Vince so powerfully that his life would never be the same. After this experience, Vince became a Christian and dedicated his life to the Lord. In that same month, Vince received a book from his Christian Grandma called *"The Secret of His Power."* This book was about a famous miracle-working Evangelist named Smith Wigglesworth. God used this book to prepare Vince for ministry. God also used Smith's testimony found in another book called *"Apostle of Faith"* to talk to him about things He wanted to do through him in his latter years.

Vince decided to go to a Christian high school in his senior year. At this school, Vince was introduced to a seasoned Evangelist who took local churches to feed the poor and evangelize. Vince found out he lived near the Evangelist and started traveling with him. During this time, Vince became his right-hand man and saw many amazing miracles on the streets through this ministry. This ministry was called to train the Church on evangelizing with power. Vince traveled up and down the West Coast, ministering to the homeless and helpless while equipping the Church. Vince has a big heart for the poor, homeless, and hurting people.

Within a short time, Vince heard from God to attend Bible College. Through confirmation from God and a miracle of his tuition being paid for, Vince started to study the Bible more deeply at this Bible College. Vince's foundational training from the Word of God during this time was priceless. Vince ended up graduating as the Valedictorian from this Bible College.

After Bible College, Vince started ministering to kids at a Christian school, taught Sunday School, and functioned in the local church. Vince later moved into full-time ministry and was an assistant Pastor at a local Church for five years during the mid-'90s.

As an assistant Pastor, Vince visited a Church where the Prophet Kim Clement was ministering. Prophet Kim Clement pulled Vince out of the crowd and prophesied over him. In that prophecy, God told Vince through Kim Clement that He would use him mightily and needed to prepare himself.

Vince later worked in the marketplace, where he is the CEO and part-owner of Agora Advantage. God called Vince to the marketplace, but Vince knew that he would be called back into full-time ministry later in life. Agora Advantage has been a fantastic opportunity where Vince has grown in many ways. As a sign from God, Vince was voted in as the CEO of Agora Advantage on the Day of Pentecost.

As Vince neared the prophesied time that God would bring him back into full-time ministry, he began seeking the Lord more deeply. During this time, Vince had another unforgettable encounter with God regarding the Ark of the Covenant. God gave Vince a vision of four men carrying the Ark of the

Covenant into a Church. The Holy Spirit spoke to Vince and said, "Wherever you read Ark of the Covenant in the Old Testament, think Holy Spirit. Wherever you read Holy Spirit in the New Testament, think Ark of the Covenant. Put the two together, and you will know Me." Vince went and studied these two subjects everyplace he could find them in the Bible, and he received tremendous insight into understanding the Holy Spirit.

God also revealed to Vince a prophetic way to study the Bible from this encounter. Vince went on to spend years in the Word of God, studying different subjects of the Bible as the Holy Spirit led him. At the leading of the Holy Spirit, Vince researched every place a word or phrase was found from the Old and New Testaments. Vince has currently done over four hundred of these studies, some of which took months to complete. The revelations that came out of these studies were life-changing. Vince wrote down all these teachings and revelations, which make up many of the truths he writes about in his books and messages today. Vince found that when you study a subject everywhere it is located in the Bible you can receive the full counsel of God on that subject. Vince also received many dreams and visitations from God during this time.

Vince has a unique calling where he can preach, teach, prophecy, move in the gifts of the Spirit, bring healing, and perform miracles by the power of the Holy Spirit. Vince is called to help the body of Christ come into their destiny and High Calling.

Currently, Vince resides in Northern California with his wife, Eunice, and their two dogs enjoying the blessings of God.

INVITE VINCE TO SPEAK

VISIT

WWW.VINCEBAKERMINISTRIES.COM

ADDITIONAL BOOK BY
<u>VINCE BAKER</u>

ADDITIONAL BOOK BY
<u>VINCE BAKER</u>

www.amazon.com/author/vincebaker

www.VinceBakerMinistries.com

ADDITIONAL BOOK BY
<u>VINCE BAKER</u>

www.amazon.com/author/vincebaker

www.VinceBakerMinistries.com

ADDITIONAL BOOK BY
VINCE BAKER

www.amazon.com/author/vincebaker

www.VinceBakerMinistries.com

ADDITIONAL BOOK BY
<u>VINCE BAKER</u>

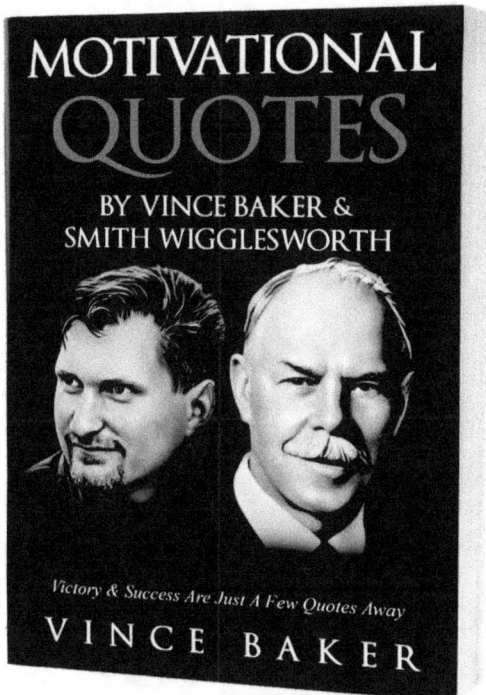

www.ingramcontent.com/pod-product-compliance
Lightning Source LLC
Chambersburg PA
CBHW071709120626
46550CB00001B/155